# Expert Learning
## for
## Law Students

# Expert Learning
# for
# Law Students

THIRD EDITION

## Michael Hunter Schwartz
Professor of Law and Dean,
University of the Pacific McGeorge School of Law

## Paula J. Manning
Professor of Law, Western State College of Law

CAROLINA ACADEMIC PRESS
Durham, North Carolina

**Library of Congress Cataloging-in-Publication Data**
Names: Schwartz, Michael Hunter, author. | Manning, Paula J., author.
Title: Expert learning for law students / Michael Hunter Schwartz and Paula
  J. Manning.
Description: Third edition. | Durham, North Carolina : Carolina Academic
  Press, LLC, [2017] | Includes bibliographical references and index.
Identifiers: LCCN 2017011855 | ISBN 9781611639650 (alk. paper)
Subjects: LCSH: Law students—United States—Handbooks, manuals, etc. |
  Law—Study and teaching—United States.
Classification: LCC KF283 .S354 2017 | DDC 340.071/173—dc23
LC record available at https://lccn.loc.gov/2017011855


e-ISBN  978-1-5310-0517-7


CAROLINA ACADEMIC PRESS, LLC
700 Kent Street
Durham, North Carolina 27701
Telephone (919) 489-7486
Fax (919) 493-5668
www.caplaw.com


Printed in the United States of America
2020 Printing

# Contents

# Preface

In the 10 years since the second edition of this text little has changed about the predictive value of LSAT scores and undergraduate grades; they still do not really tell you whether a particular student will succeed in law school. Some law students who have high LSAT scores and excellent undergraduate grades continue to fail out of law school. Some law students who have lower LSAT scores and lower undergraduate grades continue to graduate at or near the top of their law school classes. And some students who study incredibly hard still do poorly in law school. On the other hand, there have been a number of new developments in our understanding of learning theory and human psychology and at many law schools there have been significant changes, in teaching and curriculum, responsive to this understanding. As a result, this new edition of *Expert Learning* retains the core original materials which have helped hundreds of law students to excel in law school, and become "Expert Law Students" while reimagining the text for today's students and classroom.

The goal of this text is to help you succeed in law school by becoming an "Expert Law Student". Expert law students study differently. Not necessarily harder, but differently. Any law professor can spot the expert law students. These students approach their law studies with confidence, resourcefulness, diligence and planning. They are in control of their own learning, figuring out for themselves what they need to do to learn law. They know when they understand and know when they need help, and they even prepare better for meetings with their professors and ask better questions. They do better in law school than their peers, seem to have an easier time of it, and enjoy the experience more. Importantly, expert learning can be taught—which means all students have the power to become an "Expert Law Student".

The text is organized into two parts. Part I provides background information about expert learning. It describes what expert learners do, and how it differs from other study and learning strategies. Part II focuses on specific learning strategies needed by new law students. This edition places greater emphasis on the law school learning process, helping students to understand the connection between pre-class assignments, in-class instruction and post-class study, and how these tasks relate to exam performance. This edition also includes a number of new sections, including sections devoted to developing the right mindset to improve performance, organizing information to improve exam writing, a new way of understanding the connections and differences between thinking and writing; and integrated reflection questions designed to stimulate the type of reflective learning required for significant improvement in any discipline.

This preface would not be complete without an acknowledging colleagues and students who have contributed to the development of the ideas and materials in this edition, including Rory Badahur, Lisa Blasser, Kris Franklin, Russell McClain, Corie Rosen and Erik Oh.

# Part I

# Basic Principles

# Chapter 1

# Introduction to Expert Learning

There is a better way to study law, to prepare for the bar exam, to learn anything at all. That way, known as "Expert Learning," allows students to learn more, learn better and perform better than their peers. Expert learning, however, is not magic. You hold all the power within yourself to decide whether you wish to become an expert learner; you must be willing to make the necessary demands on yourself.

Expert learners have three characteristics:

1. They **actively engage** with the material to be learned. They are *not* passive readers/listeners.

2. They **take responsibility** for their own learning. They view learning as something they do for themselves, not as something that is done for them or to them.

3. They **practice "self-regulated learning"**; they use specific processes to guide their own learning.

This third criterion, **Self-Regulated Learning** (SRL), may be a new concept for you; it is best understood as a cycle, consisting of three phases: (1) the **forethought** phase, a **planning phase**, where the student decides what to learn and how to learn it; (2) the **performance** phase, a **monitoring and implementing phase**, where the student puts the plan into action while constantly assessing whether he or she is "getting it"; and (3) the **reflection** phase, an **evaluation phase**, where the student determines whether the plan has produced efficient and optimal learning.

- **Phase 1 (forethought):** The planning phase of SRL sets the stage for learning. During this phase, the student analyzes the learning task, sets learning goals (making sure these goals are very clear) and plans learning strategies (by considering a variety of ways to approach the learning task).

- **Phase 2 (performance):** During the monitoring and implementing phase, the student implements the plan and makes sure he or she is making progress toward the learning goals.

- **Phase 3 (reflection):** During the evaluation phase, the student determines how well the chosen strategies worked and how those strategies might be improved.

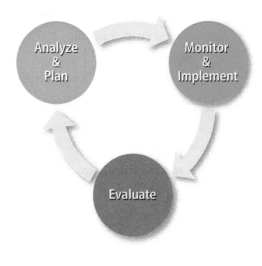

When you engage in this cycle of planning, implementation, monitoring and evaluating, it causes you to be constantly reflecting on your learning. Students who do this take control over their own learning and become experts not only in the general principles of learning, but also in what learning approaches work best for them. These students also become experts in knowing when they are learning—and when they are not; they also know how to get the help they need when they are not learning.

## What Is the Benefit of Becoming an Expert Learner?

Expert learners learn more, get better grades, remember what they have learned longer and enjoy learning more. Studies conducted at every level of education have reached the same conclusion. Self-Regulated Learning (SRL) skills are a better predictor of educational success than traditional measures of aptitude, such as the SAT and LSAT. In fact, studies of law students, medical students, students working towards graduate degrees in statistics, undergraduate students and even high school and younger students have found that students who use even one aspect of SRL, such as goal setting, invoking self-efficacy or self-monitoring, outperform those who do not. In short, expert learning can help you achieve your goal of succeeding in law school.

## What Expert Learners Know and Do

Years of academic studies of expert learning and expert learners have helped educational psychologists develop a prototype of expert learners—a list of the skills and knowledge that expert learners possess. Expert learners:

- ❑ Control their own learning processes
- ❑ Are active, not passive, in their approach to learning
- ❑ Are motivated (i.e., enjoy learning, have specific short-term and long-term goals, etc.)
- ❑ Are disciplined (i.e., have learned good habits and use them consistently)
- ❑ Know their own strengths and weaknesses
- ❑ Initiate opportunities to learn—rather than waiting for assigned learning tasks
- ❑ Set specific learning goals for themselves
- ❑ Have a large repertoire of learning strategies from which to choose
- ❑ Know both *what* to learn and *how* to learn
- ❑ Plan their approach to learning

❑ Monitor their learning while it's happening (i.e., notice when they're not learning and adjust their learning approach)

❑ Are not afraid of failure or difficulty, and can adapt to successes and failures

❑ Select challenging tasks that stretch their abilities

❑ Consistently reflect upon their choices and how well they are learning

❑ Evaluate the effectiveness of learning approaches and strategies

❑ Use learning strategies selectively and strategically

❑ Attribute failures to correctable causes and attribute successes to personal competence

---

**PAUSE. THINK. ACT.** Look at the list of the characteristics of expert learners. Check the boxes of the items that currently describe you. Now take a moment to think about the following:
- In what ways do you already do things that expert self-regulated learners do?
- In what ways do you not do the things expert learners do?
- What will you do to improve your expert learning skills?

---

# Taking the Next Steps

You can be an expert learner. Students who have never even considered engaging in self-regulation can learn to be experts. In fact, with the proper instruction, students can make expert learning a part of who they are. Students who develop and implement expert learning skills report that it changes not only how they study, but also how they work and live (because both work and life require continuous learning). This book is designed to help you do just that; by reading the materials, completing the exercises, and following the steps described in the following chapters, you can become an expert learner and law student.

---

**PAUSE. THINK. ACT.** Why do you want to be an expert learner? How will it help you meet your current goals? How can you improve as a learner based on what you have read so far?

# Chapter 2

# Becoming an Expert Learner

Law school is the beginning of your professional career. Take a minute to think about what that means.

Professionals are held to higher standards. Professionals in every discipline—athletics, music, medicine, and yes, law, are required to perform at a higher level, to exhibit more skill than non-professionals. Because law school is the beginning of your professional training, the demands are greater and the expectations are higher. Perhaps during your undergraduate career, you were able to get by with little preparation, perhaps cramming at the last minute or using short-cuts. You may not have needed to be an expert learner to succeed, and even excel. Do not expect that to be true in law school. You are no longer just a student. You are a professional in training. You will be expected to learn and apply vast amounts of information, under pressure and time constraints, with far less performance feedback than you are likely used to receiving.

The good news is that you have it within you to do everything required to succeed. In fact, you very likely possess at least some of the characteristics of an expert learner—and those you don't yet possess can be developed and improved. All it takes is commitment and concerted effort on your part.

## The Characteristics of a Self-Regulated Learner

Expert learners are Self-Regulated Learners. They actively control their behavior, motivation and thinking as they are engaging in academic tasks. The following is a list of characteristics of self-regulated learners.

Self-regulated Learners:

- view academic learning as something they do for themselves rather than as something that is done to or for them
- believe academic learning is a proactive activity, requiring self-initiated motivation
- set goals
- monitor what they are doing and are honest in their assessment
- employ strategic thinking about their learning
- are interested in the subject matter
- are well-prepared
- are ready with comments, questions, ideas, and insights
- identify problems and solve them

- are not afraid to fail or to admit they do not understand
- are driven to rectify failure and to construct understanding

---

**PAUSE. THINK. ACT.** Review the list of characteristics of self-regulated learners. Think about your own learning experiences. Rate yourself on a scale of 1–5, with 1 being "I do not yet do this" and 5 being "I almost always do this." Which areas need the most improvement? Which are areas of strength?

---

# Expert Learning Step by Step

As you know from chapter one, expert learners engage in the SRL cycle, which involves three phases: *forethought, performance* and *reflection,* each of which has multiple components. Each of the phases is detailed below, but before you begin to learn about each of the phases, it is important to understand how your mindset impacts your ability to be a self-regulated or expert learner.

## Step One: Mindset Matters

Self-efficacy has been proven to be a particularly powerful predictor of educational success. Self-efficacy is your belief that you have the ability to successfully master an academic task. It is a critical component of SRL because it is what drives the self-regulated learning cycle.

It ensures you will continue to reflect on and alter your learning strategies when something you are doing is not producing the desired results. It is the belief that if you persist, you will be able to improve or achieve the results you desire. In short, unless you believe your efforts will pay off, you will not persist when things are challenging or when you fail—and you will likely select tasks that are easy for you, so that you do not risk the chance of failure. Unfortunately, unless you are willing to select tasks that are challenging for you, and at which you may fail, you are limiting your learning potential.

Mindset and attribution style, the next two topics, play key roles in developing and maintaining self-efficacy.

### Choose Your Mindset: Growth Requires Effort, not Ability

Your mindset impacts your self-efficacy. Students with growth mindsets are far more likely to persist in the face of difficulties or failure. They are more likely to select the types of activities that produce growth and learning. Thus, they are more likely to be successful in law school. Since mindset can be learned, you can choose to adopt a growth mindset.

Students with growth mindsets perceive intelligence as something that can be developed and increased; they perceive education as an opportunity to encounter challenges that will produce intellectual growth. Students with fixed mindsets perceive intelligence as a fixed quality—an innate ability; they perceive education as a way to measure how much of that quality the student has.

Students with a growth mindset view having to work hard as a necessary part of improving skills. As a result, such students are not afraid to select tasks that are challenging, and that may even result in failure. Students with a fixed mindset view having to work hard as an indication they do not have the right amount of fixed ability and are not capable of performing the task. As a result, such students will select only those tasks they are already good at—to demonstrate they possess the required intelligence already. Not only do they select easy tasks, but fixed mindset students also may choose to not work hard on a challenging task so they can attribute their failures to laziness (not working hard enough), rather than lack of ability.

**Only students with a growth mindset have the potential to improve** because mastery of anything, including law, requires deliberate practice—extraordinary, purposeful and sustained effort over a long period of time, with a focus on improving weaknesses—and only students who view working hard on challenging tasks as a way to become more effective will engage in this type of practice.

| Growth Mindset | Fixed Mindset |
|---|---|
| • Prefers challenge over success (Selects difficult tasks that may result in failure) | • Prefers success over challenge (Selects tasks where failure is unlikely) |
| • Views hard work, and even struggle, as a necessary part of improving skills | • Gives insufficient effort so that failures can be attributed to lack of effort, rather than lack of ability |
| • Views failure as necessary for learning and growth | • Views failure as indicative of a lack of ability |

> **PAUSE. THINK. ACT.** What is your mindset? Do you select challenging tasks, even when there is a risk you might fail? Do you select tasks which force you to work hard? Do you see struggle, difficulty and even failure as a necessary part of growing as a learner?

### Attribution Style: Temporary, Specific and Changeable Errors — Attributing Failures to Correctable Causes

Attribution style is the way a person uses language to explain the causes of events. Your attribution style also impacts your self-efficacy. Whether you perceive yourself as capable of being or becoming competent at tasks, and whether you will persist in the face of difficulty or failure also depends, to a large extent, on your attribution style. Students with optimistic attribution styles are far more likely to persist in the face of difficulties or failure. They are also more likely to select the types of activities that produce growth and learning. Thus, they are also more likely to be successful in law school. Like mindset, attribution style can be learned; you can choose to adopt an attribution style that will help you succeed.

Students who characterize negative events, difficulties and failures as:

- permanent (unchangeable)
- pervasive (rather than limited to the particular context); and
- the result of a personal failure because of some unfixable, internal flaw

are exhibiting a pessimistic attribution style. Here are some examples of statements from a student with a pessimistic attribution style:

> *I am a terrible writer.*
> *I've always been bad at writing.*
> *I will always struggle.*
> *Everyone else is smarter than I am.*
> *I just do not understand this course.*

Students with this attribution style usually cannot see themselves as able to become effective with additional effort, and they do not persist in the face of difficulty or failure. Conversely, students who characterize negative events, difficulties and failures as:

- temporary;
- specific to the context;
- attributable to a particular failing or problem; and
- changeable

are exhibiting an optimistic attribution style. Here are some examples of statements from students with optimistic attribution styles:

> *This legal writing assignment didn't go so well, I need to pay more attention to citation.*

*I haven't mastered the IRAC writing style yet.*
*I can do better; I just need to work harder at understanding how these rules for joinder work.*

Students with this attribution style usually see themselves as able to become effective by exerting more effort.

Students with an optimistic attribution style persist in the face of difficulty; students with a pessimistic learning style avoid tasks that are difficult, and give up in the face of failure. Because law school is challenging, even for students who were very successful as undergraduates, persistence is critical for success—which is why attribution style is important.

---

**PAUSE. THINK. ACT.** How do you view your own failures? As an opportunity for growth? As fixable with further effort? What is your current attribution style? Do you need to make changes in how you think about negative events?

---

## Step Two: Planning to Succeed— The Forethought Phase

The **forethought phase** consists of all the thinking you should do before you begin a learning task. You might think about it as the preparation phase, but don't be misled, these activities are just as important as actually doing the tasks, and each of the activities in the forethought phase improve educational results.

The purpose of the forethought phase is to prepare yourself to begin learning. You must come to grips with what you need to learn and how you will go about doing so. The forethought phase includes five activities or sub-phases:

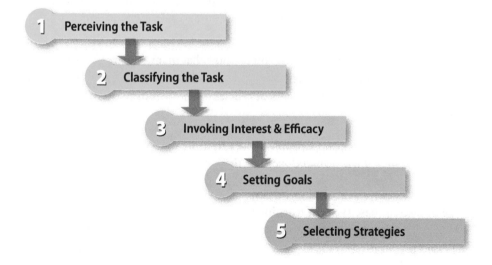

1. Perceiving the Task
2. Classifying the Task
3. Invoking Interest & Efficacy
4. Setting Goals
5. Selecting Strategies

The forethought phase should be seen as a process. The expert learner moves through this process in a fairly linear, straightforward way. In many ways, you may perceive this phase as a process of simply being explicit, of forcing yourself to make conscious, thoughtful decisions about your study plans, as opposed to "just studying." In fact, in the beginning, you may feel that some of these steps require you to be excessively conscious, to act unnaturally. You may even feel these acts are needlessly time consuming at first. If so, one of your goals for the first semester of law school should be to use the steps so frequently that the steps become natural and speedy.

> **ENGAGE.** As you read about each of the steps in the forethought phase, plan one of your law school assignments.

### 1: Perceive the Task

At the outset of a learning experience, all learners, expert and otherwise, perceive the task. In other words, they recognize that a task has been required of them. For example, before you start an assignment you usually read about it in a syllabus or on a course website. As a student who is or will be going to law school, you almost certainly are skilled at performing this task.

At this stage you must determine (a) that you need to do something (get ready for an examination, read a textbook, memorize course material) and (b) your deadline for completing the task. For example, a syllabus for a Criminal Law class might include the following two entries (among many others):

Week 1     The Mental State          pp. 118–165
Week 8     Midterm Examination

To succeed in this course, you need to perceive that the first entry is a reading assignment related to something called "The Mental State" and the other entry is a disclosure of when you will be taking your midterm. The midterm examination is an assignment of all the tasks necessary to be prepared to take the examination by the eighth week of class.

It may or may not be surprising for you to know that many students get so wrapped up in the week-to-week assignments of law school that they fail to engage in the activities which prepare them for the most crucial tasks—examinations.

*Since few professors assign preparation activities (they just schedule tests), students must sequence and schedule exam preparation activities on their own, complete them on their own and monitor their effectiveness on their own.*

Because successful preparation for law school examinations requires students to engage in each of these types of learning tasks, each is explored in depth later in this book. Try not to get so caught up in your day-to-day law school tasks that you postpone exam preparation to the last few days before your exams. While that approach may have worked well for you in college, it won't work well in law school.

In the first weeks of law school, you will receive many assignments and have significant and seemingly overwhelming demands placed on your time. Consequently, you will need to take time to make sure you have planned how your studying will get done.

---

Turn to the assignment you are planning and answer the following: (1) *What is the assignment?* (2) *By when must it be completed?*

---

## 2: Classify the Task

Having perceived a task, expert learners think about what is involved in performing the task. To classify the learning task, note the type(s) of skill(s) required by the task (e.g., reading for understanding, memorizing, problem-solving, writing) and the subject area of the task (e.g., history, geology). You are probably skilled at perceiving tasks and have likely classified tasks before, although you may not have done so at the level necessary for law school and law practice success.

Not all learning tasks are alike, and different tasks require different learning strategies. Expert learners take vastly different approaches depending upon whether they are reading an economics textbook, writing a paper, researching a question, memorizing formulae in preparation for a chemistry test or learning a new musical piece to play on a musical instrument. For example, a law school reading assignment might require organizational strategies, such as outlining rules or creating graphic organizers depicting the relationships among the concepts you are learning, and might require comprehension strategies, such as pre-reading and questioning. Similarly, a law school writing task, even during an examination, might require different organizational strategies than you have used in the past and would require editing strategies. Finally, a memorization task might require selection from a wide variety of strategies, such as putting the information into your own words (elaboration), rehearsal (reviewing and reciting information), or even using mnemonics or images to create associations, the choice of which would depend upon your purpose in memorizing, your planned use of the memorized information, and your possession of contextual information.

By classifying the learning task at the outset, you can make it easier for you to later decide which learning strategies would be most effective. The first classification is a simple one, requiring less than five seconds—identifying the subject area in which the task falls. A somewhat harder classification involves identifying the nature of the assignment. Law school learning tasks do not vary as much as college tasks vary. However, in law school, you will have multiple tasks to complete every single day and so must determine exactly what each task demands so that you can select the strategy best suited to successfully and efficiently complete each task.

Law school learning tasks fall within one of five categories: reading comprehension, research, synthesis, problem-solving and exam preparation (which includes organizing information, issue spotting, application of rules to facts, applying and distinguishing cases, and memorization). The discussion below describes in general terms these various types of learning activities. This discussion does not describe how to perform these tasks—that discussion will come later in this book. At this stage, you just need enough information so that you are able to classify the types of learning tasks you will be performing in law school.

- **Reading Comprehension:** Reading comprehension tasks in law school most often involve reading and understanding court opinions and statutes. These assignments are the typical day-to-day assignments students receive from their law professors. Law professors give these assignments and expect the students not only to read the cases and rules but also to understand them. This may mean reading material from an unassigned source (called a supplemental source) as a means to provide context for the assigned reading.

- **Research:** Research involves discovering what the applicable law is. Typically, it involves working through a procedure to find what governs the next step (or, more accurately, the next branch of steps) of the procedure. For example, if, during an early step, the student learns of an applicable statute, the student would then find the statute and cases applying the statute. On the other hand, if the student determines there is no applicable statute, he or she will have to search an index of cases organized by subject area.

- **Synthesis:** Synthesis, in the law school context, refers to making sense of materials (usually a set of cases) which appear to address the same subject; each case may add information about the application of the applicable law, and/or may appear to present conflicts. It involves reconciling the additional information and/or the conflicts among the cases or recognizing that the cases cannot be reconciled. Synthesis tasks are typically an implicit, rather than an explicit, part of law school assignments. In legal writing or first-year professional skills courses, students usually must reconcile a set of cases as part of a larger problem-solving, hypothetical-based writing task. In other words, in such courses, students are given a hypothetical set of facts. Their task, in part, is to research and find the relevant statutes and court opinions. Once the student has found the relevant statutes and court opinions, the student must make sense of them, reconciling or at least understanding any potential conflicts among them. Once she does so, she is able to use the cases and statutes to analyze the hypothetical facts. Likewise, a law school examination is usually a hypothetical set of facts. Students must make sense of the cases they read before taking the exam, so they can use the cases to analyze the hypothetical set of facts.

- **Problem Solving:** The entire process of reading a hypothetical set of facts, determining the body of applicable law (or, more likely, the bodies of applicable law), researching and synthesizing the law (or using the law as the student has learned and synthesized it throughout a course), and then analyzing how lawyers representing each of the hypothetical parties would argue the analysis of the facts to obtain the desired outcome is collectively referred to as problem-solving. Typically, as noted above, the student is given only the hypothetical set of facts and then is asked to analyze those facts as lawyers representing all the parties described in the facts would do. Law school papers and examinations, as well as bar examinations, almost exclusively test students' problem-solving skills.

- **Exam Preparation:** Exam preparation includes the reading comprehension, synthesis and problem-solving tasks described above and five other main tasks: organization, concept learning, principle learning, memorization and exam writing. Because successful preparation for law school examinations requires students to engage in each of these types of learning tasks, each is explored in depth later in this book.

## Exercise 2-1

The exercise reflected in the table below was designed to make sure you can correctly classify typical law school assignments. For each of the following excerpts from law school syllabi, classify each learning task implicated. For each of these excerpts, more than one learning task will be implicated.

| Question No. | Course | Week | Topic(s) | Assignment | Learning Tasks Implicated (check each task implicated) |
|---|---|---|---|---|---|
| 2-1.1 | Contracts | Week 5 | Damages for Breach of Contract | *Hawkins* (pp. 3–7); *Sullivan* (pp. 7–8); *Groves* (pp. 11–18); *Peevyhouse* (pp. 19–22); *Johnson* (pp. 22–25); *Dix Construction* (pp. 36–39) | ☐ Reading Comprehension<br>☐ Research<br>☐ Synthesis<br>☐ Problem Solving<br>☐ Memorization<br>☐ Organization<br>☐ Concept Learning<br>☐ Principle Learning<br>☐ Legal Writing |
| 2-1.2 | Legal Research and Writing | Week 7 | Objective Memorandum | Research the issues raised in the client letter distributed in class and prepare an objective memo analyzing the issues | ☐ Reading Comprehension<br>☐ Research<br>☐ Synthesis<br>☐ Problem Solving<br>☐ Memorization<br>☐ Organization<br>☐ Concept Learning<br>☐ Principle Learning<br>☐ Legal Writing |
| 2-1.3 | Torts | Week 15 | Final Examination | None | ☐ Reading Comprehension<br>☐ Research<br>☐ Synthesis<br>☐ Problem Solving<br>☐ Memorization<br>☐ Organization<br>☐ Concept Learning<br>☐ Principle Learning<br>☐ Legal Writing |

> Turn to the assignment you are planning and answer the following:
>   (1) *What is the subject area in which the task falls?*
>   (2) *What types of learning are involved?*

### 3: Invoke Your Interest and Self-Efficacy

This is the step that is best correlated with student success. Ironically, this is the step students are most likely to skip. Some law students find it awkward or artificial to force themselves to think about why they are interested in what they are learning and why they believe they will succeed in learning it. Unfortunately, giving short shrift to this step is a big mistake. It may seem to you like the least significant step, but it may in fact be the most significant one.

> *There are literally thousands of studies showing that students who get themselves interested in what they are learning (self-interest) and who believe they will succeed in learning (self-efficacy) outperform those who do not.*

There are even studies showing that students who receive false positive information about their capability outperformed students who do not receive such information or who received negative information. These results make sense because learning is a product of effort, persistence and strategy selection. Students who are interested in the subject matter and believe they will learn are more likely to try hard, to persist in the face of the inevitable difficulties in learning anything new, and to try alternative strategies if their initial strategy choices prove erroneous. As a result of this effort, persistence and strategic behavior, the students are more likely to learn what they need to learn. They then develop greater interest in what they are learning (because the understanding they gain makes the material more interesting) and greater self-efficacy (because they have succeeded) and therefore study more, persist more and use more strategic behaviors. In other words, self-interest and self-efficacy create a cycle of learning that leads to success in learning enterprises.

### The Self-Interest/Self-Efficacy/Better Studying/Better Results Cycle

## Invoke Your Interest

Novice learners focus only on whether they find the task intrinsically interesting. Expert self-regulated learners consciously create interest in the task by figuring out why the task is important for the course they are studying and for meeting their own educational goals (e.g., becoming a lawyer). An expert learner would regard reading this book as interesting because learning how to learn is important for any academic endeavor, and because learning how to be a self-regulated learner will help them succeed in law school.

Students can invoke self-interest in a number of ways—by tapping into the reasons they are performing tasks. Here are four common reasons students might be interested in law school tasks:

1. **An interest in law that led them to attend law school.** Everything you do in law school is part of a process of getting ready to be a successful lawyer. Most people chose to attend law school because becoming a lawyer was a dream. Recalling that dream often helps students find interest in what they are learning.

2. **The excitement and challenge particular to law school learning.** Learning in law school is a challenge for almost everyone. It is much like learning to play a sport or a musical instrument well, because it requires hard work and a lot of practice and is not easy to master. At the same time, learning in law school is exciting. At least part of the discussion throughout law school revolves around questions of what the law should be. For example, law students might discuss why, given that the Constitution has no explicit mention of a right to privacy, we have such a right. Most people seldom have time to contemplate these questions in their day-to-day lives.

3. **Imagining using law school learning right now and in the future as a lawyer.** This process does require some thought. For example, students who plan to practice criminal law or family law or environmental law may have difficulty developing interest in their study of contract law. They can do so, however, by recognizing that, in their day-to-day activities, they are making dozens of contracts (contracts to buy homes, cars, groceries, dinners, medical and dental services, etc.), for which knowledge of contract law may help in some way. Moreover, lawyers who practice criminal law sign contracts with their clients and their employers (the District Attorney's or Public Defender's offices, for example) and on behalf of their clients or the public (plea agreements). Similarly, family law practitioners not only sign client and employment contracts, but also draft custody and divorce agreements. Environmental lawyers make contracts with clients, employers and, on behalf of their clients, contracts with governmental regulatory agencies, such as the Environmental Protection Agency (EPA). Considering how they will use what they are leaning helps students develop an interest in it.

4. **An interest in learning for its own sake.** Attend any grade school class and you will find classrooms full of students who are excited by learning because growth,

change and success are rewards in themselves. In fact, many law students who wait a few years after graduating from college before attending law school report that the absence from school taught them to appreciate the excitement of learning. Studies of students who are expert learners suggest that expert learners enjoy learning for its own sake much more than their peers do.

---

Turn to the assignment you are planning and answer the following:
  (1) *Why am I interested in this material? Why do I care about doing this task?*
  (2) *What's the point of learning this material? How will I use it now or in the future?*
  (3) *Why do I want to become a lawyer? How will mastering this task help me do that?*

---

## Invoke Self-Efficacy

Expert learners *consciously* invoke self-efficacy. This is simply is a matter of identifying past successes and drawing analogies between those successes and particular law school tasks. All that is required for this step is to recall something you have done that was difficult at first, but at which you eventually succeeded.

Nearly all of us can point to a past experience where we struggled to learn to do something, but eventually succeeded — a sport, a musical instrument, calculus, philosophy, a job task. We can recall the struggle, the need for hours and hours of practice, and the self-doubt. Hopefully, we can also recall the triumph of succeeding. When we remember the struggle and the success, it helps us to remember that we are capable of succeeding in the face of difficulties, so that we persevere when new difficulties are presented.

Invoking self-efficacy is more a matter of remembering to do so than a matter of intellectual struggle. Try this exercise right now: Remember something you have learned that did not come easy to you at first. What made it hard? How did you manage to learn? How did learning it make you feel?

---

Turn to the assignment you are planning and answer the following:
  (1) *When have I successfully learned something similar or similarly difficult?*
  (2) *How did I succeed at that task?*
  (3) *How did that success make me feel?*
  (4) *Why will I succeed in learning this material?*

---

## 4: Set a Learning Goal

After you have decided you want to learn and that you will succeed at doing it, you are ready to set learning goals. A goal is a specific outcome you desire. Expert self-regulated learners generally set mastery learning goals that, most commonly, focus on learning the material as well as possible, rather than solely on their grade. Expert learners set goals that have specific standards by which they will measure whether they master the material. These goals are short term and moderately difficult to achieve.

The process of setting achievable, challenging goals, and breaking them into manageable sub-goals where necessary, is a process that serves us well in all phases of our lives. We benefit when we create a plan of action and a standard for measuring whether we have achieved it. In educational settings, goal setting is a crucial prerequisite to success. Students perform better when they set appropriate goals and use those goals to monitor their achievement.

Effective goals must be all of following:

1) **Concrete**
2) **Short-term**
3) **Challenging**
4) **Realistic (i.e., achievable)**

Turn to the assignment you are planning and set a learning goal. Next, evaluate your goal in light of the following discussion.

### Goal Setting Rule #1: Goals Must Be Concrete

A goal must describe behaviors or actions and have explicit criteria for its achievement so you can know what to do to achieve it. An abstract life goal, for example: "I will exercise more," gives little guidance. What constitutes exercise? Is playing ball with a child exercise? Is weight-lifting exercise? How frequently must the person exercise to be able to say she is exercising "more"? Does "more" refer to the duration of each exercise experience or the number of exercise experiences per week or month? A goal which describes actions and has explicit criteria would be: "I will do aerobic exercise for twenty-five minutes three times per week." Now, the speaker knows what constitutes exercise, how much exercise is minimally required each time and how often she should do it.

Likewise, an abstract educational goal such as: "I will learn the rules for Civil Procedure," is also problematic because it fails to give the student a method for knowing what she should know and be able to do when she's done. What does "learn" mean? Must the student be able to recite from memory or select them from a list? Must she be able to explain how the rules apply or apply them to a new situation? How accurate must her recitation be? How will she know if she has accurately "learned" the "rules"? A goal which describes actions and has explicit criteria, and that would capture the same basic idea as the original "learn the rules of Civil Procedure" goal would be:

1. By the end of the first unit of instruction (two weeks), I will be able to list the ways to establish subject matter jurisdiction in federal court. For each of those ways I will be able to recite the required elements and paraphrase what is required with 100% accuracy, compared with the Federal Rules, rules from my casebook and notes I have taken during class.

2.  By the end of the first unit of instruction (two weeks), I will be able to review a hypothetical fact pattern and identify the type of subject matter jurisdiction that is in issue, with 100% accuracy, based on the answers to those hypotheticals.

3.  By the end of the first unit of instruction (two weeks), I will be able to apply the correct rule for subject matter jurisdiction to the issues I have spotted in a hypothetical and determine whether a court has such jurisdiction, with 80% accuracy, based on the answer to the hypothetical.

4.  By the end of the first day of instruction on subject matter jurisdiction, I will identify why I am interested in learning about subject matter jurisdiction, and why I believe I will succeed at learning it.

Notice that each of these goals refers to *observable* behaviors. Note also that most have standards of performance. Some, those for which measurement is impossible because they are really goals that focus on emotions or attitudes, do not. Tasks that can be mastered perfectly, such as the recitation of the required elements, have 100% accuracy as the measure; those learning tasks that are more difficult and more complex, such as the application of the rule to resolve a hypothetical problem, have an 80% standard, reflecting that higher degree of difficulty. Also notice that these goals are for a particular topic in Civil Procedure, since learning all of the rules for Civil Procedure is such a large task that it needs to be broken up into many sub-goals, such as these. Finally, notice there are knowledge goals (e.g., the list of elements) and skill goals (e.g., issue spotting and application of the rules). Students sometimes forget to include both types of goals.

---

Evaluate your goal — is it concrete? Is it measurable? Is it specific? Do you need to revise it?

---

### Goal Setting Rule #2: The Goals Must Be Short-Term

While most people and most students set long-term goals, such as becoming a lawyer and learning everything in a course, learning goals must be short term so that you can evaluate them close in time to when you set them. This approach allows you to more effectively evaluate your learning and ensures that most study sessions are productive.

For example, the above goals all focus on what the learner would be able to do by the end of the unit of instruction in which the student will focus on the skills and knowledge in question. Of course, some goals, such as learning and understanding all the rules for Civil Procedure, or organizing all of the necessary law for a final examination into an exam approach, cannot be achieved in one session or even a few sessions. The key for such goals is to break them into short-term sub-goals, such as practicing applying a defined portion of the rules to a series of hypotheticals. Thus, for a Civil Procedure class, a student might set one goal of applying the rules relating to diversity jurisdiction (a type of federal subject matter jurisdiction) to a series of hypotheticals to test the student's understanding of the rules, and a second goal organizing the rules for diversity jurisdiction into an exam approach, and a third goal of memorizing these rules. The student could then set similar goals with respect to federal question jurisdiction (a different type of subject matter jurisdiction). Some sub-topics might even be so large that they would need to be broken down further. They key is to create manageable, concrete goals which can be accomplished in a short period of time.

> Evaluate your goal — is it short term? Is it achievable in a single session? Should it be broken down into sub-parts?

### Goal Setting Rule #3: The Goals Must Be Challenging

It is important to set challenging goals. Goals should encourage you to stretch yourself. Students who set goals that are too easy often become bored and may even lose interest before completing them.

> Evaluate your goal — is it challenging?

### Goal Setting Rule #4: The Goals Must Be Realistic

Just as the goals cannot be too easy, they also cannot be too hard or unachievable. It would be impossible, for example, to memorize everything in this chapter with 100% accuracy. Such a goal would lead to frustration and disappointment. Students need to set achievable standards. Likewise, time goals should be realistic. A 100-page law school reading assignment cannot be completed in only one or two hours. A student might be able to finish turning the pages within that time, but the student's retention and understanding would be so minimal that, in effect, most of the time would have been wasted.

> Evaluate your goal — is it realistic?

### A Few Final Thoughts about Setting Goals

Generally, goal setting requires some thought. You cannot simply look at an assignment in a law school syllabus (which may only list the pages to be read) and set a goal for it, because you may not know what it is you must learn. To create goals which describe actions and have explicit criteria, and which are challenging yet achievable, you need to look over the assigned materials and get a feel for the topic, the length of the assignment and the complexity of the topic. You also need to consider all of the steps it may take to complete your goal, and they may not be obvious from the written assignment. For example, you might need to consult a supplemental source before you begin reading the assigned cases. You also, of course, would want to consider any instructional objectives provided by the instructor. At first, this may take time, because you may be new to setting goals this way—but like every other skill, in life and in law school, with practice you will become more proficient (and efficient).

As you set goals, be sure to check them against the four criteria by which goals are measured, until you become a master at goal setting.

> Review the goal you set at the beginning of this section. If necessary, redraft your goal to conform to the guidelines in this section.

### 5: Select a Strategy

The final and crucial step of the forethought phase involves creating a specific plan. To succeed you must devise and tailor a strategic approach to achieve the goals you set. You must decide which strategies would be most productive for the task. This means you must decide: (1) the techniques you will use to learn; (2) how you will maintain focus and attention, and deal with difficulties in learning; and (3) how, when, where and with whom you will use those strategies.

#### Cognitive Strategies: What Techniques Will You Use to Learn?

There are a large number of cognitive strategies for each of the types of learning. Learning strategies are so many, so varied and so task dependent that explaining them will require the entire second half of this book. At this stage of your study, you only need to know that learning strategies are task-specific (different depending on the task), are many in number (you often have several choices for each type of learning), and are learner-specific (dependent on your learning preferences, personality type and learning goals).

There are several factors that bear on the question of which cognitive strategy would be most appropriate for any particular learning task:

- The demands of, benefits of and limitations of each possible strategy;
- Your learning goal(s);
- The time available to complete the task;
- The importance of the task relative to alternative uses of your time;
- Your learning style;

- Your personality type; and, to a lesser degree
- Your familiarity, experiences and comfort with each of the possible strategies.

Additionally, each learning experience offers you additional information about what works best for you with respect to a particular learning task; that information is crucial to future technique selections. In fact, the most successful students will alter the techniques they learn in this book both as they are using them and in planning future learning activities, based on the results they obtain.

In short, more than anything else, expert learners are expert in how they learn best. While you will be developing that expertise through your activities in reading this book and as you apply the skills to learning activities in law school classes, to your work, and to your personal life, you will not complete your conversion into the status of learning expert for about one year—after having had the chance to hone your learning strategies through trial, error and adaptation.

### Motivational Strategies: How Will You Maintain Focus and Attention and Deal with Difficulties?

Within certain parameters, motivational strategies are a matter of personal preference and control. You are in the best position to know what will motivate you to get started on your studying and what you should say to yourself while you are studying to help you stay focused. You also need to plan for those moments when you are having difficulty focusing on your work, and when you feel tired, burned out, anxious, etc. Some of the techniques already described in this section—like invoking self-interest (reminding yourself why the task is important to you) and ensuring your are in the right mindset (focused on effort, mindful that struggle and difficulty is part of learning, not evidence that you are not capable), are techniques that address some of these issues, some of the time. It also helps to break up tasks into a series of achievable short-term goals, so the tasks before you are manageable, rather than daunting. Nevertheless, there may be times where those techniques are not working as well as you may have hoped.

Many students find it helpful to plan their own rewards for completing certain steps in a learning process, such as planning a ten-minute break to take a walk, or for a phone call to a friend or loved one, after finishing reading some defined portion of materials, or completing some other specific task. You might also find that despite your efforts to maintain balance, it has been a long time since you have done the things that made you happy before coming to law school—you might want to consider whether you still do those things (run, or work out, or read for pleasure). Working these things back into your routine, and even using them as rewards for finished work, can help you stay motivated—and more importantly, balanced.

Another effective technique is to use self-talk—things you say to yourself to keep you on task and focused—such as: "First, I will do _____, then I will do _____" or "Keep your eyes on the prize (the law school diploma)" or "I know I can do this; this is just like when I _____." Or "Stop being so negative, you can do this, it's just like _____."

### Environmental Strategies: Where, How, When, and with Whom Should You Study?

Like motivational strategies, environmental strategies are also a matter of personal preference and control. Once again, you are in the best position to know what materials you need to study and where, when, how long and with whom you should study. But don't be surprised if you have to adapt your strategies or develop new ones if you find the strategies you used as an undergraduate no longer work for you. Remember that law is a profession, and professionals must practice and perform at a higher level.

### Where Will You Study?

You probably already have preferences for where you study — you may prefer a quiet, solitary location, or one that is loud, with some distractions. Expert learners are able to evaluate whether a particular environment is helping or hindering them from achieving their goals — and they adjust accordingly. For example, if you need a quiet place to study, and the law school's law library proves distracting because peers and friends interfere with your focus or distract you from studying, you may want to change locations. Expert learners also vary their study location — because studying in a variety of locations, using a variety of methods, can aid in retention of material. The key is to monitor your learning — and whether your choice of study location is an effective choice for the tasks you are performing. Only you will know if your study space is effective — and only if you monitor how well it is working, and accurately assess the strengths and weaknesses of your selection.

---

**PAUSE. THINK. ACT.** Plan your study space: What are your possible options? What are the strengths and weaknesses of each option?

---

### How Will You Allocate Your Study Time?

There are best practices in terms of the amount and length of time for study, however, mere time on task is not a predictor of success. While students who do not put in sufficient time and effort will most certainly struggle to succeed in law school, every law professor knows of a student who studied endlessly, but who did not do well in law school because her studying was not productive. This is why it is critical to understand the importance of each task, and weigh that against the amount of time you have available to study.

### How Important Is the Task?

To effectively allocate time, students must be able to accurately assess the importance of each task — both to know how much time to allocate, and to be able to prioritize each task. For example, while students need to be prepared for class to help retain new learning and to benefit from the opportunity for in-class feedback from the professor, it is important not to assign disproportionate value to the experience of appearing smart to the professor and peers in class. Consequently, you should not prepare for class in a way that interferes with the other learning activities you should be doing.

> Many new law students devote so much time to class preparation (reading and briefing cases) that they fail to make time to engage in activities to consolidate their learning, such as reviewing their class notes, outlining the course or creating exam approaches, or writing practice exams—all of which bear a much greater relationship to performance on law school examinations. Expert learners do not make this mistake.

Take care not to fall into the trap of many new law students, who let case reading and briefing consume all of their time, and who fail to do the study and practice that are essential to exam success—like taking practice exams and creating exam approaches.

### How Frequently Should You Engage in the Task?

Expert learners space their learning activities out over time, rather than trying to cram all their studying together at once. Spaced study produces better and more efficient learning—you will learn more, retain the material for longer, and be able to recall the information you need, faster and with greater accuracy if you give yourself time between study sessions, and return to material several times, over several days or weeks. In addition to being a superior method for retaining information, spaced study also allows you to:

- identify gaps in your understanding and skills while there is still time to rectify them;
- build your skills, by ensuring you have time to obtain and then implement feedback;
- rest before your examinations (law school tests require creative thought and you are more likely to perform better on such tests if you are well-rested)

Also, remember that for law school, the goal is not just to remember the information for your exams, but to store the information in long term memory, because the material will be covered again on the bar exam, and potentially when you begin practicing law. You are more likely to retain information for the long term if you space your learning.

### How Much Time Should You Spend?

Law school classes require incredible amounts of work; in general, new law students devote 3 or 4 hours outside of class for every one hour in class, for each of their law school subjects.

Stop for a moment and think about what that means. If you are enrolled in 15 units (a typical first semester load) this means law school will required about 60 hours per week, minimum, of your time outside of class: 15 hours in class + 45–60 hours of outside study = 60–75 hours per week. Because of the heavy workload, almost all law students feel pressed for time.

Calculate your weekly hours:

number of units: _____ × 3 = _____ (number of hours for study)
                          + _____ (number of hours in class)
                          = _____ (total weekly hours devoted to law school)

Of course all students are different — the correct amount of time for any learning task is the time it takes you to develop mastery. If you have a learning disability which impairs your reading speed, you may need to devote one and a half to twice as many hours to your studies as is recommended above. For this reason, you may want to consider a reduced number of units — so you have sufficient hours in the week to devote to your studies.

### How Will You Get It All Done?

You have likely never needed to devote such a significant number of hours to your studies. For this reason, you may never have needed to use a calendar, or write down a "to do" list. Even if that has been true for you in the past, you will want to consider a new strategy.

> Law school requires you to be skilled at time management; if you do not consciously plan your time, you will almost certainly fall behind and fail to successfully complete the necessary tasks.

You can use any type of calendaring system. If you have difficulty planning your time, or you feel like you are falling behind, or are not able to accomplish all of the tasks you need to complete, you may want to use the step by step guide set out below, in addition to following these guidelines for effective time management:

- **Be detailed and specific.** Calendars that contain very little information, e.g., "read for contracts," are neither helpful nor effective. Be sure you write down exactly what you plan to do, and how much time you are allotting for the task, e.g., read Contracts pages 114–121 and brief cases (list case names), 10:00 a.m. to 1:30 p.m.

- **Hold yourself accountable, reflect and revise.** In the beginning, you may not be very good at estimating how long tasks take, but it is important to take a guess and schedule each task, then reflect on how well you estimated the time it would take, and then adjust your calendar for the next day or week. By being specific about time, holding yourself accountable and reflecting on how to better schedule your time, you will ultimately improve. However, if you fail to do these things, you will likely never learn to accurately assess how long such tasks will take.

- **Assess your performance, and revise your calendar based on your assessment.** Especially in the beginning, you may find it difficult to assess how much time each task will take to complete. For example, the reading assignments may seem short, but because of the complexity of the material, they may take many hours to complete. *Be willing to adjust and adapt.* Change any aspect of your schedule that is not working for you.

- **Work backward from deadlines.** Successful time managers start with deadlines and a list of all the tasks involved in accomplishing a particular goal. They assign each task to a specific day and time and build in time for the inevitable struggles involved in performing complex, difficult tasks. In law school, working backwards from deadlines insures that you will finish tasks with plenty of time for revisions and necessary help.

- **Work on the most challenging work when you are freshest.** Be sure to spend your time as if it's a precious commodity. Figuring out new, difficult material is more challenging than converting a course outline to flashcards for memorization purposes. Writing practice exams requires more mental energy than checking the accuracy of your citation form. Plan accordingly.

- **Safeguard your time.** Say no to people and activities that interfere with your designated study times.

---

### Creating Calendars That Work: A Step by Step Plan

This guide will give you an idea of the activities you should be doing to prepare before, during and after class. These activities are covered in the chapters that follow. The guide also helps you implement many of the skills and strategies discussed in this chapter.

**STEP ONE**—**select your style.** Start with a day by day, week by week or month style calendar (you can print any of these from your electronic calendaring software or various websites, draw your own on a sheet of paper, or use your computer or smartphone).

**STEP TWO**—**the non-negotiables.** Fill in your class times—by hour and day—and any other commitments over which you have no scheduling control (i.e., work).

**STEP THREE**—**assigned material.** Review the syllabi from each of your courses to obtain your assignments, including the number of pages you will have to read (per course) each week. Add in the estimated time(s) on the days that you will complete your reading, briefing and other assignments for each of your classes. *Include the exact number of pages you intend to complete for each time period, during the time you intend to study for that class.*

**STEP FOUR**—**pre-class review time.** Block off 15–20 minutes before every class to review your briefs/outlines/notes to re-familiarize yourself with the material that will be covered in class. If you have two or three classes in a row (with no or minimal time before one or more of your classes), allocate enough time prior to the first class to review for all of the classes scheduled that day.

STEP FIVE—post-class review time. Block off 30–60 minutes after each class (or 2 hours at the end of the day, if you have classes back to back) to review your lecture notes, your outlines and briefs, and to refer to supplemental materials if you have questions.

- Make notes about any areas of confusion and add to your calendar or to-do list the task of figuring it out. Make a plan and set aside time in your calendar to utilize a supplemental guide, consult a study group, re-read the material, or make an appointment with your professor to discuss the unclear topic. Be sure you understand every issue—how it will be tested and how the law is applied.

- Edit and summarize your notes. Be sure the information you have in your notes/briefs/outlines accurately captures what you need to know and understand for your exams.

- While the information is fresh in your memory, start organizing and creating your essay approaches from the material covered in class; organize all potentially testable issues. This is the hardest part of your study process because it forces you to have a deep understanding of the material, but if it is done regularly, you can focus all of your efforts at the end of the semester on practicing application of the law.

STEP SIX—practice time. Schedule at least 2 hours per subject for practice—either essay writing, working through examples in supplemental materials, or writing out responses to the practice hypos and other materials provide by your professor. *Part of this time should always include writing practice.*

STEP SEVEN—balance. Add in exercise, work, family/spouse time and daily living. For example, block off four hours on Saturday or a few hours every night or every other night for your family. It may sound strange or unfeeling to schedule family time, however, planning the time (1) makes it more likely you will be able to do it; and (2) alleviates some of the guilt you may feel both when you are away from your family, and when you are away from your studies, because you know you have time for both.

STEP EIGHT—rewards. Set up "rewards" for yourself for completing all of your scheduled activities—allow yourself to do things that are fun when you've successfully done all of your work for the week.

STEP NINE—communication. Email or give a copy of your weekly calendar to your parents, friends, spouse and other important people in your life so: (1) they have an understanding of what you are doing and (2) they know when to expect your undivided attention. This will help them understand your work load, and the effort required to succeed in law school. It will also help them to "ease off" and not call, email and text you during the time you really should be concentrating your efforts on studying.

**STEP TEN**—reflect and reassign.

- Be sure to keep track of how long it actually takes you to complete assignments so you can more accurately calendar time from week to week.

- If you do not accurately assess your time, and you do not finish in the time you have allotted on your calendar, you will need to block out additional time on your calendar to finish the assignment. *If you had planned to do something else once you finished, do not simply continue with the assignment until you are finished, since this will put you behind on other assignments; instead, move to the next scheduled assignment, and come back to the incomplete assignment and finish it during the newly scheduled time.*

- If you fail to complete something during a week, move it to the next week. Reflect on why you were not able to reach your goals. Did you allocate sufficient time? Do you need to spend more time each week? Did you use your time productively? Should you change locations? Study groups? Should you shut off your phone? Turn off your wi-fi? Change what you do to other times of day when you are more effective?

\* This plan is based on a handout originally developed by our colleague, Professor Lisa Blasser.

### A Note for Procrastinators

If you have a tendency to procrastinate, this discussion is for you. It is helpful to start with an understanding of the causes of procrastination. There are several causes, including perfectionism, fear of failure, difficulty in estimating the time required for a task, and an inability to distinguish between important tasks and essential tasks. Procrastinators tend to underestimate the time required to complete a task and overestimate the non-existent benefits of being backed against the wall time-wise. In fact, procrastinators perform below their capabilities, enjoy the process less, and suffer from higher levels of exhaustion, substance abuse and illness.

The most important thing a procrastinator can do is to start a task—not plan the task or discuss the task or travel to a place to do the task, but start the task. Other useful things you can to do to minimize your procrastination inclination include:

- label your reasons for not getting started for what they are—excuses,

- identify the causes of your choice to procrastinate the particular task you are procrastinating,

- confront your self-doubts, false beliefs, and perfectionism, and

- use activities you enjoy—television, movies, hanging out with friends, etc.—as rewards for completing tasks you need to complete rather than as procrastination activities.

### With Whom Will You Study?

Finally, you will need to choose when to study with others. Other students, as described later in this book, are an excellent source of practice and feedback as part of exam preparation activities. Peers also are helpful sources for dealing with areas of confusion and getting the necessary social and emotional support. Seeking such help from peers is highly correlated with educational achievement. Moreover, students benefit even more from helping their peers; if you are forced to understand something well enough to explain it to your peers, you must attain a high level of mastery, making this activity one of the most productive learning enterprises in which students can engage. For this reason, nearly all students need to include peer work in their study plans.

Such activities can become counter-productive, however, if you select peers who are not as committed to their own learning as you are and therefore are unwilling to do their share of the necessary work, or if you become embroiled in social conflicts with those peers, or if the presence of peers distracts you from doing those tasks on which you must work alone. Expert students recognize when peer studying is necessary and appropriate and when it may be a distraction, and they adjust accordingly.

---

Create a specific plan for completing your selected assignment.

   (1) **What** learning strategies will you use:

      a. What techniques will you use to learn?

      b. Is there a way to work with your learning style, personality type, etc.?

   (2) **Where** will you study?

   (3) **When** will you do the task—time and timing:

      a. How much time do you have to complete the task ?

      b. How important is the task (relative to other tasks)? Given your other tasks, how much time should you spend on this task?

      c. What deadlines do you need to meet? When must this be completed? What other deadlines do you have?

      d. What day and time will you do this task? When will you take breaks?

      e. Is this a complicated task? Will it require sustained concentration? If so, are you doing it when you are freshest?

   (4) **With whom** will you study?

      a. Should you do this task with someone else?

> b. Who should that be?
>
> (5) **How** will you approach the task and deal with difficulty:
>
> a. What will you do if you are having difficulty focusing on your work (i.e., you feel tired, burned out, anxious, etc.)?
>
> b. How will you reward yourself for completing the task?

## Step Three: Getting It Done, the Performance Phase

The performance phase is the implementation phase of SRL—where you do the work you have been planning. There are three tasks that make up this phase:

1. Attention-focusing,
2. Implementation
3. Self-monitoring.

Unlike the forethought phase, the performance phase is not a set of independent, successive steps. Instead, each of the three tasks—attention-focusing, implementation and self-monitoring—may occur at the same time, or one at a time, but in no particular order. In other words, while you are implementing your learning strategies, you should also focus your attention and monitor your learning progress. For the purposes of learning how to do each of these tasks, however, it is helpful to consider the tasks independently.

### 1. Attention-Focusing

You need to track your attention whenever you are engaged in learning, regardless of whether you are reading a text or participating in a classroom experience. Unless you successfully focus your attention on the learning task, the new learning never even reaches your short-term memory.

Almost all of us have had the experience of engaging in pseudo-studying. Pseudo-studying is an activity that looks like studying from the outside, but actually involves no learning. For example, many of us have had the experience of reading a page in a textbook over and over again without taking in any information, or we have spent hours in the library supposedly studying with a friend, but actually devoting most of the time to socializing. In college, such wastes of time are not always problematic; in law school, however, frequent pseudo-studying results in poor performance.

Pseudo-studying is usually a result of poor attention-monitoring which is caused by boredom, fatigue or self-doubt. Expert learners do not, therefore, allow themselves to be distracted by these things. They use one or more of the following techniques to focus their attention:

- Follow each step of a procedure, in order, checking off each step as they go;
- Verbalize (out loud) what they are about to do;

- Develop mental images of what they are trying to do as they are doing it;
- Praise themselves as they work.

**PAUSE. THINK. ACT.** Why do these techniques help learners focus their attention? Which techniques have you used in the past? Why did they work for you?

### 2. Implementation

This part of the performance phase involves actually performing the learning tasks. Later sections of the book describe the learning strategies most helpful to law students, explains how to perform them, and identifies the strengths, weaknesses and uses of the strategies. At this stage of your study of SRL, you simply need to be aware that this part of the performance phase involves performing those activities.

### 3. Self-Monitoring

In the context of the performance phase, the most significant distinction between novice learners and their expert peers is that the experts more closely and more accurately self-monitor their learning. Expert learners self-monitor five things:

1) Comprehension
2) Efficiency
3) Environment
4) Help-seeking, and
5) Attention

*Monitoring Comprehension.* Expert students can tell when they are getting it and when they are not. They use this information to alter their approaches before they get poor grades. Many naïve learners, in contrast, overestimate their understanding and therefore fail to study as thoroughly as they need to study. In law school, there may be little or no feedback—therefore, you will need to find ways to test for understanding (such as supplemental sources and practice materials). One way to do this is to find a source which requires you to commit to an answer, and then allows you to evaluate your choice by comparing it with a correct answer.

*Monitoring Efficiency.* Evaluate how long you have been studying and how much effort that studying is requiring. Weigh those two factors against the importance of the learning task. Streamline activities when it is appropriate to do so, alter your strategies to make your process more effective, and prepare yourself for the time and effort certain difficult tasks will require. This is an important step in effectively managing your time.

*Monitoring Environmental Strategies.* Pay attention to *where* you are studying, *when* you are studying (including the time taken for study breaks) and *with whom* you are studying. Expert learners make sure that they actually study when they had planned to study, that they take scheduled breaks to allow themselves spaced learning experiences, that the location they have chosen to study facilitates their learning and that their study partners enhance their learning.

*Help-Seeking.* Difficulties arise for all learners in all educational settings. Identify your comprehension difficulties and get the help you need from instructors and peers. Expert learners keep asking different peers and instructors until they are sure they understand. Some peers and even some teachers are better than others in providing such help; expert learners find out who is good at helping and act accordingly.

*Monitoring Attention.* Unfocused study is, generally, a waste of time because it does not produce learning. Make sure you are able to pay attention (e.g., not too tired, do not need a study break, are not studying in a location which is distracting).

---

**ENGAGE.** Review the steps for Creating Calendars that Work, from earlier in this chapter. Can you identify the self-monitoring tasks?

---

Once students become expert at self-monitoring, much of the monitoring occurs offline (on a less conscious level). Expert self-regulated learners are always vigilant about their comprehension and their efficiency, as a result, self-monitoring requires less conscious effort.

The monitoring process often causes expert learners to change or modify their approaches and techniques during the learning process. Expert learners do not merely observe their learning; they evaluate it with a purpose in mind—achieving their learning goals. Consequently, expert learners change their approaches whenever their self-monitoring reveals that those approaches are not working.

---

**PAUSE. THINK. ACT.** Recall a learning experience that did not go as well as you would have liked. Was there a point in time before you received your grade when you knew things were not going well?

If "yes," how did you know? Why were you unable to address the issue(s) productively?

If "no," why do you think you were unaware that you were having a learning difficulty?

---

## Step Four: Pause. Think. Act. The Reflection Phase

Expert learners know the value of stopping to think about what they have done. Novices may skip this stage entirely, or devote very little time or energy to the task. Stop for a moment and reflect on this: Have you been devoting sufficient time to the "Pause. Think. Act." boxes throughout this chapter? Have you actually thought about and answered each of the questions to the best of your ability? Have you thought about the implications of your answers both for your future learning and law school success? If your answer is "no," ask yourself why you ignored or under-performed on the reflection phase—and whether that is something you should continue doing. If your answer is "yes," congratulations—you have already demonstrated a willingness to use reflective learning skills—skills that will be critical to your future success.

> *The reflection phase of the cycle guides you as to future learning. When you reflect on what you did and how effective it was, it helps you plan and improve future learning activities.*

The reflection phase plays a large role in determining the success or failure of future learning. During the self-reflection phase, expert learners evaluate their learning outcomes and figure out the causes of those outcomes. Thus, the reflection phase reinforces expert learners' sense that learning is a matter of planning, strategic choice and persistence—rather than a matter of innate ability.

Students only really become expert learners when they take full control over their own learning process, devising learning strategies that make sense for their particular set of preferences and understandings. Like the forethought phase, it is easy to contemplate omitting the reflection phase but it is not wise to do so. Although the learning task is over at this point, and you may already be anticipating the next learning task and want to move on, failing to reflect usually equates to failing to improve.

In the reflection phase you analyze:

- what you did
- how you did it
- how well you did it
- why you did as well as you did
- how you feel about how you did, and
- how you will do things even better in the future

This phase includes four facets:

1. **Self-evaluation,**
2. **Attribution,**
3. **Reaction, and**
4. **Adaptation**

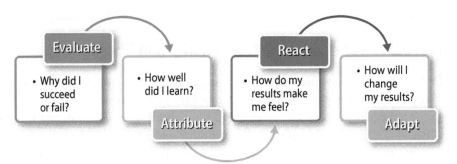

## 1. Self-Evaluation

One of the easiest ways to distinguish expert learners from novices is their efforts at self-evaluation. Expert learners evaluate how they are doing, immediately after they have completed their learning activities, and they do it accurately. There are some key differences between expert learners' and novice learners' self-evaluation skills. For example:

| Expert learners: | Novice learners: |
| --- | --- |
| • Frequently evaluate their learning, | • Seldom evaluate their learning, |
| • in multiple ways, | • use only one way, |
| • objectively, and | • subjectively, and |
| • according to explicit criteria | • not according to explicit criteria |

These differences influence all of the other steps of the reflection phase, enhancing the expert learners' sense of empowerment, as they figure out the causes of their successes and failures, celebrate their successes, and determine how to correct any failures. Sadly, the differences also explain the novice learners' feelings of discouragement and powerlessness.

Expert learners assess their learning experiences in four ways:

(1) *internally*, on their own;
(2) *externally*, through formal or self-imposed assessment events;
(3) for *accuracy*, by comparing their predicted outcomes with their actual outcomes; and
(4) for *efficiency*—by weighing their outcomes against their goals and the time and effort the learning required.

**After learning new material, you should assess yourself using the same criteria.**

**You can do so by following these steps:**

(1) Internal Evaluation

> **PAUSE. THINK. ACT.** Ask yourself: How Well Do I Think I Learned? Did I achieve my learning goals? Have I mastered the material?

This evaluation is really the only one possible in real world contexts, such as the practice of law, making it particularly crucial that you learn to accurately evaluate your learning. In fact, internal self-evaluation is one of the techniques used by expert practicing attorneys to help them avoid malpractice. Expert attorneys know when they know something and, more importantly, they know when they do not know. This knowledge guides expert practitioners in how they practice law, informing many decisions, such as decisions about which cases to take and which to reject, decisions as to when to ask for help with a client's problem and when to keep struggling to figure it out, and decisions as to when to do more research and when the research process is complete. It requires you to be objective, and honest with yourself.

## (2) External Evaluation

> **PAUSE. THINK. ACT.** Test your knowledge on a practice test or problem. Then ask yourself: How Well Did I Perform?

Expert learners seek out opportunities to test their knowledge. They conduct an external, objective evaluation—so they can hold themselves accountable for what they know and don't know. They take practice tests, for example, whenever it is possible to do so and they request professorial or peer evaluation of their efforts or they evaluate their efforts themselves. Expert learners are the students who choose to take the optional tests and do the optional exercises. Novice learners, in contrast, miss these opportunities or even consciously try to avoid them because they fear poor results, think they are not ready to take such tests, may not see the value in such activities or are overconfident.

As part of this assessment, expert learners know that they need to accurately calibrate their understanding. Experts are more likely to write out their answers, rather than simply think them through—so they can truly assess what they did not know—by comparing their actual answers to the rubric or explanation. They also know being tested on material is a powerful way to enhance their retention of the material—and is a far better way to memorize and store information than simply reading, re-reading or repeating information.

Opportunities for such practice and feedback are available from many different sources. Many law schools provide students with copies of past essay exams and answers. In addition, the common law school practice of forming study groups creates opportunities for peer testing and feedback. Finally, students can test themselves using a variety of supplemental sources which contain sample questions and answers, practice multiple choice and short answer problems, and sample hypotheticals.

## (3) Accuracy Evaluation

> **PAUSE. THINK. ACT.** After you perform on a self-test or other test (an external evaluation), compare your performance with your internal evaluation. Ask yourself: how accurately did I predict my assessment results?

Expert learners self-evaluate by reflecting on the accuracy of their internal self-assessment. Because, as explained above, internal self-evaluation is such a crucial skill for practitioners in all fields, expert learners use reflective evaluation to help them fine-tune their self-assessment skills. This is another reason external evaluation is so critical—it allows the learner to compare their internal evaluation with objective criteria from the external assessment. Each time you take a practice test or a graded exam, you have the opportunity for accuracy evaluation—by comparing how you thought you did with how you actually performed and evaluating whether and to what extent your internal evaluation was accurate.

### (4) Efficiency Evaluation

> **PAUSE. THINK. ACT.** Ask yourself: Given my goal and my results, did I spend my time wisely? How did this task help me accomplish my goals? Is this the best way to do that? Should I increase or decrease the amount of time or effort I spend on this task in the future?

At this stage of the self-evaluation process, the learner weighs:

| the degree to which her results suggest she has achieved her goals, and the importance of the activity | vs. | the time and effort she used in implementing her learning strategy, and the time she has available |
|---|---|---|

An optimal set of learning strategies (environmental, motivational and cognitive) not only produces learning, but also is as efficient as possible. Because law students, like everyone else, only have a limited amount of time, they need to assess their learning strategies not only for whether they produced optimal learning but also for whether the strategies caused the student to learn the material as quickly as possible. In this sense, expert learners act as their own efficiency experts.

## 2. Attribution

Having evaluated their performance, expert learners develop explanations for why they performed well or poorly. These explanations are called attributions. Expert learners are much more likely to attribute failures to things they can correct—such as insufficient effort or selecting the wrong learning technique(s). This leads expert learners to try again, and to try harder when they fail. In contrast, novice learners are more likely to attribute their failures to a lack of ability and, therefore, are more likely to give up and stop trying.

As you may have guessed, attributions are important to law school success because they greatly influence persistence. Some learning tasks, particularly tasks that involve the development of high-level intellectual skills (such as legal analysis) require many SRL cycles to develop mastery. Like learning to play a sport or a musical instrument, learning to perform legal analysis often involves multiple instances of trial and error, a good deal of struggle, and very often, failure. Because novices believe successes and failures are caused by ability, they are likely to give up and stop trying if they fail to learn on the first try. In contrast, expert learners, who recognize that their failures are due to correctable causes, and who expect that some learning tasks will require many SRL cycles, persevere, and eventually succeed.

### *Attribution Style — Once Again, Mindset Matters*

As you can see, how you view your own successes and failures is critical to your success. Attributing success or failure to ability, rather than effort, does not serve you well. It can lead you to give up or to fail to study or to be over-confident if you do not believe great effort is a necessary part of success. On the other hand, understanding that effort and persistence is what ultimately leads to mastery and success helps to create a cycle of positive and dedicated learning, and ultimately, positive results.

Take a minute to think about your attribution style. Think about how you react when you perform poorly. Answer the following questions:

1.  When you experience failure do you typically think:
    a.  This is difficult, but it will get better with practice; or
    b.  I am never going to be good at this.

2.  When you receive a really bad grade, or negative feedback, do you typically view the failure as being:
    a.  About the specific problem (e.g., I need to work on my grammar and spelling); or
    b.  About something beyond the assignment (e.g., I am not a good writer).

3.  If you've given something your very best effort, and you still do not succeed, which are you more likely to think:
    a.  I still am not getting it, but this is fixable with some additional effort and feedback; or
    b.  I am just not good at this and never will be, I'll try something else.

For each question, the "a" answer is an example of an optimistic attribution style, which is characterized by statements that view failures as temporary, specific to the context, and fixable with further effort. They evidence hopefulness—a belief that if you persist you will improve. Students who adapt this style are more likely to persist when things are difficult. They are most likely to be or to become expert learners. The "b" answer for each question is an example of a pessimistic attribution style which is characterized by statements that view failures as permanent, pervasive (bigger than they actually are) and personal (the result of some unfixable ability related problem). Students who exhibit this style are likely to believe that even with additional effort, the results will not change—so they do not persist. They are not likely to be or to become expert learners.

The good news is that you can alter your attribution style. There is no real magic to making attributions. It is merely a question of self-awareness and attitude. You have to be aware of how you think and feel, and choose to frame your thoughts so that you adopt an optimistic attribution style.

### Attribution Accuracy

Successful learning also requires that you learn to make accurate attributions, because accuracy helps ensure that future learning efforts succeed. The keys to making accurate attributions are reflection and brainstorming.

Give yourself time to reflect on your just-completed learning process. When you reflect: re-trace your learning process from beginning to end, looking for errors and inefficiencies; consider the difficulty of the learning task and whether you did not learn simply because the task requires cycling through several or even many attempts to learn.

Brainstorm the possibilities. Human error is just as much a part of the learning process as it is of anything else in life. Each phase of the SRL cycle involves possibilities for miscalculation. Also, some failures to learn are inevitable given the nature of the learning task.

Review your process with a checklist of possible causes in mind. Here is one such checklist:

**Possible problems in the forethought phase**
- Did not set appropriate goal
  - Did not set any goal
  - Goal did not follow guidelines
- Incorrectly classified the task
- Did not invoke self-efficacy
- Did not develop interest/did not determine why I needed to learn the material
- Poor motivational strategy choices (could not stay motivated because: _____)
- Poor environmental choices
  - bad location
  - timing
  - too long without break
  - poor choice of study partners
  - other _____
- Poor cognitive strategy choices

**Possible problems in the performance phase**
- Incorrect use of strategies
- Did not maintain focused attention
- Did not self-monitor (failed to spot problems during the learning process)
- Did not persist

**Possible problems in the reflection phase**
- Did not pursue opportunities for self-assessment
  - Did not take advantage of opportunity for practice and feedback

      ◦ Did not create opportunity for practice and feedback
      ◦ Did not assess learning using any objective criteria
    • Incorrectly assessed how well I learned
      ◦ Did not assess learning using objective criteria

In addition to the checklist, be sure to take time to think about why you made the choices you made—and what you will do differently in the future.

### 3. Reaction

Reactions are the emotional feelings you have in response to your results and your attributions. Expert learners generally feel better about themselves as learners, even when they encounter learning difficulties, and therefore are more likely to persist until they succeed.

Since expert learners typically attribute failures to correctable causes, and not to a lack of ability, they do not have a negative self-reaction when they experience failure. Expert learners retain their sense of self-efficacy, regardless of their outcomes. Conversely, novice learners perceive failures to learn as personal defeats, as saying something about their intelligence or capacity to learn—which produces negative emotions, including feelings of incompetence. Novice learners' self-efficacy depends on positive outcomes and therefore is considerably more vulnerable—it essentially disappears when inevitable learning failures occur. Since expert learners believe the causes of poor learning outcomes are fixable with further effort, they tend to perceive themselves as able and competent, whereas novice learners, who believe poor learning outcomes are the result of unfixable, personal issues, often do not.

### 4. Adaptation

The adaptation step is where you identify solutions and make adjustments for future learning. It is much easier to make learners aware of the need to engage in this process than to explain how to do it. Ultimately, you are the expert in your own learning. You are in the best position to figure out the causes and the solutions for your failures to learn, or inefficiencies in the learning process. There are, however, three things you should remember:

1. Measure your performance by how well you have achieved your own learning goals—not by what others have achieved.

2. Keep what is working—and change what isn't. In many instances, there is no failure to learn at all and therefore no need for adaptation. In others, you will not have fallen very far short of your learning goals and therefore a major overhaul is unnecessary. If the learning deficiency is a small one, only a small adjustment is appropriate. In still other situations, the issue is one of efficiency, not effectiveness, and again only small adjustments may be in order.

3. Excellence is a worthy aspiration, but perfection is not. Sometimes a desire to be perfect can keep you from making any gains at all or can slow down your progress by making you inefficient. Rather than changing every aspect of the

learning process after a failure, expert learners know that they may need several SRL cycles to master a difficult learning task, so unless the whole process went wrong from the outset, they make small adjustments and plan to keep adjusting as they develop more information from their practice.

## Step Five: Continuing the Cycle — On to the Next Forethought Phase

Learning, whether it is self-regulated or not, requires persistence, thoughtfulness and a high degree of motivation. Expert learners possess this motivation, because they know they will eventually learn. As they cycle through the reflection phase, they anticipate the forethought phase, developing a belief that with further effort they will succeed and making strategic plans that will influence how they go about the performance phase. The degree to which students engage in self-regulated learning determines, ultimately, not only whether learning occurs, but also whether the learner enjoys the process and sees the learning experience as a positive or a negative one. SRL allows students to command their own learning and to ensure that they achieve the goals that led them to enter the academic enterprise in the first place.

---

**PAUSE. THINK. ACT.**
1. What aspects of the SRL cycle make sense to you? Why? (What have you observed in your life as a student that makes you believe that these aspects will work for your law school studies?)
2. What aspects of the SRL cycle do not make sense to you? Why? (What have you observed in your life as a student that makes you believe that these aspects will not work for your law school studies?)
3. Is there anything you can do differently to improve your ability to learn and succeed in law school? How do you plan to implement these changes?

---

# Chapter 3

# Understanding Your Personal Style

Expert learners know themselves well. They know how to learn. They know what strategies work best to produce learning. They know how they *personally* learn best and how they prefer to learn.

Your learning style and personality type are significant considerations in evaluating your strategy options. Stop for a moment and try this: cross your arms. Fold them in front of you as if you intend to signal you don't like what you are hearing. Wait for a moment. Now cross them the other way. Did that feel strange? Was it awkward to try crossing them differently? Stop and think about what this means. You probably have an arm crossing preference. One way feels more comfortable than the other. All things being equal you would probably prefer to cross your arms in the way that feels more comfortable.

Learning preferences are similar. We all have ways of learning, interacting with others, and taking in information that feel comfortable for us. It doesn't mean we can't use other strategies (or cross our arms a different way); it just means that all things being equal, we prefer to use the strategies that are most comfortable. And often this is exactly what we should do—because it is most efficient. For example, if you find you retain information best when you have an example of how a concept works, you should record and remember, or even create examples of concepts to help you retain your learning. On the other hand, sometimes your preferences and comfort zones can lead you to select strategies that would be unproductive or inefficient—and in those instances, you will need to use a different method, one that may not feel as comfortable, but that is a better fit for the circumstances. For example, you may prefer to learn by hearing, but sometimes information is only provided in a written format, and there is no opportunity to read it out loud. In such cases, you will need to adapt—to cross your arms differently. Also, it is a good idea to learn information using more than one method (both "with type" and "against type"), because it produces the best learning. When you learn using more than one method, it creates new "paths" to the information—making it easier for you to retrieve it in different contexts and in stressful situations, like during law school exams, when you may feel "stuck" or overwhelmed.

Personality types and learning styles do not describe students' strengths or weaknesses in terms of whether they will succeed as learners, especially because no particular type or style is better or worse for learning anything. Law school itself involves activities that meet the preferences of most people, regardless of their learning style.

Moreover, results from such assessments produce, at most, a set of suggestions or ideas; they give students guidance in their preferences, not mandates for how they should go about being students. In other words, a particular personality type or learning style is not a box that limits students to particular approaches but, rather, a guide that points students towards particular approaches that, all things being equal, may increase a student's efficiency and enjoyment.

# Personality Types: An Introduction

Psychologists use the term **personality type** to describe the basic psychological, social and perceptual characteristics that a person brings to the learning environment. Personality typing has been the subject of literally hundreds of studies. There are many tests designed to classify people's personality types, most of which are based, in large or small part, on the Myers-Briggs Type Indicator (MBTI). These tests classify you according to four matched sets of preferences:

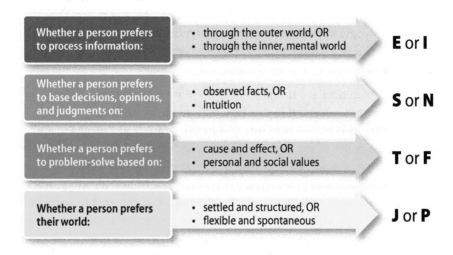

These characteristics give insights into a student's core approaches to learning. It is important to remember that no person falls into any classification entirely or prefers everything to be structured only one way. These classifications indicate preferences, not exclusive categories. Here's a bit more information about these categories.

## Information Processing: E and I

The first classification deals with how you process new information, and where you prefer to focus your attention in the learning process. You are classified as an extrovert (E) or as an introvert (I). Extroverts prefer to think aloud, enjoy projects more than tests and enjoy engaging in peer teaching. They prefer action and are goal-oriented and innovative. Introverts are reflective and observational. They enjoy abstract reasoning and time for reflection, and they require time to think before speaking.

## Problem Solving: S or N

The second classification deals with how you approach solving a problem, how you prefer to acquire information, how you find out information about the world around you. You are classified either as sensing (S) or intuitive (N). Sensing people prefer to work with observable facts within what is given. They are realistic and practical and can handle and work with large numbers of facts. Intuitive people tend to look at the big picture and try to grasp the essential patterns and concepts, but are impatient with details. They enjoy complexity and follow their inspirations, regardless of data.

## Forming Opinions and Drawing Conclusions: T or F

The third classification deals with how you make decisions, reach conclusions and form opinions. You are classified as either thinking (T) or feeling (F). Persons who rely on a thinking approach strive to make decisions objectively; they like to weigh evidence, seek objective truth and discover the logic of things. People who rely on a feeling approach base their decisions on their values or the values of others. While feeling people tend to be sympathetic and kind in dealing with people, they do not base their decisions on emotions. Feeling people base their decisions on whether the chosen result is consistent with their values.

## Structuring the "Outside" World: J or P

The fourth and final classification deals with how you interact with the outside world or bring structure to your life. You are classified as either focused on judgment (J) or as focused on perception (P). People who prefer a judging approach prefer their lives to be planned, organized and ordered. They like to make decisions, complete projects and regulate and control their lives. Persons who are focused on perception enjoy living flexibly and spontaneously. They like to adjust their goals and plans "on the fly" and prefer general parameters to rules.

### Implications for Learning

Each of these categories has implications for learning. For example, sensing students should strive to find, through their peers, their instructors or supplemental materials, both concrete examples of and the practical implications of the concepts they are learning. They should strive to find the procedural aspects of the skills they are learning and to find multiple opportunities for drill and practice. Students who are intuitive need to force themselves to attend to facts and details and to focus in class. In addition, they need to force themselves to develop the rationales for their insights.

As you can see, your four category type can help you identify strengths and weaknesses in your learning process. Additionally, knowing your study partner's or study groups' type(s) and understanding the strengths and weaknesses of those types can help you as well. For example, if your group is composed of entire of one type — for example you are all sensing — you may all have the same weaknesses. By picking study partners with different types, you allow yourselves to see things from a different perspective — and catch things you might otherwise miss. By understanding how each person's type impacts their study, you can also understand how to help the group (and you) make the most of each interaction.

Now that you understand the basics of the typologies, you are ready to take an MBTI test. There are many free online versions of the MBTI-type test. Two such websites are: http://www.humanmetrics.com/cgi-win/JTypes1.htm and http://www.personalitytype.com/quiz.html. At the conclusion of the test you will be given a four-letter code that reflects your classification for each pair described above; you will also be given an indication of the strength of those classifications. Both websites also provide some helpful information about the implications of your personality type.

---

**PAUSE. THINK. ACT.** Using one of the above links, take the test. Read about the implications of your type. Find your four-letter personality type on the list below and read the additional information. Ask yourself: How might my personality type influence how I go about studying law?

---

Below is some information about learning preferences according to the corresponding four-letter code. This is a very brief look at the potential strengths and weakness for law school studying of each four-letter classification. For a detailed discussion of the implications of your type on law school studying, the book *Juris Types*, by Don and Marty Peters, is an excellent source.

## ISTJ

ISTJs possess some important strengths for their law school studies. They are serious about their studies, and get their work done. They do their work accurately and methodically and are thoughtful. Such discipline and thoughtfulness are keys to success in law school because the workload is so demanding. ISTJs tend to analyze legal issues logically and systematically and to use the evidence described in fact patterns well. They are less likely to become stressed during examinations.

ISTJs, however, need to guard against focusing so hard at mastering each of the trees of legal subjects (each of the rules of law) that they lose sight of the forest (the big picture of the area of law they are learning). They also need to open themselves up to change; all learning involves change and, therefore, unless inhibited, ISTJs tendency to resist change may inhibit their development of lawyering skills. In working with other students on projects and in study groups, ISTJs need to force themselves to listen to peers who have more creative and innovative ideas and to express their appreciation for the people with whom they are working rather than keeping such feelings to themselves. On examinations, they need to resist their inclination to see only one side of issues.

## ISTP

ISTPs also possess analytical and practical strengths that are likely to prove helpful with their law school studies and tests. They tend to be logical and fact-focused, a crucial pair of skills on law school exams. They also are seldom procrastinators and therefore are likely to timely complete all of their law school work. Likewise, ISTPs are often efficient, in the sense that they strive to find the best way of limiting the amount of effort required for each task. They are curious, and they are effective at finding the core of things.

ISTPs' search for efficiency, though, may lead them to cut necessary corners. They need to force themselves to carefully plan their studies and law school assignments and then to stick to that plan. Because ISTPs tend to get bored easily, they need to commit themselves to peers, such as members of their study groups, to make sure they complete the necessary work. Finally, ISTPs need to open up to their peers and professors, especially if and when they are struggling with their law school studies (and most law students do struggle at times), or they may not get the help they need.

## ISFJ

ISFJs possess great common sense, focus well on facts and have great memories for the many nitty-gritty details of some bodies of law. All of these skills are helpful on law school exams, particularly law school multiple-choice tests. ISFJs are hard working and diligent, are great planners and follow-through on their plans, helpful attributes given the workload demands of law school. They also generally work well in groups because they tend to be helpful and warm.

They are risks, however, in being an ISFJ law student. ISFJs need to budget extra time for tasks because they are likely to spend a lot of time on planning and do each task so meticulously. ISFJs need to carefully select their study partners because they sometimes get taken advantage of and too often try to rescue others in trouble. They also have a tendency to be too literal and, consequently, to miss subtleties. Finally, they need to force themselves to think more globally on assignments and essay exams and, by doing so, develop the less obvious approaches and arguments.

## ISFP

ISFPs make good study group members because they are sensitive to others, patient and flexible. They are interested and enthusiastic learners and are excellent at enjoying the learning moment for itself. For this reason, they usually set good short-term learning goals, plan strategies for achieving those goals and achieve them in one setting. They tend to be very hard workers. They have particular skills in adaptation and improvisation, both of which are excellent attributes for law students, almost all of whom by necessity develop new ways of learning.

ISFPs need to guard against their tendency to see feedback as discouragement rather than as a tool for getting better. On law school essay exams and papers, they need to make sure they analyze objectively and with skepticism. A key to law school success for ISFPs is planning and organizing their study time and study resources.

## INTJ

INTJ's natural inclination towards perfectionism is their gift (and their curse, as explained below). It is a gift, because it drives them to mastery and causes them to take full responsibility for their own success, two critical attributes of successful law students. So much of traditional law school instruction requires students to self-teach; INTJs are well equipped for these demands. INTJs are great at developing original legal arguments and ideas and learn legal theory readily. They have insight and vision and are very energetic.

INTJ's perfectionism is their curse, because perfection in learning endeavors as difficult as law school is nearly impossible, and, as a result, there is some risk INTJs will be too hard on themselves and their law school peers. Another issue is that INTJs tend to miss details and ignore common sense when either conflicts with their original ideas. As a result, on law school exams, they may develop and make an original argument at the expense of making the obvious, necessary and sometimes better argument. They also tend to miss out on the benefits of learning from others, and, given their inclination towards single-mindedness, the choice to work alone is likely to interfere with their success. Finally, when they do work in groups, to be productive, contributing members, INTJs need to respect the feelings of others, even if they regard those feelings as illogical.

## INTP

INTPs are intellectual, logical and, at times, creative at a brilliant level. These are great attributes for a law student. INTPs also are precise and insist upon logic. They enjoy the type of hairsplitting that is sometimes necessary to correctly analyze legal issues. They work well independently. INTPs' skill in finding flaws in arguments and ideas is an excellent tool for reading court opinions and self-editing their law school essays and papers.

On the other hand, INTPs tend to be impatient with details and sometimes lack follow-through; they may not finish all of their law school assignments, class preparation or exam studying. They have a tendency to get stuck on small flaws and not finish what they have started; as a result, their grades suffer, because deadlines in law school tend to be enforced through severe penalties. Finally, because some of INTPs' ideas are complex, they sometimes have trouble communicating them to others; because law school essays and papers succeed only to the extent readers can follow the argument, INTPs need to be careful to explain all the steps of their reasoning.

## INFJ

INFJs possess strengths that, when harnessed, can help them succeed in law school. They tend to be intense, committed and idealistic. They are original thinkers and delve deeply into situations, making it easier for them to identify difficult legal issues and develop more in-depth arguments on law school exams and papers. They make good leaders and work well on group projects.

INFJs' focus, however, can tend to develop into an unhelpful single mindedness. On law school examinations, they need to make sure they attend to all the facts and not just those that support their theories. They need to make sure they take care of the routine tasks of law school and not just the activities they find stimulating. They need to make sure they analyze everything objectively. They need to be open to feedback and avoid hypersensitivity.

## INFP

People who are INFPs possess excellent long-range vision, and they have many skills necessary to manage their law school workload: flexibility, adaptability and commitment to their long-term goals. They communicate well in writing and prefer that mode. They can be very convincing, a trait helpful in nearly all law school writing.

INFPs need to make sure they are being logical and fact driven when taking law school exams. They tend to procrastinate the operational aspects of projects, such as law school papers, and they spend too much time refining and polishing their ideas and not enough time actually researching, writing, and editing. Because they tend to be perfectionists and self-critical, INFPs need to guard against feelings of inadequacy, remain open to feedback and avoid translating failures in learning, which are a normal part of law school, into negatives.

## ESTJ

ESTJs possess many skills that are readily adaptable to law school studies. Their conscientiousness, enjoyment of structure, and strong memorization and organizational skills ensure they finish their law school projects on time and done well. They are logical, objective and analytical, and, therefore, in law school, they quickly develop legal reasoning skills.

ESTJs are less comfortable with and struggle more to understand legal theory. They have a tendency towards being rigid and have trouble seeing gray areas, which, given the difficult and ambiguous legal problems on law school exams and assigned as law school papers, is a significant problem. By becoming more adaptable and listening to others' ideas (particularly the ideas of people who are very different from them), they can gain insights they might have had trouble seeing on their own and thereby harness their skills, limit their potential issues and excel in law school.

## ESTP

ESTPs have particular skill in understanding underlying principles, making it easier for them to understand legal rules and their application. They are effective in group settings, because they tend to be outgoing and diplomatic. They do well with high stress situations, like law school, because they are easy-going and realistic. They also pay attention to details, a helpful trait for a detail-oriented field like law. Finally, they tend to be high-energy people.

ESTPs must discipline themselves into planning; their tendency to move from putting out the fire on one task to putting out the fire on another task simply will not work in law school and will be even less effective on the bar exam. They need to budget their time, limit their commitments or risk being overrun and overwhelmed by the demands of law school. Finally, they need to discipline themselves to complete the boring details. In short, for ESTPs, law school success is all about time management, goal setting and self-discipline.

## ESFJ

ESFJs, being people persons, both work well in law school study groups and feel a strong need to participate in them. Their study group peers appreciate their conscientiousness and graciousness, and the ESFJs satisfy their craving for connection and relationships in the context of law school, which tends to be a competitive and individualistic environment. ESFJs are great at identifying and remembering facts and are very well organized, two crucial traits for law school success.

ESFJs tend to place others ahead of themselves, an extremely risky behavior in law school, where time and energy are such precious commodities. They also must force themselves to overcome their natural reluctance to ask for help when they need it and to be open to constructive criticism. Finally, they need to slow themselves down from time-to-time to make sure they have analyzed legal problems fully and from all angles; in particular, they should try to look for new or different ways of doing things.

## ESFP

ESFPs are realistic, have good common sense and are good observers. They adapt well to new environments, so their transition to the law school world is not as difficult as it is for some of their peers. Because they get along well with others, they make good group members. They also are persuasive, an important skill for most law school courses, and they are excellent at details.

ESFPs, however, have difficulty disciplining themselves to the workload demands of law school. They do well when they use organizational and time management strategies to help them set goals and achieve them. By doing so, ESFPs can strike an appropriate balance between work and play and between social concerns and educational needs. When they do not discipline themselves, on the other hand, ESFPs are at risk for not finishing tasks, or even law school itself. ESFPs learn best from hands-on experiences and therefore should strive to find the practical applications of what they are learning in their first-year coursework and seek out clinical and other real-world learning experiences later in law school.

## ENTJ

ENTJs make great leaders of study groups—they have lots of vision, are great long-term planners and organize people very well. They are logical and driven; consequently, both legal reasoning and the workload necessary to develop the skill come naturally to them. They work efficiently, research well and enjoy theory, truth and mastery.

Because ENTJs are so focused, they sometimes move too quickly and miss information. Their leadership inclinations can be problematic for group projects, because they sometimes ignore the input of others. They need to force themselves to seek feedback and then force themselves to learn from it. Thus, for ENTJs, their rule of thumb should be, "don't miss out on information."

## ENTP

ENTPs do not shy away from the challenges of law school; rather, they enjoy them. They are enthusiastic learners and enjoy new ideas and multiple possibilities, which law professors love to introduce regularly into class discussions. Of all their skills, ENTPs' analytical skills, their ability to recognize flaws in arguments readily and to intuit arguments on both sides of issues, most directly translates to law school success.

ENTPs do worse with the mundane aspects of law school. They have a hard time with the details, the day-to-day labor, and they ignore the easy and best way to do things because they prefer innovation for its own sake. They are more likely to skip the preparation so they can go right to the aspect of a task that interests them. Unfortunately, in law school, the details and the sweat matter as much as the ideas, so ENTPs must discipline themselves.

## ENFJ

ENFJs have the natural organizational skills and ability to see beyond the obvious that are typical of successful law students. They also possess the ability to be consistently productive and responsible about their work, which enables them to finish their work in law school and do it well. They are people lovers and value relationships, making them cooperative study group members. They also read people well.

ENFJs' people focus can be their undoing in law school. They sometimes become overworked or disillusioned when things are not working well. They do not always address their own needs and, as a result, their studies may suffer. They need to be careful not to make assumptions and to make sure they have and understand all the facts. They also need to force themselves to learn from criticism rather than becoming upset by it.

### ENFP

ENFPs possess excellent pattern recognition skills and therefore have the potential to be excellent at identifying legal issues, both on exams and in law practice. They also are original thinkers and notice details better than most, both of which are critical to success on law school exams. They also are sensitive, adaptive and resourceful.

ENFPs, however, often lose interest or focus once they have hatched their original idea. They need to develop time management and organizational skills to make sure they take care of everything they need to do to ready themselves for exams and to write and edit their law school papers. They greatly need to focus on follow-through, because it does not come naturally to them. They prefer to work with others and benefit greatly from working with people who possess better discipline and attention to the details involved in finishing any project, even if that project is getting ready for an examination.

If you are interested in learning more about the implications of your four-letter code, there are numerous websites from which you can learn more about your type, including the following:

http://typelogic.com/
http:///knowyourtype.com/intro.html
http://www.wncc.nevada.edu/studentservices/counseling/styles_types/2_
16_personality_types.html
http://www.capt.org/Using_Type/Workplace.cfm

## Learning Styles: An Introduction

Learning style refers to your preferences in how you acquire new learning. There are numerous learning style classifications, none of which yet has prevalence among educators. While knowing your learning preferences can assist you in understanding how you prefer to absorb and assimilate information, it is not a mandate for how you should learn. More importantly, no particular learning style is more or less conducive to success.

There are a number of different inventories for classifying learning styles. For example, one set of classifications, known as VARK, which refers to four categories of learning styles: Visual, Aural, Read/write and Kinesthetic, classifies absorption preferences (how you prefer to "take in" or absorb information). In other words, some people enjoy and absorb information best from graphic images, some from reading text and writing about what they are learning, some from hearing the information, and some from practical examples and experiences. There is also a fifth learning style, multi-modal, meaning the student learns readily in several of the modes. Here is a "snapshot" of each style:

- **Visual learners** prefer to "see" concepts, they like all forms of graphic organizers, including flowcharts, concept maps, hierarchy charts and comparison charts. They need to translate written and spoken information into graphic form and then translate their graphics into the written and spoken word.

- **Aural learners** (also known as "auditory learners") prefer to learn from hearing. They like to hear their instructors, their peers and even themselves speak. In fact, they often must read written materials aloud to remember them. They also like to participate in group activities in which group members discuss what they have been learning.

- **Read/write learners** prefer the printed word. They like to learn from text, including text books and other written materials and to express themselves in writing as well.

- **Kinesthetic learners** learn best through experience, not only by touching and feeling, but also through the experience of applying what they are learning about, which can include actual, exemplary or simulated experience. They also like to learn through movement.

- **Multi-modal learners** may prefer two, three or even all four strategies. There is even some evidence that multi-modal learners prefer using multiple strategies for each learning experience.

The VARK website, located at: http://www.vark-learn.com includes the online assessment instrument on which these materials are based. The site also includes additional information about the four categories, and printable "help sheets" which offer suggestions as to how your particular learning style might influence your approach to studying.

Law school requires you to absorb an enormous amount of information. More importantly you must be able to store and recall that information long after your exams are over—for the bar exam, and for law practice. For this reason, you will want to know your preferences for absorbing information—and you will want to be aware of those preferences so that you can vary your strategies (work against "type").

---

**PAUSE. THINK. ACT.** Go to http://www.vark-learn.com. Take the online assessment to determine your absorption preferences. Once you have identified your preference, read the "help sheets" then ask yourself: What have I learned about my learning preferences? How might my learning preferences influence how I go about studying law?

There are a number of other inventories, all of which help learners to understand preferences. Below is a list of some of those inventories:

- http://www.metamath.com/lsweb/fourls.htm (uses categories identical to the VARK categories in all ways other than their labels, also provides some excellent study recommendations)

- http://www.learning-styles-online.com/overview/ (discusses seven different learning styles and provides links for inventory and strategies)

- http://facultyweb.cortland.edu/andersmd/learning/Kolb.htm (assigns a student to one of four learning style categories depending on whether the student is more oriented towards feeling or thinking and whether she is more comfortable doing something new on her own or watching someone else do it first)

- http://www.nwlink.com/~donclark/hrd/styles.html#kolb (addresses Kolb's ideas as well as all the other theories addressed above and more)

# Part II

# Becoming an Expert Law Student

# Chapter 4

# Law School Expectations

To be in a position to apply expert learning principles to your legal education, you first need to know what you can expect to encounter in law school. In law school, professor expectations of students are high. Students who take command over their own education, who act upon their learning rather than passively receiving it, excel. In many respects, your only choice is whether to take control over your learning or to perform far below your capability.

Law school teaching, testing and feedback methods are dramatically different from the methods you have encountered so far in your academic career. In this section, you will learn about those methods as well as how to best succeed in the law school environment by developing critical class preparation, study and exam taking skills.

## Law School Basics — The Goals of Legal Education

During law school you will be expected to:

- acquire enormous amounts of knowledge;
- demonstrate your skill in applying that knowledge;
- develop proficiency in using those skills; and
- develop your professional identity.

### Acquiring Knowledge in Law School

What you need to know at this early stage of your legal education is that law school instruction and testing require you to acquire enormous amounts of knowledge. You need to learn a vast repertoire of new terminology, hundreds of rules of law and case holdings, legal policy and theory (the reasons underlying the rules and holdings), and the mental steps involved in performing a wide variety of skills. You also need to learn how all this information is interrelated. You will be expected to retain this information even after your classes end, because it is information you will need for the bar exam, and for practice.

### Acquiring Skills in Law School

Even if you learn perfectly every bit of information presented to you in your texts and classes, you still may fail to do well in law school. This seeming contradiction is not really a contradiction at all and, in fact, it is the single most important thing you need to know about the goals of legal education.

> *Although knowledge is crucial to success in law school, the goal of legal education is to teach you skills. You must be able to apply the knowledge you acquire, and you must be able to do it effectively, in writing.*

This point is crucial and often overlooked by new law students. Almost every law school professor will tell you that every year there are students who are shocked at the low grades they receive. Students will usually say something like, "But I understood the material," or "I knew the law cold." These students understood that they had to assimilate vast amounts of knowledge to succeed in law school. They failed to realize, however, that such knowledge was not enough—it was only the starting point.

Law school requires you to acquire a lot of knowledge, but, for the most part, your exams and papers are not evaluated on whether you have learned it. Rather, law school examinations and papers require you to demonstrate your skills in applying that knowledge to new situations. To understand this relationship between skills and knowledge, forget about law school for a moment. Think about a skill that you have learned, such as playing the piano, performing a sport (such as basketball) or even doing long division. In each instance, knowledge was crucial. In piano, you needed to know, among other things, what the musical notes are and where each note is located on your piano. In basketball, you needed to know all the rules of the game and how the game is played. To do long division, you needed to know what a division problem looks like, each of the steps involved in performing long division, and the order in which you must perform those steps.

In each of these settings, however, such knowledge is not enough to be able to perform the skills. To perform the necessary skills—playing the piano or basketball, or doing long division—you also need to practice performing the skill and obtain feedback on how you were performing. And the skills do not come quickly nor easily. In learning piano, you need to spend endless hours practicing both on your own and while a piano teacher watches, listens and gives feedback on the positioning of hands and fingers, use of the pedals and transitions between notes. To learn to play basketball, you need to devote countless hours practicing your shooting, passing, rebounding and defending both on your own and while a coach watches and gives feedback on the positioning of your hands, arms, feet and eyes, your assessment of what is happening during plays and games, your anticipation of what was about to happen, and the positioning of your body in relation to the other players with whom you were playing. Even long division requires you to practice hundreds of long division problems, both on your own and while a teacher (and/or parent) watches and gives feedback on your computations (the dividing, multiplying and subtracting involved in doing long division), on the extent to which you followed the procedure required to perform long division (e.g., did you remember the correct next step) and on how to check your work for accuracy (such as by multiplying your result by the dividend).

From this discussion, a pattern or set of best practices for acquiring new skills should be evident to you. Acquiring new skills requires you to:

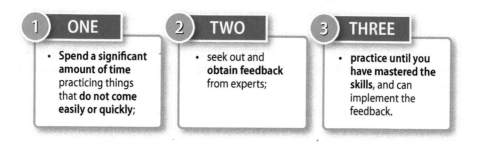

**1) ONE**
- **Spend a significant amount of time** practicing things that **do not come easily or quickly;**

**2) TWO**
- seek out and **obtain feedback** from experts;

**3) THREE**
- **practice until you have mastered the skills,** and can implement the feedback.

In law school, while students must learn many skills, the principal skills they must learn are: legal reasoning (sometimes called "thinking like a lawyer") and expressing that reasoning orally and, predominately, in writing. As you will learn in these materials, these are multi-faceted skills. Like other skills, they require you to possess vast stores of knowledge—but knowledge alone is not enough. You must learn to combine and use knowledge in ways that, while similar to skills you already possess, are unique. For this reason, for most students, law school skills come neither quickly nor easily; they are the product of countless hours of study and practice and require you to make frequent efforts to obtain feedback from your peers and professors, and to calibrate your own understanding—by using supplemental materials that help you accurately self-assess your progress.

## Developing a Professional Identity— Acquiring Values in Law School

Most law schools also strive to teach certain values to their students. The following values are those most commonly emphasized in legal education: (1) professionalism, (2) service to others, to the profession and to the community, (3) sensitivity to the differences among us and (4) lifelong learning.

Law professors try to inculcate these values in students by making them a focus of a course, a class session or a discussion; by modeling those values; by including specific graduation requirements believed to help students develop those values; and by structuring learning activities that allow the students to develop the values on their own. During law school you will reflect on what it means to be a member of the legal profession and you will begin to establish your professional identity— in your interactions with faculty, other students and members of the legal profession.

# The Skills, Knowledge and Values Law Schools Assume You Already Possess

Although law schools strive to teach skills, knowledge and values to their students, they also assume that you already possess certain skills, knowledge and values necessary to make it possible for you to learn what you need to learn in law school. Those skills, knowledge and values fall within five major categories: reading comprehension skills, writing skills, learning skills, knowledge about the legal system and openness to being taught.

- **Reading Comprehension Skills:** Law schools assume that entering law students possess excellent reading comprehension skills. Law students must digest enormous amounts of reading material in short periods of time. The reading material is abstract, complicated, and, sometimes, dry. Much of it includes language that is either unfamiliar to non-lawyers or uses familiar language in unfamiliar ways. For this reason, new law students should devote particular attention to the information in the next chapter about how successful law students and lawyers read and understand court opinions.

  Note that while reading comprehension is an important skill, there is no evidence that very high reading speeds help you do well in law school; however, slower reading skills can be an issue. It is a good idea to know what your reading speed is, and if you read less than 250 words per minute, to consider getting some help. There are a variety of online reading speed assessments, as well as smartphone "apps," which can help you determine your reading speed and, if necessary, improve that speed. Some of these resources are listed in the references at the end of this book.

- **Writing Skills:** Law schools assume students enter law school with excellent writing skills. Specifically, law schools assume that entering students possess excellent knowledge and skill regarding grammar, usage, paragraphing, punctuation, organization and other related writing skills. You therefore need to either possess those skills, or you need to work to enhance your existing skills before you start law school. Fortunately, if you need help in this area there are many resources available to you, some of which are listed in the references at the end of this book.

- **Learning Skills:** Law schools assume that you possess excellent learning skills, including organization, memorization, examination preparation and other learning skills. This book addresses how you will need to develop those learning skills to account for the increased difficulty of learning in law school.

- **Legal Civics:** Law schools assume you possess basic knowledge of legal civics, including knowledge of how cases move through our legal system, court hierarchies, the concepts of precedent and appeal, how statutes become law, the roles lawyers commonly play and the work they do, the state and federal constitutions and their roles within our legal system, and the relationships between federal and state law and between our state and federal court systems. Fortunately, any of the legal civics resources identified in the references at the end of this book should be sufficient to help fill in any gaps in your knowledge in any of these areas.

- **Teachability:** Finally, law schools assume you are teachable. In other words, because law school skills, at least in some respects, are unique and difficult to learn, law students need to be open to feedback, eager to learn, willing to change and unafraid of criticism. The most successful law students do not fear criticism but, instead, welcome it.

---

**PAUSE. THINK. ACT.** Look at the list of skills in the previous section. Rate yourself in each category. Do you already possess these skills? Do you need to acquire or develop any of these skills? Make a plan to address any skills deficiencies.

---

# Taking the Next Step:
# Doing What Expert Law Students Do

Expert law students understand how to prepare before class, engage during class and synthesize what they've learned after class — to prepare themselves for law school exams, and ultimately, the bar exam. The first thing to understand is that these tasks are interrelated. What you do before class impacts how well you are able to engage during class, which impacts how well you will be able to synthesize material after class and then prepare for and succeed on your examinations. Unfortunately, this relationship is not always clear to new law students, at least in part because there is a fairly substantial disconnect between the way most law professors teach and how they test. For this reason, you may not initially understand this relationship or focus your energy on those things that are most productive. This section of the book is intended to help you make the most of the process and direct your attention to the tasks that are most likely to help you succeed.

# Chapter 5

# Starting Off Right: What to Do *Before* Class Begins

If you plan to succeed in law school, it begins with the work you do before you step into the classroom. Many students who were successful in college were able to succeed without having to work very hard and without doing their reading assignments before they attended class. Law school is different. Whereas in college classes, professors devote considerable classroom time to re-explaining the knowledge already explained in the assigned reading and other materials for the course, in law school classes, professors start with the assumption that all the students in the class can acquire knowledge from texts and therefore focus classroom time on student skill development. Law professors generally assume students have acquired most of the knowledge they need to acquire from the text and focus on developing students' lawyering and analytical skills. Consequently, if you fail to prepare for class, you will not be able to follow the class discussion.

Expert law students recognize that they will learn little in class if they show up unprepared, and they understand they must show up prepared, because they must master the material. Unlike most undergraduate courses, where students may have been given "study sheets" or guidance as to what topics would be on their exams, in law school courses, no such guidance is given. Students are expected to master every topic assigned in the course.

Expert law students understand that classroom learning is ultimately a matter of taking control—and such control starts long before the scheduled start time for class. Thus, expert law students set explicit, mastery learning goals, read the assigned materials, brief the assigned cases, review and synthesize their notes from the previous class, plan for the upcoming class, and use practice materials to assess their strengths and weaknesses. In preparation for each class, expert learners plan the structure of their class notes, how they will focus their attention, and the questions they expect to be answered by the class discussion. This chapter covers the steps you should take to engage in each of these tasks—and prepare yourself for class the way expert law students do.

## Step One: Read Like an Expert

When you arrive to class, you must be prepared to discuss and use the material you've been assigned to read—which means you must learn to read for understanding and with an eye toward how your reading will apply to future situations. Also, you must do your reading before each class starts. Remember that law school professors do not spend time telling you about what you should have read. They expect you will show up ready to apply the reading—and class discussion will be focused on teaching you to use what you've read. If you are not prepared, and have not done the reading, you will not be able to follow class discussion, and you will not learn the skills you must master for your exams, and for practice. In law school you will read to:

- develop knowledge and understanding of the subject area you are studying, and the substantive rules of law;
- understand the material well enough to apply what you learn to future disputes;
- develop a new professional vocabulary and an understanding of how the legal system works; and
- develop your ability to think in the way that characterizes legal decision-making.

Most of your reading for law school will consist of appellate court cases—also known as opinions. An opinion is a published document created by a judge, or a set of judges acting together, in which the author describes the nature and facts of the dispute before the court, the parties, the relevant rules of law and precedents (past decided court opinions), the court's decision, and the reasons for the court's decision. Law school texts, frequently called "casebooks," consist mostly of court opinions that the editors of the casebook have selected, edited and organized. A case may be selected for a textbook because it established an important new rule, because its results or reasoning have had particular influence on other courts, because of its notoriety or its interesting facts, because the court's discussion of the issues was particularly insightful, or sometimes because the court's discussion was lacking in insight, poorly reasoned or badly decided. As you read a court opinion, it is often productive to try to figure out why the casebook editor selected the case. Casebook editors seldom include the full text of the cases they use, choosing to edit cases to focus on the point the textbook author hopes you will learn.

Students and lawyers read cases as source material for rules and holdings, to help them understand the application of the rules to particular facts, as springboards for discussing the policy rationales for the rules and the case outcome, and as models from which hypothetical variations can be taken. Consequently, expertise in reading cases is crucial to student success.

Successful law students read cases differently than their less successful peers. Successful Law students are expert case readers. These students understand a good deal of time in law school is spent reading—and law school reading is very different from other reading. Your goal should be to become an expert at reading legal materials, including cases. As you develop expertise, you'll read more efficiently, and you'll be better able to participate in class discussions, to prepare for exams, and to keep your life balanced. You can begin to develop expert reading skills by understanding what expert readers do.[1]

---

1. A good portion of this section is based on material from: RUTH MCKINNEY, READING LIKE A LAWYER (Carolina Academic Press), an excellent text for any student interested in improving legal reading skills.

# 1. Expert Readers Make Sure They Know Something About the Subject Before They Begin Reading the Case

Many new law students feel as though they have no idea what parts of the case are important, or what they are supposed to get from the cases. As a result, they have trouble understanding their reading. Expert law students on the other hand, either already have an understanding of the subject matter, or develop knowledge about the subject matter before reading the cases, and then armed with that background knowledge, are able to read efficiently and effectively.

Knowing something about the subject matter makes it easier to understand new information and recall it later. The new information is stored in the brain through the connection to this prior knowledge. Expert law students gather this knowledge from a variety of sources.

**Before they read cases** on a new topic, expert law students:

(a) review the syllabus and casebook table of contents;
(b) read and think about the introductory materials in the casebook;
(c) read a supplemental source which explains the topic; and
(d) read the notes, problems and questions that follow or precede the case.

These materials, problems and questions are designed to help you understand the purpose for including the case in the text, as well as to provide you context and purpose for reading the materials. Each of these sources are described below.

## (a) Using Course Syllabi and Casebook Tables of Contents

Students can gain a feel for the organization of a set of cases by looking at their course syllabus and the table of contents of their casebook. The syllabus, for example, may list assigned materials by topic. Similarly, the authors of casebooks often list topics in their table of contents. Students can draw tentative inferences and gain insight into the structure of the subject, as well as information about what will be covered in the cases they read, from the syllabus and the casebook table of contents. For example, most first year students study a tort called Intentional Infliction of Emotional Distress. In most torts texts that tort would be listed like this:

I. Intentional Torts
    a. The meaning of intent
    b. Intentional Torts to the Person
        i. Assault
        ii. Battery
        iii. False Imprisonment
        iv. Intentional Infliction of Emotional Distress
    c. Intentional Torts to Property
        i. Conversion
        ii. Trespass to Land
        iii. Trespass to Chattel

     d.  Privileges
        i.   Consent
        ii.  Necessity
        iii. Self-Defense
        iv. Defense of Others

From this table of contents, you should come to understand that Intentional In-fliction of Emotional Distress is one of seven intentional torts; that it is one of the four intentional torts against a person (vs. against property); and that it requires intent.

If the professor's syllabus and the table of contents of the outline prove unhelpful, students can find similar information in the table of contents in a hornbook (a large text explaining in detail an entire subject area, like contracts law), a commercial outline (a shorter book, depicting, usually in outline form, the major points of law in an area) or some other supplemental text. Frequently, law school professors will list their preferred supplemental sources in the course syllabus as recommended or optional texts. When they do, it is a good idea to treat these texts as required reading. Students can gain valuable insight into both the substance of the material they are about to cover, as well as an understanding of how the topics are organized, by reviewing such texts.

### (b) Using Introductory Information

Practicing lawyers seldom read cases in a new area of law before they have read some type of practice guide or other materials designed to acquaint the lawyer with the area of law. Similarly, students should not read cases until they have some information about the area of law covered by the case(s). A good source of such information is usually the introduction to the chapter or chapter section in which the assigned cases fall. Even if the introductory reading is not assigned, it is worth reading. The introduction may provide an overview of the subject area, and, in some cases, may outline the key legal principles the student will be learning. Often, these sections give students guidance as to the connections between what they have read and what they are about to read, making it easier for students to connect their new learning to prior material as well as predict what they will be learning from the cases they are about to read. Some introductory sections will even articulate the prevailing rule and identify major policy concerns with respect to the assigned topic. When a casebook does not provide such introductory material, or when the introductory material does not effectively convey information about the topic, it can be helpful to read about the subject area in a hornbook or other supplemental text.

### (c) Using Supplemental Resources

There are many supplemental sources available to law students, which are described in more detail in chapter 8. For purposes of preparing yourself for reading assigned cases, the supplemental sources that are useful are hornbooks and other summaries of the law. These type of supplements often include discussions of key cases, including many of the cases found in casebooks. They may even include a summary of the principle for which the case stands and a discussion of how the case fits into the selected course topics. Reading hornbooks and/or other supplements which summarize the law, before reading the cases, can help students discern the reasons that the casebook authors included the cases in their casebooks (and the reason students have been assigned the particular case). Hornbooks also usually identify when there is a disagreement among the state courts regarding a particular point of law and the rules the differing courts have adopted. This information allows students to consider the possibility that the case was included because the author of the casebook, or the professor assigning the case, disagrees with the opinion. If so, the students can anticipate that their professor may ask them to critique the case and argue whether it was a good decision as a matter of public policy. In many cases, the author of your casebook may have authored a supplemental source, like a hornbook, or your professor may have recommended a source as optional or recommended reading. Expert law students treat these recommendations as required reading, because they know that reading such a source can help them make sense of difficult material.

One caveat is worth noting—some law faculty may express distaste or outright hostility to the use of supplemental texts. Part of this concern stems from the fact that, by necessity, every law school class only addresses a portion of the particular body of law under study. It would be impossible, in fact, to cover all of contracts or torts or civil procedure law, even in a two-semester course. Thus, some professors have a well-founded concern that their students will either confuse themselves by knowing more law than they need to know or by learning the wrong portion of the body of law. This is why it is important to read the material that covers the topic you are assigned, even if the case you are assigned is listed in multiple areas of the hornbook or other supplement. These concerns, however, do not relate to the reason for recommending the use of supplements as a source of general knowledge about the subject matter. Even the most strident anti-supplemental source professor is unlikely to object to the idea of reading a hornbook for the sole purpose of developing prior knowledge so that the case reading experience is more productive. And remember, it is also a good idea to choose supplements that are recommended by the professor teaching your course—since they will likely have vetted many of the available sources to find one that is in line with their teaching of the topic.

### (d) Starting with the Questions and Notes That Follow the Case(s)

Prior knowledge can also be acquired from the questions and comments that follow the case or the set of cases. The questions after the case frequently make reading the case easier. The questions may state the issue in the case and give the student some guidance as to the structure of the analytical approach of the opinion, describe critical points or weaknesses in the court's reasoning, provide historical context for the opinion, set forth a key basis for the court's decision and even point out information the court ignored or arguments the court chose not to address. Most reading comprehension experts actually recommend that students read such questions first, regardless of the subject matter being studied—so that students can orient themselves to the critical issues. Students who read the questions first have a great advantage — because they know what is important before they even begin reading.

## 2. Expert Readers Understand Their Purpose for Reading Cases — And How They Will Use What They Learn

Lawyers analyze and use a court opinion by focusing on the outcome in the case (how the court resolved the issue presented to the court) and the court's reasoning (the explanation for the court's decision) which help the lawyer to predict how other courts might use the opinion to resolve future disputes. Similarly, expert readers focus on understanding how and why the court reached its decision, so they will be apply to apply what they have learned to predict future outcomes — including the hypotheticals and problems presented by the professor during class, and on law school exams.

In the first few weeks of law school, it can be difficult to remember that the primary point of reading any case is to understand the main idea of the case — and how it will apply to future disputes. This is because law professors typically have more than one goal in mind when they discuss cases with you during those initial weeks.

First, they want you to become part of the legal discourse community — this means developing the vocabulary you will need when you are a lawyer. Lawyers have a language of their own; the sooner you learn this language, the better off you will be, because you will be more adept at reading and understanding cases and other materials. It is for this reason that law professors may ask you to define every unfamiliar word and every word used in an unfamiliar way — even if the word is not one you needed to know to understand the court's decision and reasoning.

Another goal is to teach you to about the legal process — the procedure parties must go through to resolve disputes within the legal system. You need to understand this procedure, because you will be navigating this system when you become a lawyer, and because the procedural posture of the case impacts how an appellate court can view the case — for example, the court reviews an appeal from a trial with great deference to the trial court's determinations about the facts.

Yet another goal is to teach you to be detail oriented — because lawyers must pay very close attention to details. In law, one word — or one comma — can make a big difference in meaning. Lawyers (and judges, and law school professors) work very hard to be as precise as possible in their writing, although even they often fail. Lawyers expend so much effort on precision because slight nuances in meaning can change the legal implications of what the lawyer has written. To teach you to be detail oriented, law professors may focus on details in the case they know you will have overlooked. When a professor focuses on a detail in the case which you overlooked, it is important for you to assess whether you missed the detail because you did not understand it's significance to the court's decision, or whether it is a detail related to one of the other goals — like developing your vocabulary or understanding of the legal process. If you miss details because you are not paying sufficient attention or because you did not understand the court's decision or reasoning, you must take care to alter your strategies so that it does not continue to happen.

Each of these goals requires you to pay attention to things in the case that may not be related to the main idea (or the court's ultimate decision or reasoning); if you find you are spending all or most of your time and attention on these things—looking up words, understanding the procedural history or posture, and paying attention to every detail of a case—and as a result you are forgetting to read for the main idea of the case, you will need to adjust your strategies. Law school exams will not focus on these other goals, but instead will focus on the parts of the case that will be used to resolve future disputes—and these are typically all related to the main idea. For this reason, it is important that you quickly develop your legal vocabulary, understanding of the legal process, and ability to understand what makes a particular detail legally significant—or not. This way you can spend your time understanding how the case will apply in the future, and begin reading like a lawyer. In fact, expert case readers, including lawyers, are able to move quickly to the parts of the case that will help them achieve their goal—because expert case readers have already developed their vocabulary, understand the procedural details automatically, and can distinguish between legally significant and legally insignificant facts. This is true because expert readers have typically spent thousands of hours reading cases. Keep this in mind when you inevitably find case reading to be a challenging skill; although you will improve a great deal during the first semester, it will take years of practice to completely master.

## 3. Expert Readers Read for the Main Idea, While Still Understanding That They May Need to Attend to Many Small Concepts (and Details) to Grasp the Main Idea

When you read a case, pay attention to the headings in the text to understand why the case is included—i.e., the main point the author hopes you will learn and understand. In addition, pay attention to the facts and details the court relied on in reaching the decision, including the reasons articulated by the court and any examples or other cases the court compares with the facts of the dispute presently before the court. Remember that questions and notes at the beginning or end of the reading are intended to help you evaluate whether you understood the material, including the main idea and key details. When you are finished reading a case, it is a good idea to try to summarize the main point of the case in a few sentences, to assess whether you understood the main idea.

As a novice legal reader, you will encounter terminology that you have not seen before, as well as terminology that is familiar, but seems to have special meaning in the context of legal reading. Most students, even relatively novice learners, have developed strategies for dealing with an unfamiliar term or word. As a general rule, most readers either simply infer meaning from the context in which the word appears or ignore the word. On the one hand, legal reading is no different. Getting bogged down on a word-by-word level can cause a student to lose sight of the big picture, the principle for which the case stands. This level of understanding, the ability to understand what a court's opinion is trying to teach future parties, is essential and cannot be sacrificed in an obsessive focus on details.

On the other hand, part of becoming a lawyer means becoming part of the legal discourse community—by learning key terms that are part of lawyers' everyday language. Mastering the terminology from the outset, by looking up and committing to memory new terminology and new meanings for those familiar words used in an unfamiliar way, makes future case reading efforts easier and quicker. As you develop this vocabulary, it will improve your reading comprehension and speed and make class discussion and preparation more manageable. In addition, you will be better equipped to communicate in the manner that characterizes legal thinking and writing. Mastery of legal terminology helps students write better case briefs, legal writing papers, and essay examination answers. For these reasons, until you learn the terminology, you should look up any new or unfamiliar term, or any familiar term which appears to have special meaning—but understand that those words may not relate to the main idea of the reading.

Note that developing a professional vocabulary does not mean that your everyday language and writing should be filled with legalese (legal terms that are unfamiliar to lay persons), but rather that you should understand such terms when you hear and read them so that you do not have to stop and think about what they mean in order to understand the materials you will read and work with in your everyday practice. When you speak or write, however, you will want to make your written work as clear as possible and that may mean communicating your ideas without using unnecessary legal terminology.

## 4. Expert Readers Pay Attention to Important Details, Including Words That Have Special Meaning in the Context of the Reading

Experts in case reading are more likely than novices to note the date of an opinion, the status of the parties, the court issuing the opinion and the author of the opinion. Experts do so because they know that legal decision-making can be influenced by all of these factors. For example, judges, like everyone else, are influenced by the society in which they live. To understand some decisions, therefore, one needs to consider the date on which the court made the decision because the date will suggest the historical context (e.g., war or peace), the economic situation (e.g., The Great Depression) or technological developments (e.g., developments that make it easy for parties to quickly communicate even if they reside great distances from each other) that may have influenced the decision. Likewise, expert case readers consider the identities and statuses of the parties (e.g., whether they are powerful or powerless, famous or infamous), the court that issued the opinion (e.g., a lower court in a conservative state such as Alabama or a higher court in a progressive state such as New York), and the author of the opinion (some judges are famous for their innovations or for the high quality of their opinions).

## 5. Expert Readers Read to Understand How the Case Will Apply to Future Disputes

Each of the cases you read is intended to apply not only to the dispute in the case you are reading but also to future disputes; cases establish precedent to be followed by courts in deciding future cases.

Expert case readers keep in mind, even before they start reading cases, that court opinions do not state absolute truths. Rather, court opinions are really just pieces of persuasive writing in which the author (a judge) is trying to convince his or her audience (lawyers, other judges and law professors) that the decision he or she is describing is a correct one. This is why students should not see themselves in a passive role, receiving wisdom from judges through court opinions. Successful law students adopt an active role as they get ready to read, planning to develop for themselves an understanding of what the opinion means—and how they can use that information in the future.

Successful students recognize that case reading is a matter of interpretation, not unlike the interpretation of a poem or novel. To understand this point, look at the image below. As you do, decide whether you think it is a picture of an old woman or a young woman:

The picture is arguably of a young woman whose head is turned to the right. It is also arguably a picture of an old woman who is looking down. You might be familiar with this optical illusion, and so you might see both the young and the old woman. If you do not see both images, this YouTube video may help: https://www.youtube.com/watch?v=7f1G6Nx5VDw.

The point is that whether the woman is old or young is subject to interpretation—it is a matter of perspective. Cases are similar. Contained within each case is a number of possible interpretations; your job as a lawyer is to persuade the court to "see" the case (or set of cases) from your perspective. You can imagine how this works in practice if you imagine how two lawyers (representing opposing parties to a lawsuit) would deal with the same case precedent. It is very likely one lawyer will perceive the precedent as favorable to his or her client, and the other lawyer will perceive the precedent as unfavorable. The lawyers will try to convince the judge to interpret the decision in a way that favors their respective client — to "see" the case from the lawyer's perspective. In other words, you will use this skill in practice when you apply the reasoning from the cases you read to the problems your clients face, to predict what the court will do, or to persuade the court to rule for your client.

The following chapters explain in detail how to perform this skill — the skill of helping the court to "see" a case from your client's perspective. For now, know that expert readers read cases with this goal in mind — they think about how the case might be used in future contexts — noting the general principles, rules, facts, policy and other information the court relies on, or emphasizes, in arriving at its decision; thinking about what differences might present themselves in a future dispute; and deciding whether and why those differences would change the court's decision. Understanding why the court reached its decision will help you predict the outcome of future disputes the court will hear (including those involving your clients). While you are reading, you should think about:

(1) understanding how the court applied the rules;
(2) what facts or policy or other considerations influenced the court's decision; and
(3) what differences presented by a new dispute might change the court's decision.

If you can answer these questions about the case, you will be able to respond effectively to questions about future cases, including the hypotheticals posed during class discussion and on your exams. To help you with this process, as you read each case, you might want to think about (and answer) the following questions:

- If I changed _____ (a key fact in the case) to _____ (a different fact), would the court have reached the same result? (Students should ask this question in multiple forms to generate their own hypotheticals, both hypotheticals that would result in the same conclusion the court reached in its opinion and hypotheticals that would result in the opposite conclusion.)

- What could the losing party have argued to change the result? (Often courts make it sound as if the result in the case was inevitable, but, of course, a lawyer representing the losing party thought the question was close enough that the case warranted an appeal, and sometimes the question divides the judges and results in a dissenting opinion.)

- What reason(s) did the court give for reaching the result? Which facts did the court use to support the reason(s)?

## 6. Expert Readers Interact with the Text — And Form Their Own Opinions

Expert readers engage in a dialogue with court opinions. As they read, they evaluate the opinion, looking for flaws in the courts' reasoning, descriptions of the facts, statements of law and assertions about the public interests implicated by the parties' dispute. They even argue with the opinions, making notes on their casebooks indicating their disagreements.

This is not meant to suggest that students must force themselves to disagree with decisions or that they should alter their understandings of court opinions to fit their values. What it does mean is that students should not see themselves in a passive role, receiving wisdom from judges through court opinions. Rather, successful law students adopt an active role as they get ready to read, planning to develop for themselves an understanding of what the opinion means—and how it can be used in the future.

Notice that these comments reflect a view of court opinions that is typical of expert law students (as explained above): courts do not simply report "truth" but, instead, construct meaning. Students are free to do the same and, in fact, should question the court's version of the truth.

As you read each case, you should ask yourself: Did the court reach the correct conclusion? Why or why not?

## 7. Expert Readers Acknowledge Personal Reactions

Expert readers have personal reactions to their reading. In law school, you may not be encouraged to voice your personal feelings in class (you may even be discouraged from having or acknowledging personal feelings), but ignoring or dismissing your personal reactions can slow down your reading process, so you should continue to acknowledge personal reactions even if they do not have an outlet in the classroom. If you visualize what is going on, rather than merely moving from word to word, and allow yourself to have personal reactions to what you read—your reading skills will improve. So take note of your own ideas and feelings—even when you are not able to express those ideas and feelings in the classroom.

## 8. Expert Readers "Loop" through Their Text

Novice case readers are much more likely to simply read through the case from beginning to end, highlighting things they feel are important as they read. In many instances, the student ends up highlighting so much that the student has not actually accomplished the goal that led the student to use a highlighting pen: reducing the case to a more manageable amount of material. Expert readers are more likely to read every court opinion more than once. During the first reading, which may involve a good deal of "skimming" the material, expert law students are simply trying to get a feel for the overall story and how the case comes out. Once they have this information, expert readers are able to read the case again, and focus on what is important, slowing down to attend to the key details and moving quickly through the material that does not address the main idea of the case. During the first read, expert readers put down their highlighting pen and write a few comments, choosing instead to absorb the main idea—and save the highlighting or note taking until they have some understanding of what they are reading.

## 9. Expert Readers Take Notes While They Read

Expert readers take notes so that they are able to remember information about the cases and can discuss and apply the concepts they have learned. Experts readers know that they will need to recall what they were thinking when the case is discussed in class—so they take notes to remind them about their thinking process and understanding of the case. Experts also take notes because they know that trying to remember everything while they are reading overtaxes their memory and makes reading slower.

One way to make sense of difficult aspects of cases is to use representation imagery. This means drawing a diagram, timeline, or other visual representation of what is happening in the case. This can be a particularly useful tool for organizing a convoluted set of facts—such as cases involving complicated party relationships, intricate contractual relations, or a difficult-to-follow series of events.

## 10. Expert Readers Understand the Connection between Case Reading and Class Discussion

Expert readers understand that the assigned reading is just one part of an interrelated experience. The reading you are assigned before class begins is related to the discussion that follows in class. Your class session will not usually be a review of what you have read, but a discussion of how the reading applies in new and different contexts. You will be expected to analyze a new situation, and predict what the outcome would be if the cases you've read were applied to the new situation. This is why it is essential for you to have read and thought about the material before coming to class.

---

**PAUSE. THINK. ACT.** An excerpt from a law school text, representing a typical reading assignment, appears in Appendix B. There is supplemental material from a hornbook type supplemental source (which you will learn more about in chapter 8), included in Appendix C. Following the ten points set out above, read the materials. After you have finished, evaluate your strengths and weaknesses in light of the ten points.

---

## A Final Thought About Case Reading

There is no question that, in the beginning, learning to read cases will involve considerable effort. In fact, most law professors expect new law students to spend hundreds of hours, particularly in their first year of law school, developing their case reading skills. The investment of time is a good one. The only way to develop good case reading skills is to practice reading cases following the strategies described in this section. If you take shortcuts, you will not develop these skills during law school — which will make you a less effective new lawyer.

# Step Two: Brief Like an Expert

Most legally trained readers (which includes your professor) think about cases in terms of the specific types of information that are included in traditional case briefs. Therefore, you really do need to read and brief all of the cases in your assignments before each class session starts. It is worth noting, at the outset, that case reading is more closely connected to success in law school than case briefing, likely because a brief is simply a record of what you learned during your reading.

It is important to put briefing into perspective. Few, if any, professors assign grades to their students' case briefs, or test briefing skills on examinations — which is why you should insure you are not devoting all of your time to reading and briefing, and ignoring other crucial skills. However, even though briefs are not graded, their creation is not a meaningless exercise. A case brief helps impose structure on a court opinion by reorganizing the opinion into the categories common to every opinion — and to legal decision-making. The end result of a good case brief is a product students can use to participate effectively during class, and to prepare for examinations. The process of briefing also helps you to learn to quickly and accurately identify the information from a case which is helpful to you as a lawyer.

There is one absolute with respect to case briefing: while there are commercial sources of case briefs for most casebooks, expert law students do not use them. Expert students know that learning requires active efforts on their part and that briefing cases on their own is an active experience, whereas reading someone else's case briefs is a passive one. As important is the fact that there are no commercial case briefs for cases when you are a lawyer. If you do not learn how to decipher cases yourself during law school, you will not possess this skill when you graduate — and there will be no commercial briefs to turn to.

Expert law students recognize three important things about their briefing efforts even before they start writing them:

1. A good case brief starts with a careful, thoughtful, active reading of a case using the strategies described in the previous section.

2. A case brief is a tool for learning; it is a written record of your understanding of the key components of a case.

3. Different professors demand different things from students' case briefs. Expert law students adjust accordingly. These differences are reflected in the kinds of questions their professors ask during classroom discussions and in the professors' expectations in terms of student performance on examinations.

Very few law professors care about what students actually have written in their briefs; rather, they care about how students respond to their questions. Some professors want students to perform in class as if they have created detailed briefs that include each of the elements described below, and more. Others want much less. Moreover, professors vary in the parts of the brief or opinion they emphasize. These differences reflect, in some instances, professor idiosyncrasies and, in others, differences among legal experts as to what is important in cases and what law students should be learning.

When you discuss concepts and cases in class and in practice, you may or may not be asked about the traditional parts of a case brief. However, most legally trained readers (including your professor) will probably be thinking in terms of the specific types of information that are included in traditional case briefs. Even if you do not write out a traditional brief for each case, it is important that you have identified and thought about each of these pieces so that you are prepared to participate in class discussion and so that you practice thinking about cases the way a legally trained reader will.

# The Anatomy of a Case Brief — The Traditional Components

Below is a list and description of the parts of a traditional case brief. You should be aware that the categories are easy enough to describe, but may not always be easy to identify or draft; case briefing is an example of a skill that requires many, many learning cycles to master.

## 1. The Heading or Citation

*This tells you where you can find the case.*

The citation includes the following information about where the student can find the opinion: the name of the reporter (a "reporter" is a hardcover book that includes the full texts of certain specified court opinions), the number of the series within that reporter (e.g., first, second or third series), the number of the volume within that series and the page number on which the case begins. It also tells the reader the court that decided the opinion.

For example, the *Parker* case has, among its citations, this citation:

$$3 \text{ Cal. 3d } 176$$

Vol.   Reporter   Series   Page
No.                          No.

This citation tells the reader that she can find this case in volume 3 of the third series of the California Reports, on page 176.

You will learn how to cite cases and other materials in your legal writing class, and you will most likely become quite proficient at it after just a single semester. Most expert law students also include the page number of the casebook where they case is found, so they can easily find the case if called on to do so in class.

## 2. The Parties

*These are the people or entities involved in the conflict described in the case, as well as the broader descriptions of the parties which allow you to carry the case forward to new situations.*

You should identify the parties by (1) name, (2) designation in the case (e.g., Plaintiff, Appellant, Petitioner, Respondent, Guardian Ad Litem, etc.), and (3) category. Judges, lawyers and professors think about how the cases they read will apply to future cases. They tend to think of the broader category of each party (e.g., seller, buyer, employer, employee, custodial parent, police officer, internet provider, etc.) because it helps them to think about the types of situations the case will apply to in the future. In practice, you will usually read cases in an effort to determine how a court might rule in your client's case or to find a case that helps you persuade the court to rule for your client. You will rarely find a case that is exactly like yours, and instead will have to look to similar cases to predict the outcome in your case. It helps to learn to think about parties and cases in terms of broad categories, rather than as limited to the exact facts in the case you are reading, and to think about how the case will apply to new and different contexts.

## 3. The Procedural History (Sometimes Called the Procedural Facts)

*This is what happened to the case before it got to the court writing the opinion you are reading.*

Procedural facts are all the facts relating to how the case moved through the legal system. Procedural facts describe what the parties, the judges and the jury did with the dispute within the legal system. Procedural facts begin once the parties enter the judicial system. In other words, once a person initiates a lawsuit or once the prosecuting attorney decides to file a criminal complaint, the procedural facts have begun. The procedural facts end with the appeal to the court issuing the opinion under study.

## 4. The Legally Significant "Conflict" Facts

*These are the facts that created the conflict and that the court considers when resolving the conflict. For some faculty and classes, this will include procedural facts.*

The conflict facts are all the events that transpired before someone involved the courts. They often include information about who did what to whom, when, why, and where. Nearly all law professors expect students to include facts in their case briefs; some will spend little or no class time on fact recitations, while others will focus considerable time teaching students to create proper fact recitations.

Nearly all law professors expect students to include only the relevant facts in their briefs. For example, a party's career status may or may not be relevant. The fact that a person is a lawyer would be relevant to a case discussing the legal significance of that party telling a lie to obtain property from a client and irrelevant to a case discussing whether a party who crashed his car into the lawyer's car failed to drive his car with the requisite degree of care. Likewise, some actions, while interesting to the reader, may be legally irrelevant. The fact that someone was a famous baseball player is probably irrelevant to a statement of facts about a criminal prosecution of that person for arson.

A fact is relevant if (1) it is one of the facts upon which the court based its decision or (2) a reasonable person would need to know the fact to be able to understand the court's decision. Most students find it helpful to draft the facts section last, after they have written the other sections.

Expert law students avoid simply copying the wording and sequence used by the court; instead, they write the facts in their own words—using the court's words only when the exact wording is significant. As is true of all learning experiences, people learn more when they act upon the materials than they do when they simply copy the materials. Writing facts in your own words requires active learning, which improves retention, and helps you recognize when you are not understanding the material. More importantly, while most opinions include a recitation of facts early on in the opinion, that recitation is often both over- and under-inclusive. It is over-inclusive because judges have no restrictions on what they include and often include irrelevant facts. It is under-inclusive because judges often omit facts altogether that are problematic for their decisions (those facts can sometimes be found in a dissenting opinion). Expert law students, therefore, do not simply mindlessly copy and paste the courts' initial statements of facts; they develop their own.

## 5. The Issue or Question Presented

*This is the legal question the court is answering or resolving.*

A case may have more than one issue (and more than one holding and more than one rationale). Sometimes, the task of identifying issues is a difficult one, particularly for novice law students. As you try to identify the issue or question presented, first consider the topic heading of your casebook. Next, consider where the court focuses its attention—where it focuses most of its discussion, and applies the facts to the rule. Finally, consider what new point the case teaches. Each of these considerations should help you identify the precise issue raised by the case.

Issue statements are commonly formulated in one of two ways, depending on the professor's preferences. Professors who emphasize holdings, rather than issues may not ask for issue statements at all, or may be satisfied with very general issue statements. Professors who emphasize issue statements may prefer students create fact-laden, precise issue statements. Professors also vary on the degree to which the factual descriptions within an issue statement should be the actual facts of the case or generalized statements of those facts, although a preference for the former is more common. For the first few weeks, until you understand each professor's preference, you may want to first create fact-laden, detailed and case specific issue statements (often called narrow issue statements) and then consider how the statements might be modified to meet the preferences of professors who prefer issues to be stated in a manner that is less confined to the specific facts of the case, and draft a second, broader, less case specific issue statement (often called a broad issue statement), and take both to class. Drafting both types of issue statements will also help you begin to understand how to manipulate the case the way a lawyer would (focusing the issue the way the lawyer hopes the court will "see" the case).

## 6. The Holding

*This is the court's decision — the answer to the issue or question presented, and sometimes the reasons for that decision.*

The term holding is a bit confusing for new law students, at least partly because law professors use the term to mean different things. The outcome and reasoning are sometimes referred to as the holding. Sometimes the term holding is used to indicate the rule and reasoning the court uses to answer the question presented. Still other times, the term holding is used to indicate only the final outcome — i.e., the answer to the question presented, but not the statement of reasons for the decision. In this text, the term holding will be used to include the answer to the question presented (the outcome), as well as the rule and reasoning used by the court to reach that answer.

Although law professors do not agree on the precise meaning of the term holding, they do agree that to sufficiently demonstrate understanding of a case, a student must be able to state the court's decision and explain the basis for that decision. It will be up to you to determine what your professor labels that information.

In most instances, the breadth of a holding, meaning the degree to which it can be generalized, is an educated and reasoned "guess" at what future courts will "see." For lawyers, the holding is the basis of the lawyer's argument. Recall the prior discussion about how lawyers work with precedents. Lawyers try to get the court to "see" the case from the lawyer's perspective. Therefore, in legal documents like motions and briefs, case holdings are drafted to reflect the way the lawyer wants the court to view the precedent. Sometimes courts explicitly state a holding, and sometimes courts do not. In either case, a lawyer's task includes defining that holding — the statement of the precedential effect of the opinion — in a way that favors the lawyer's client. Remember that the breadth of a holding is speculative; a lawyer will not know with certainty how a future court will "see" a case until the court deciding the client's case adopts one side's perspective — and issues a ruling.

Holdings are statements, not questions — they express what the court actually decided; also, holdings are usually expressed in the present tense. Holdings drafted by lawyers typically identify the key applicable principle of law (the rule), the facts that were critical to the court's conclusion, and the court's reasoning. These are the types of holdings which are useful for students in legal writing courses and on law school exams. Like issue statements, holdings may be drafted narrowly and broadly. As with issue statements, it helps if you draft one of each — to evaluate whether you are able to manipulate the case the way a lawyer would.

Finally, know that if there are multiple issues in the case, expert students develop multiple holdings — one for each issue the court addresses in the opinion.

## 7. The Rule

*This is the legal principle applied by the court to answer or resolve the issue or question presented. A rule can be carried forward to resolve similar conflicts in the future.*

Rules are usually easy to identify. They are statements setting forth the applicable law in a particular situation. For each issue, there will be one or more applicable rules. Usually rules are followed by a citation to a case, a statute or some other legal authority, such as a law review article, a hornbook or a treatise. It is important to make sure you identify the precise rule(s) on which the court is relying in resolving the issue. For example, the full text version of the *Parker* majority opinion states the following eight rules. As you read each rule, decide whether it should be included in the rule section of the case brief.

1. "[T]he matter to be determined by the trial court on a motion for summary judgment is whether facts have been presented that give rise to a triable factual issue."

2. "Summary judgment is proper only if the affidavits or declarations in support of the moving party would be sufficient to sustain a judgment in his favor and the opponent does not by affidavit show facts sufficient to present a triable issue of fact."

3. "The affidavits of the moving party are strictly construed and doubts as to the propriety of summary judgment should be resolved against granting the motion."

4. "The moving party cannot depend upon allegations in his own pleadings to cure deficient affidavits, nor can his adversary rely upon his own pleadings in lieu or in support of affidavits in opposition to a motion; however, a party can rely on his adversary's pleadings to establish facts not contained in his own affidavits."

5. "[T]he court may consider facts stipulated to by the parties and facts which are properly the subject of judicial notice."

6. "[T]he measure of recovery by a wrongfully discharged employee is the amount of salary agreed upon for the period of service, less the amount which the employer affirmatively proves the employee has earned or with reasonable effort might have earned from other employment."

7. "[B]efore projected earnings from other employment opportunities not sought or accepted by the discharged employee can be applied in mitigation, the employer must show that the other employment was comparable, or substantially similar, to that of which the employee has been deprived; the employee's rejection of or failure to seek other available employment of a different or inferior kind may not be resorted to in order to mitigate damages."

Rule 7 is really the only rule that directly responds to the issue and is a basis for the court's ruling. It is helpful to include Rule 6, however, because it provides context for understanding Rule 7.

## 8. The Paraphrase

*The paraphrase is a restatement of the rule in your own words.*

Expert learners know that being able to translate a principle (of law, of science or of math) into one's own words shows that the student understands it. In fact, expert learners use this task as a way of monitoring their comprehension; if they cannot state the rule in their own words, they *know* they do not understand it and need to either re-read the case, obtain help from a peer or their instructor or read more about the rule in a supplemental text. A few points are important about paraphrases. First, your paraphrase must accurately capture the rule. Second, where the exact words chosen by the court are significant to its holding, your paraphrase should include those words.

## 9. The Reasoning

*This is the court's train of thought as it reaches the answer to the issue presented. Sometimes this section includes an analysis of policy issues that influenced the court. This section (alone or when drafted as part of the holding) can be carried forward to determine whether and how the case should be applied to future conflicts.*

The reasoning section should include both the rationale and the application of the rule. A rationale explains the court's reasons for reaching its decision and therefore is sometimes called the court's reasoning. The rationale includes any public policy supporting the court's decision. Public policy is the social good served by a rule of law or by a precedent. In some cases, courts explicitly identify and discuss the public policy implications of both the rules they state and their holdings. However, in other cases, courts do not explain the public policy implications of the rule on which they rely. The often-challenging task for the student, therefore, is to figure out what social good the court must have had in mind.

Sometimes, students can identify unstated policy considerations (rationales) by simply thinking about why the court must have thought that its decision was a good one for society. Another, similar way to get at the policy is to consider who the prevailing party is and guess why other similarly situated parties (e.g., employees, prisoners, purchasers of land, etc.) might believe the decision was a good one. For example, employees might see a decision which prevents employers from forcing employees to take jobs they do not like as replacements for jobs the employers promised as a good decision because it preserves employees' freedom to decide for themselves what they wish to do.

It is also helpful to consider alternative decisions the court could have made and the social good those alternative decisions might have served. Keep in mind that public policies are really arguments about what behavior should be encouraged, and such arguments almost always come in matched sets. In other words, although opinions often make it sound as if there is only one social good at stake in any particular case, deciding a case usually requires judges to select from competing social goods (public policies). Five policy trade-offs common to legal decision-making are:

1. Certainty and predictability v. flexibility and justice
2. Encouraging competition vs. preserving individuals' rights
3. Allowing freedom of action vs. protecting society
4. Encouraging economically efficient behavior vs. preserving individuals' rights
5. Punishing and discouraging socially undesirable behavior vs. preserving individual rights

This list of policies—predictability, justice, encouraging competition, preserving individual rights, allowing freedom of action, protecting society, encouraging economically efficient behavior, punishment, and deterrence—serves as a sort of smorgasbord from which students may select in identifying the policies implicated by a particular decision. When briefing a case, students should identify both the policy adopted by the court and its traded-off match.

The application is the court's explanation of how the rule was applied to the facts to reach the result and therefore is also sometimes called the court's reasoning. Application involves two distinct techniques—application of rules to facts and the court's treatment of prior precedent. In explaining decisions, students need to understand how the court applied the rule to the facts of the case. In other words, students should explain why it is that the rule the court stated warranted the result the court reached. This explanation involves identifying the key facts and explaining what aspect(s) of the facts caused the court to conclude that the factual situation required by the rule *was* present in the case or *was not* present in the case.

The application also involves the court's treatment of prior precedent which the court must apply or distinguish. Finding where the court has applied or distinguished prior precedent(s) is fairly straightforward. Courts always apply or distinguish a precedent immediately after stating the name of the precedent case, describing the key facts of that case, and articulating a holding for that precedent. The author then either applies it or distinguishes the stated precedent.

It is important, of course, to know the difference between applying a precedent and distinguishing a precedent. Judges (and lawyers when they make arguments to judges) *apply* precedents that reached favorable results, i.e., results similar to those they want to reach in the present case. Applying a precedent involves identifying similarities between the precedent and the case for which the court is writing an opinion and then explaining why those similarities justify reaching the same result as in the precedent case. Judges (and lawyers) *distinguish* precedents that reached unfavorable results, i.e., results opposite to the results they wish to reach in the present case. Distinguishing a precedent therefore involves identifying differences between the precedent case and the case for which the court is writing the opinion and then explaining why the difference(s) justify reaching a different result than the court reached in the precedent case.

Sometimes, the majority and dissenting opinions conflict on whether the precedents are similar enough to apply them to the case before the court. In some opinions, courts apply some precedents and distinguish others.

In the next few chapters you will have the opportunity to practice the skill of applying and distinguishing case precedent, in the context of the law school classroom, examinations and other writing assignments.

## 10. Concurring and Dissenting Opinions

*A dissenting opinion is an opinion written by a judge who disagrees with the conclusion reached by the other judges. A concurring opinion is an opinion authored by a judge who agrees with the conclusion reached by the other judges but has different or additional reasons for reaching that conclusion.*

Not every opinion has a dissenting or concurring opinion, but when they do, students must summarize the key points in any dissent or concurrence. The student's task, when confronted with a concurrence or a dissent, is to *identify* the points of dispute between the majority opinion and the dissent or concurrence and *explain* the dissenting or concurring view. A dissenting or concurring opinion may disagree with the majority opinion's description of the applicable law, its characterization of the facts, its statement of public policy or its application of law to fact or of precedent to fact.

## 11. Your Own Ideas

*These are the thoughts, feelings and questions that you have as you read the case.*

Remember that although you may not have time to voice your thoughts and feelings in class, you should not ignore them; keeping notes of the thoughts and feelings that emerge as you read a case helps you focus, keeps you invested in what you read, clarifies your thinking, and encourages you to find patterns. It also helps you to remember what you have read, so that you can apply it later — in class discussion and on examinations.

## 12. Synthesis

*This is the final step, where you think about how the case you are reading relates to other cases you've read and fits into the "big picture" of the course.*

The final step in case briefing is not a piece you will necessarily include in your brief, and yet it may be the most important thing you do during the briefing process. For each case you read, it is important to develop a working hypothesis about the point of the case and how it fits into the course as a whole. This will help you to understand how the cases that you read are related to one another, to other topics and to the course as a whole, rather than to view each case in isolation. Sometimes this process is called synthesis. It is easier to begin this process if you wait until you have read the first few cases in each of your courses.

First, you should know that sometimes cases are actually in conflict and are irreconcilable because they show different jurisdictions' approaches to deciding the issue—and the point of the casebook is to teach you both positions. The term jurisdiction in this context refers to the court system in which a case is decided. For example, one case may have been decided under California law and the other under New York law. In this situation, the conflict between the two cases stems from the fact that the two jurisdictions simply have adopted conflicting rules. Other times, the cases will appear to be in conflict but are actually reconcilable. There are a number of ways to reconcile cases, including the following:

(1) The conflict may be explained as a historical issue. One decision may reflect the law as it was in the past and one may reflect the current version of the law. In other words, if both decisions come from the same jurisdiction, it may be because that jurisdiction changed the law at some point. In fact, even if the two decisions come from different jurisdictions, they still may reflect an older rule and a newer rule.

(2) The conflict may derive from factual differences between the two cases that required the courts to adopt a different rule.

(3) The two cases may have different outcomes, and may appear to have reached different conclusions, but may in fact be following the same reasoning or employing the same social policy considerations.

### *Case Briefing Exercise*

On the next page you will find a case briefing exercise designed to help you identify the pieces of a case brief.[2]

Draw a line to connect the labels in the left hand column with the corresponding examples of those concepts, from a sample brief written for *Parker v. Twentieth Century Fox Corp.*, in the right hand column. Some of the labels have more than one example, and some of the examples do not have a corresponding label—to make the exercise more challenging and make it difficult to answer via process of elimination. The answers are in Appendix D.

---

2. This exercise is based on an exercise first distributed by our colleague, Professor Rory Badahur.

Parker (Plaintiff/Appellee/Actress-Employee); Twentieth Century Fox Corp. (Defendant/Appellant/Movie Studio-Employer)

Parker (Plaintiff/Appellee/Employee) filed suit for breach of contract. Plaintiff moved for summary judgment. The motion was granted and the lower court awarded Parker a judgment in the amount of the agreed compensation under her written contract with Twentieth Century Fox Corp. (Defendant/Appellant/Employer); Defendant appealed. Appellate court concluded

**Heading**

trial court correctly ruled in plaintiff's favor. Lower court judgment affirmed.

[T]he measure of recovery by a wrongfully discharged employee is the amount of salary agreed upon for the period of service, less the amount which the employer affirmatively proves the employee has earned or with reasonable effort might have earned from other employment.

**Parties**

However, before projected earnings from other employment opportunities not sought or accepted by the discharged employee can be applied in mitigation, the employer must show that the other employment was comparable, or substantially similar, to that of which the employee has been deprived; the employee's rejection of or failure to seek other available employment of a different or inferior kind may not be resorted to in order to mitigate damages.

**Procedural History**

Parker is entitled to summary judgment and award of her guaranteed compensation because she did not have to mitigate her damages by accepting Defendant's offer for a role in a different movie genre, filmed in a different location, which impaired or eliminated her rights to director and screen play approval because that offer was different and inferior to the original offer.

**Facts**

Where an employer breaches an employment contract, the employee will be entitled to the amount she would have earned under the contract, minus the amount the employer proves she could have made from other comparable or substantially similar employment. An employee does not have to accept a different or inferior offer of employment to mitigate her damages under an employment contract when the employer breaches that contract.

**Question Presented**

Whether Plaintiff employee's damages from Defendant-employer's breach of contract should be reduced because Defendant-employer's substitute offer of employment for a role in a movie of a different genre, which was to be filmed in a different location was comparable or substantially similar to the role offered to the Plaintiff-employee in the employment contract such that Plaintiff's refusal to accept the new offer was an unreasonable refusal to mitigate her damages.

**Holding**

A straight dramatic role in a western taking place in an opal mine, to be filmed in Australia is not the equivalent of or substantially similar to the lead in a song and dance production, to be filmed in Los Angeles and calling on the actress' talents as a dancer. And an offer eliminating or impairing director and screenplay approvals is inferior. Since the substitute role was different and inferior, Parker is not required to accept it to mitigate her damages. It would be unfair to allow an employer to breach a contract and then not have to pay for the breach by offering

**Rule**

employment different from what they contracted to do—an employer would have no incentive to abide by the contract.

Plaintiff, Parker, an actress, entered a contract to play the female lead in a musical called Bloomer Girl, which was to be filmed in Los Angeles, California. Parker was "guaranteed compensation"

**Reasoning**

amounting to $750,000. Under the contract, Parker also had the right to approve the film director, the dance director and the screenplay. Defendant Fox, the movie studio, decided not to make the film, and notified Parker they were not going to comply with the contract. Fox offered Parker a role for the same compensation, in a dramatic western called Big Country, Big Man, to be filmed in Australia. The new offer did not give Parker approval over the director or screenplay. Parker did not accept the offer. Parker filed an action seeking recovery of the guaranteed compensation.

*Parker v. Twentieth Century-Fox Film Corp.*, 3 Cal. 3d 176 (1970).

Parker is entitled to damages from Defendant's breach of the employment contract because an employee does not have to accept a different or inferior offer of employment to mitigate their damages resulting from an employer's breach of an employment contract.

**PAUSE. THINK. ACT.** After you review the answers to the matching exercise, answer the following questions:

1. Which example(s) are missing a label? What label should be applied?

2. Is the sample Question Presented a broad version or a narrow version? Try drafting versions that are broader and versions that are narrower than the example.

3. Are the sample Holdings broad versions or narrow versions? Try drafting versions that are broader and versions that are narrower than the examples.

4. Which sections contain information that is not found explicitly in the case? Where does this information come from?

5. What sections described in the case briefing materials are missing from this exercise? Try drafting those sections.

6. What policy reasons explain the outcome in this case?

7. How might you improve upon some of the case brief examples? Try redrafting the examples you would like to improve.

## Some Final thoughts about Reading and Briefing

Case reading and briefing are skills that are quite difficult to master. Most new law students do not really achieve mastery in their first semester or even their first year of law school. Reading like a lawyer requires tremendous amounts of practice. Full-time law students literally read hundreds of court opinions in their first year. Expert law students recognize that this difficulty and need for practice are simply part of the learning process, not unlike the thousands of hours of practice required to master a musical instrument or a sport. Expert law students recognize that learning to read and brief are not a matter of aptitude but, rather, a matter of strategic, deliberate practice.

# Step Three: Deconstruct the Rules

Soon after you start law school, you must become adept at understanding and using rules. Because lawyers use rules to analyze legal problems, and law school exams test students' development of the skills involved in applying rules to facts, rules are a unit of instruction with which students must become comfortable.

Law school exams assume that you, as a law student, can break rules into their subparts so that you are able to apply each subpart to a hypothetical factual situation. This means that in addition to being able to identify the rule from a case, statute or other material, a law student (and a lawyer) must be able to separate the rule into its component parts and identify and understand what exactly must be proven to satisfy the rule. This process is called rule deconstruction—because you are taking the rule apart.

This process requires an extraordinary degree of attention to detail. To deconstruct a rule, you must first identify each part and subpart of the rule. You must then examine the language of the rule to determine the significance of that part or subpart. It is important to be able to identify, for example, whether that part or subpart is a required element that must be proven to satisfy the rule, or whether it is a factor that may be given consideration by the court, but does not have to be proven to satisfy the rule, or whether it is an alternative to proving another required element, such that you can satisfy one of the alternatives but do not need to satisfy them all.

Lawyers need this skill for a variety of reasons. For example, when evaluating whether a client has a valid claim or defense, a lawyer might isolate each of the "parts" of that claim or defense, evaluating whether the facts presented by the client will be enough to allow the lawyer to prove each element, whether she needs additional facts to make that determination, or whether the client simply does not have a claim or defense. Lawyers also deconstruct rules as part of the process of drafting some legal documents. For example, rule deconstruction is used in the drafting of complaints, the document filed by the plaintiff to initiate a lawsuit. In many states, the complaint must identify the elements of each cause of action alleged by the plaintiff and the key facts supporting such allegations—which requires that the lawyer identify each of the elements (i.e., the required "parts" and "subparts"). As you can see, rule deconstruction is a very valuable skill.

You will likely want to deconstruct each of the rules you encounter in your courses, even if it is not specifically required or assigned by your professor—because it will help you begin to organize your examinations, and ensure you cover each of the issues your professor expects you to address on an examination. Deconstructing a rule requires that you (1) identify the parts and sub-parts of the rule; (2) understand which of the part and sub-parts must (as opposed to may) be proven to satisfy the rule; and (3) understand how the parts and sub-parts are related to one another.

## 1. Identifying the Parts and Sub-Parts of the Rule

Professors will not likely deconstruct rules for you—choosing instead to use class discussion to illustrate the different parts and sub-parts of a rule, usually by applying the rule to a set of facts and asking questions which highlight the different parts of the rule you must consider. Most professors will assume you will be able to identify all of the parts of the rule from this type of discussion. For this reason, you will want to pay close attention to class discussion to make sure you have identified each of the parts of the rule, and to see if the rule you have deconstructed is aligned with class discussion.

It may help you to know that many casebook authors include a different case for each of the parts of the rule—so you may want to think about which part of the rule is the primary focus of the case you are reading and then make a list of the components covered by each of the assigned cases.

You will probably deconstruct rules automatically by the time you become a lawyer, but initially it will take some practice. It may help you to identify the parts of the rule if, as you begin to develop this skill, you ask yourself the following questions:

- What are all the things I would have to prove for my client to prevail?
- What are all of the issues a trier of fact (judge, jury, etc.) would need to consider to determine if the rule is satisfied?
- Have any cases isolated one of the parts of the rule—and further defined it?

This process is sometimes more difficult than you may first imagine. As you practice the skill, you will become more detail oriented, and learn to examine every word, signal and punctuation mark. The following exercise will help you begin to develop this skill.

Identify each of the parts of the following definition of murder (be sure to <u>write down</u> each part separately in the blank space below—if you do the exercise in your head, you are less likely to assess your own performance accurately):

*Murder is the unlawful killing of another human*
*being with malice aforethought.*

Now compare your answer with the following answer. You very likely identified the parts as follows:

- unlawful killing
- of another human being
- with malice aforethought

Unfortunately, this does not identify each of the parts of the rule. There are actually five separate parts: (1) unlawful; (2) killing; (3) another; (4) human being; and (5) malice aforethought. Separating the rule into the required five parts is important because a prosecutor would have to prove all five of these things to prove a particular accused defendant is guilty. This means they would have to know how the court would define each of these parts. For example: "unlawful" (Does that include killings made in self-defense? In defense of one's home?), "killing" (Does that include people who would have died from natural causes anyway?), "of another" (does that mean suicide is excluded?), "human being" (Does that include an unborn fetus?), and "malice aforethought" (Does that mean it had to be planned?). If you do not separate the rule into each of these parts, there is a good chance you will miss an issue—on an exam, or even when you are a lawyer. On an exam you will simply lose points, and your grade will probably suffer. As a lawyer, it amounts to malpractice. For this reason, it is important for you to practice and ultimately master this skill.

## 2. Understand Which of the Parts and Sub-Parts Must (As Opposed to May) Be Proven

To understand exactly what must be proven to satisfy the rule, you next want to identify the type of rule structure(s) contained within the rule. The task of discerning the rule structure(s) is a crucial one to students and lawyers because lawyers use different analytical techniques in applying each type of rule structure. Rules will typically be made up of one or more of these structures:

- A **simple rule**, with a required or prohibited act and a consequence
- A list of **mandatory elements** that must be proven in order to establish the rule is met
- A set of **factors** the court may consider in making its decision, which may take the form of a list or **balancing test** requiring the court to weigh competing factors
- An either/or test allowing proof of one or more **alternatives** to satisfy the rule
- An **exception** to the general rule

These rule structures are explained in detail below. It is very common for courts and legislators to combine two or more of these structures in a single rule, however, these materials will first focus on each structure individually, and then on rules where these structures are combined.

Using pattern recognition and language interpretation will help you deconstruct the rules you encounter. Deconstructing rules involves pattern recognition in the sense that most rules follow one or more of these structures. Consequently, students can deconstruct rules by analogizing the rule before them to a prototype rule. Deconstructing rules also involves language interpretation in the sense that the distinguishing features among the various types of rule structures, in most instances, are the conjunctions used to connect the requirements (and, or, but) or the use of a "signal" word, as explained in more detail below, such as "is" for definitions and "weighs" for what lawyers call "factor tests."

In addition, many rules use what might be called "language shortcuts" which may be used to communicate more information than what the literal words state. For example, several rules you will encounter during law school include a requirement that a party have a "reasonable belief" about something. Lawyers and judges understand this requirement to communicate two requirements: (1) the party must actually or honestly believe, and (2) the party's belief must be objectively reasonable. Another common language shortcut used in rules is to preface a list of considerations with the word "include" as in "The factors courts may consider include: ..." The word "include" is a shortcut for the phrase "include but are not limited to," which means that the list which follows is incomplete and lawyers and judges are free to consider other matters not on the list.

Because the choice of **conjunctions** (and, or, but), the **punctuation** (the location of the commas), and other signals (unless, must, shall, etc.) can change the meaning of a rule, it is important to read the rule carefully and pay close attention to these details.

## Common Rule Structures

### 1. Simple Rules (If A, then Z)

Many rules simply identify an act or condition (*if A*) and its consequence (*then Z*). There are many examples of such rules outside the legal context. For example, an employer might say to a salesman, "If you want a bonus, you must exceed $500,000 in sales." Similarly, a parent might say to a child, "If you stay out past curfew, you will be grounded for one week." Both rules describe the act or condition (exceeding a dollar amount in sales, staying out past curfew) and its consequence (getting a bonus, being grounded for one week). Before reading on, take a moment and see if you can come up with a few examples.

Legal examples of simple rules include the following:

- It shall be a crime to sell alcohol to a minor
  *act = selling alcohol to a minor*
  *consequence = crime*

- In connection with a contract to construct a building, damages for delay in completion by the contractor are measured by the rental value of the completed premises for the period of the delay
  *act = delay by the contractor in completing a building construction contract*
  *consequence = payment of damages measured by the rental value.*

Many simple rules do not explicitly identify the consequence; they simply state a requirement for action or inaction; the consequence typically is addressed elsewhere, although it may be implicit. For example, a parent might say to a child, "Clean up your room right now." The required act is cleaning up the child's room and the implicit consequence for a failure to act is likely loss of a privilege. Similarly, an employer might say, "Your hours are 9:00 a.m. until 5:00 p.m." The required act is being on the job from 9–5, and the implicit consequence for failing to act (at least repeatedly) would be loss of the job.

Legal examples of this type of rule include:

- An answer to a complaint must be filed within 30 days
  *act = failing to file an answer within 30 days*
  *implicit consequence = default*

- The statute of limitations for a cause of action is one year
  *act = failing to file a lawsuit within one year*
  *implicit consequence = loss of the claim*

- The maximum speed limit on a state highway is 65 miles per hour
  *act = getting caught exceeding the speed limit*
  *implicit consequence = traffic ticket*

Applying simple rules involves assessing whether the required act or failure to act is present and then explaining the consequence. Thus, a person whom the state can prove has exceeded the speed limit suffers the consequence of a traffic ticket.

### 2. Elemental Rules (If A and B and C Are Present, then Z)

Elemental rules are the most common rules law students learn in their first-year classes. These rules are similar to simple rules in that they also include an explicit or implicit consequence if the prerequisite condition exists or does not exist. The difference is that the prerequisite condition consists of a list of requirements, *all of which must be met* for the consequence to follow. Lawyers refer to each requirement as an element.

Nearly all students are familiar with typical, non-legal examples of such rules, such as lists of requirements for papers, (e.g., the paper must be at least ten pages in length but no longer than 15 pages, must be in 12-point font, must have one-inch margins, etc.). The consequence typically is explicit (the instructor will not accept the paper or will deduct points).

Legal examples of elemental rules include the following:

- To accept an offer of a contract, the offeree must manifest assent to the terms of the offer in the proper manner. (*elements are: (1) manifestation of assent, (2) by the offeree, (3) to the terms of the offer, and (4) in the proper manner*)

- Federal courts have jurisdiction where the parties are diverse and the amount in controversy exceeds $75,000 (*elements are: (1) parties are diverse, and (2) the amount in controversy exceeds $75,000*)

- False imprisonment is the intentional confinement of another without consent. (*elements are: (1) intent to confine, (2) actual confinement, (3) the person confined must be different than the person doing the confinement, (4) the confined person did not consent, and (5) the confinement results in harm*)

- A trespasser to land may acquire title to that land if his or her possession of the land is (1) hostile, (2) exclusive, (3) continuous, (4) open and notorious, and (5) actual and lasts for the statutory period.

Notice that these rules can be expressed as a sentence: Federal courts have jurisdiction where the parties are diverse and the amount in controversy exceeds $75,000. Lawyers, however, deconstruct the rule, and translate the sentence into a set of elements: *(1) diversity, and (2) amount in controversy exceeds $75,000.* Lawyers engage in this translation process so that they can analyze each part separately. If each part is an element, the absence of any part means the rule is not satisfied. In other words, unless the amount in controversy is $75,000.01 or more, the federal court will not be able to hear the case.

When determining whether a rule is a list of mandatory elements, it is necessary to focus on the specific words used in the rule. For example, the use of the words "is" or "are" frequently signal that the words to follow are requirements rather than merely considerations. Second, the conjunction "and" usually express that the items that follow are to be added to the items that preceded them, thereby suggesting the rule has multiple mandatory requirements.

---

**PAUSE. THINK. ACT.** Review the rules in the preceding section. Identify the signals that help you determine that the rule is one with mandatory elements.

---

Applying elemental rules requires the lawyer (and law student) to demonstrate that each of the required elements exists.

### 3. Factor Rules (If A, B and C Weighed Together Justify Z, then Z)

Factor rules consist of a list of considerations that must be weighed in deciding whether the consequence is justified. These considerations are referred to as the factors. Although non-lawyers seldom use the term "factors," almost everyone has had the experience of weighing considerations in making a decision. The decision of which college or law school to attend, for example, involves weighing the cost, educational programs, and geographical location, among other things. Even more simply, the decision of which restaurant to go to for lunch may involve weighing the cost, quality and convenience of the various choices.

Factor rules are similar to elemental rules in the sense that they contain a list of considerations, each of which must be analyzed to determine whether the consequence follows. However, factor rules are different from elemental rules in one very important respect: all of the factors do not have to be present (or proven) to impose the consequence. Instead, a sufficient number of the factors must be satisfied, or, if only one or very few of the factors are satisfied, they must be the factors which carry the most weight.

You very likely already understand how factors are evaluated. Imagine for example, that you were selecting a restaurant for lunch, and you needed to be back within 30 minutes, you wanted a salad, and you didn't want to spend a lot of money. You might be willing to select an expensive restaurant that did not serve salads, if the most important factor to you was getting back in 30 minutes. On the other hand, if money was the most important factor, you might be willing to come back late so you could eat somewhere affordable. The relative importance of the factors, and not just the number of factors satisfied, is significant in determining whether a factors test has been met.

Legal examples of factor rules include the following:

- In determining whether to issue a preliminary injunction, the court weighs the strength of the party's claim on the merits, the hardship to the party requesting relief if relief were denied and the hardship to the other party if relief were granted, the extent to which the hardship to either party is compensable in money, the practicality of enforcing the order, public policy (what is best for society as a whole), and the morality of the parties' respective conduct.

- Custody shall be determined by whatever is in the best interests of the child, including: (1) the health, safety, and welfare of the child, (2) any history of abuse by one parent or any other person seeking custody, (3) the nature and amount of contact with both parents, and (4) the habitual or continual illegal use of controlled substances or habitual or continual abuse of alcohol by either parent.

- To determine whether a breach of contract is a material breach, the following circumstances are significant: (a) the extent to which the injured party will be deprived of his contract benefit; (b) the extent to which the injured party can be compensated for that lost benefit; (c) the extent to which the breaching party will suffer forfeiture; (d) the likelihood that the breaching party will cure the defect in his performance and (e) the extent to which the breaching party has acted in good faith.

As was true with respect to elemental rules, the key to recognizing a factor rule is the words used. In particular, the word "weigh" in the preliminary injunction rule, the word "including" in the custody determination rule, and the phrase "the following circumstances are significant" in the material breach rule are typical signals that a test is a factor test. Moreover, in two of the rules above, the rule for child custody and the test for material breach, the rule starts with a standard (the "best interests of the child" and "material breach") which are measured by a list of considerations which do not all need to be present to meet the standard. Although the presence of a standard does not always mean the rule will be a factor test, the use of a standard makes the need for factors to elucidate the meaning of that standard more likely, and factor rules are quite often combined with a standard that the factors attempt to measure.

Another way to see the significance of the language used is to consider what language would have signaled that the tests were elemental rules. For example, to convert the material breach rule to an elemental rule, you would have to say something about the plaintiff proving that the breach was material by showing that the injured party will be significantly deprived of the contract benefit, that the deprivation cannot be compensated, that the breaching party will not suffer significant forfeiture if the breach were deemed material, that the breaching party is unlikely to cure the defect in performance, *and* that the breaching party did not breach the contract in good faith.

Another version of a factors test is a simple balancing test—where the court weighs one factor against another factor. With such tests, rather than weighting a number of factors, the court simply decides which of the two stated factors is strongest.

Legal examples of a balancing test include the following:

- If the probative value of the evidence is outweighed by the danger of unfair prejudice, the evidence will be excluded.

- A product is defective if the risks posed by the product outweigh the benefits provided by the product.

Applying a factors test requires a lawyer to demonstrate that the factors weigh in favor of the lawyers' client. To do this, the lawyer must first be able to articulate which factor or factors should be given the most weight (and why), and then demonstrate that factor or factors is satisfied.

### 4. Alternative Rules (If A or B, then Z)

Alternative rules can be met by showing that any of the alternatives is present. Alternative rules outside the legal context are common. For example, want ads for open jobs sometimes state that applicants must either possess a particular level of educational attainment *or* a particular level of experience. Similarly, some parents impose curfew rules that require a child either to be home by the specified time or to call the parents and let the parents know the child will be late and why.

Legal examples of alternative rules include:

- A plaintiff may be awarded punitive damages if the defendant was malicious, reckless, oppressive, evil, wicked, or guilty of wanton or morally culpable conduct or showed flagrant indifference to the safety of others.

- A plaintiff in an action for breach of contract may be awarded damages for the harm caused by the breach or obtain an order requiring the breaching party to specifically perform the promise.

Crucial words which are often used to signal that a test is an alternative test are: "either" and "or."

Applying an alternative rule requires that the lawyer demonstrate that one of the alternatives is satisfied. Of course, if more than one of the alternatives is satisfied, the lawyer may wish to put forward arguments or evidence as to each satisfied alternative, to provide multiple avenues for the judge or jury to find in her client's favor. Nonetheless, the lawyer need only prove one to satisfy the rule.

### 5. Rules with Exceptions (If A, then Z, Unless B)

Human relations are so complex that, over time, courts and legislators find it necessary to create exceptions to many rules. Of course, rules with exceptions are also common outside the legal context. For example, college students are familiar with graduation requirements (the rule) that can be waived with approval of a dean or a department chair (the exception).

Examples of legal rules that have exceptions include:

- A promise to do what one is already legally obligated to do is not enforceable (*rule*), but a similar performance is if it differs from what was required in a way that reflects more than a pretense (*exception*).

- A restraint on the alienation of property is void (*rule*) unless the present and future interests both are held by charities (*exception*).

- A person who has been induced by fraudulent misrepresentations to transfer title to property may recover that property from anyone who subsequently possesses it (*rule*) unless that person was a bona-fide purchaser of the property (*exception*).

Notice that the key to categorizing rules with exceptions, as is true of categorizing all types of rules, is language. In this instance, words that often signal exceptions include "unless," "except," "but," and "but if."

When applying a rule with exceptions, the lawyer for one side is typically arguing for the application of the rule, while the lawyer for the other side is typically arguing that an exception to the rule applies, such that the consequence for the rule should not be imposed. On an examination, which usually requires a law student to examine both sides, the students would first evaluate the rule, to see if it is satisfied, and then evaluate wither the exception is satisfied, and thus, whether the consequence of the rule should or should not be imposed.

The ability to distinguish among the various types of rule structures is crucial; the chart on the following page can be used as a quick guide to help you identify the various structures.

It is very important that you do not assume that a rule is one of the structures based solely on the presence of a signal word; it is critical to read the rule, and use the language, punctuation and definitions (from other statutes, cases, class discussion and other materials) to guide you in determining the type of rule structure(s) present in any particular rule.

### 6. Combination Rules

Many rules are actually combinations of the five types of rule structures. For example, the tort battery rule is an elemental rule, but one of its elements is an alternative

| Type of Rule | Structure | Example | Signal Words |
|---|---|---|---|
| Simple Rules | if A, then Z | The maximum speed limit on a state highway is 65 miles per hour. | |
| Elemental Rules (a test with mandatory elements) | if A, B and C, then Z | Federal courts have jurisdiction where the parties are diverse and the amount in controversy exceeds $75,000. | and, with, all |
| Alternative Rules (an either/or test) | if A or B, then Z | A plaintiff may be awarded punitive damages if the defendant was malicious, reckless, oppressive, evil, wicked, or guilty of wanton or morally culpable conduct or showed flagrant indifference to the safety of others. | or, either |
| Factor Rules (a flexible standard guided by criteria or factors—including Balancing Tests; often start with a standard, and one or more of the factors can be absent without changing the result) | if A, B and C weighed together justify it, then Z if A outweighs B, then Z if A, C and F outweigh B and G, then Z | Custody shall be determined by whatever is in the best interests of the child, including: (1) the health, safety, and welfare of the child, (2) any history of abuse by one parent or any other person seeking custody, (3) the nature and amount of contact with both parents, and (4) the habitual or continual illegal use of controlled substances or habitual or continual abuse of alcohol by either parent. If the probative value of the evidence is outweighed by the danger of unfair prejudice, the evidence will be excluded. | weigh, outweigh, consider, including, factors, circumstances |
| Rules with exception(s) | If A, then Z, unless B | A restraint on the alienation of property is void unless the present and future interests both are held by charities. | except, unless, but if |

rule. Here is a typical battery rule—see if you can identify the two structures (the required elements and the alternative test):

> Battery is the intentional causing of a harmful or offensive contact with the person of another.[3]

This forcible rape statute is an example of an alternative test, where one of the alternatives includes four required elements, one of which can be satisfied with an alternative test—see if you can identify them:

---

3. The required elements are: intent, causation, contact, the contact must be with another person, and the contact must be either harmful <u>or</u> offensive—an alternative test.

Forcible rape is an act of sexual intercourse accomplished against a person's will by means of force, violence, duress, menace or fear of immediate and unlawful bodily injury on the person or another.[4]

Deciphering these rules simply requires recognizing the signals and language described in the five prior sections, and understanding that when you see a variety of these indicators that you have probably encountered a combination rule.

## 3. Understand How the Parts Are Related to One Another

The deconstructed version of the rule should help you to identify each of the issues you must consider and help you evaluate whether you can prove all of the necessary "parts." To do this, you must not only be able to identify each of the parts, but also to understand how each of the parts are related to one another. For example, as set out above, the "parts" of the stated murder rule are: (1) unlawful; (2) killing; (3) another; (4) human being; and (5) malice aforethought. Identifying each of the parts was important, but you also must understand the relationships between these parts. For example, you must understand that it is the killing which must be unlawful. As you begin to understand these relationships you may want to reorganize your outline of the rule to reflect this understanding. For example, you could organize your understanding of the murder rule this way:

Murder requires:

1) That there was a killing

2) That the killing was unlawful

3) That the killing was of a human being

4) That the human being who was killed was a person other than the one doing the killing

5) That the killing was done with malice aforethought

This organization reflects both that the killing must be unlawful, of a human being and done with malice aforethought, and that addressing whether there was a killing, before considering these other issues, would make the most sense at least in part because if there is no killing, there is no point in considering these other issues.

Deconstructed rules can and should be used for organizing your thinking and writing—including your class notes, examination answers, legal writing papers, and exam approaches. A student could use such a deconstructed rule to answer an examination question, by thinking of each piece of this deconstructed rule as the issues to consider when evaluating the examination facts (or hypotheticals posed by the professor during class). Those issues can be identified by asking this series of questions:

---

4. The fourth alternative includes four elements (fear of bodily injury, the feared bodily injury must be immediate (and not remote in time), the feared bodily injury must be unlawful, and the fear must be of one's own injury or of another's injury). Also note that this fourth element has two alternatives (one's own injury or another's injury).

Is "X" guilty of murder?
1)  Was there a killing?
2)  Was that killing unlawful?
3)  Was the killing of a human being?
4)  Was the human being who was killed a person other than "X"?
5)  Was the killing was done with malice aforethought?

These are the questions a student would need to answer on an exam testing this murder rule. These are also the questions a lawyer would ask to determine whether the elements of this murder rule are satisfied. These questions can also be turned into affirmative statements that could help a student organize a memorandum on the issue, or help a lawyer organize a motion or other document related to this topic. For example, imagine that your exam fact pattern was about X shooting Y, who is dead. You could organize the exam this way:

I.  X should be charged with murder.

    a.  X killed Y
    b.  The killing was unlawful
    c.  Y was a human being
    d.  At the time of the killing X had malice aforethought

Another point is equally crucial. Each of these requirements will have their own definitions, and sometimes additional rules (and rule structures). For example, malice aforethought (in some states) requires proof that the actor had the intent to kill, or intent to cause grievous bodily injury, or exhibited reckless disregard for great risk to human life, or committed the killing during the course of an inherently dangerous felony. Notice this is an alternative rule structure. More importantly, each of these requirements can (and should) be further defined. For example, you would need to know what acts constitute a felony, and what makes a felony inherently dangerous. In this sense, this rule for murder is like the sun in a solar system, each of the elements are planets, and some of those planets have moons. The definition is the hub from which sub-rules and sub-sub-rules emerge.

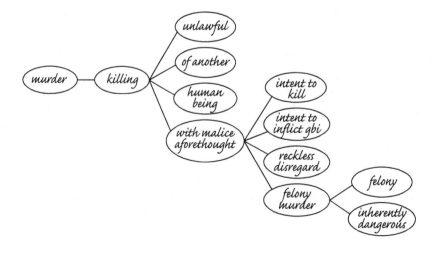

In most law school classes, students learn or must figure out for themselves the sub-rule and study court opinions addressing each of the sub- and sub-sub-rules; expert law students must then determine how the rule, sub-rule(s) and sub-sub-rules fit together and can be used to analyze hypotheticals. Much of the time, this can only be done by utilizing practice materials (described in Chapters 7 and 8) and a trial and error process, which helps the student understand all of the potentially testable issues.

There are multiple ways to organize this (and most other) statutes. If you are lucky enough to have a professor who provides you with a structure for analyzing a rule (or an examination), you should follow their instructions carefully. The key to rule deconstruction is to be certain you've identified each element so that you do not miss issues or skip analytical steps—and to organize the parts in a manner that reflects how they are related to one another.

Note that sometimes a deconstructed rule will follow the same order as the original rule, and sometimes, because it makes it easier to understand the rule, it will be in a different order. So long as the deconstructed version does not alter or change the meaning of the rule, and includes all of the parts and subparts of the rule that are necessary to resolve the issue presented, it is acceptable to order the pieces of the rule differently—assuming you have not been given a specific order by your professor.

---

**PAUSE. THINK. ACT.** Each time you deconstruct a rule, think about the following: (1) Does the deconstructed version help you to understand the rule? Why or why not? (2) Are there changes you can make that would help you better understand the rule? (Note: be sure that changes you make do not alter the original meaning of the statute.) (3) Does the deconstructed rule help you organize your thinking? (4) Will the deconstructed rule help you write an organized answer when the rule is tested?

---

## Step Four: Plan Your Notes Like an Expert

A particularly important activity for maximizing your learning from the law school classroom involves planning your notes. Expert learners do not magically produce superior notes out of thin air; their notes are the product of careful planning.

There are two main reasons why expert law students plan the structure of their notes. First, it helps them remember what they learn. Humans learn new concepts better and retain that new learning better when they understand the relationships between the new concepts and concepts they previously have studied and when they understand the relationships among the new concepts they are studying. Moreover, by planning their notes so that they fit within a structure, rather than simply recording what the instructor says without trying to fit that information within a structure, expert law students begin to develop a structure to store the new learning. In other words, if you plan the structure of your notes, you are building a storage facility in your brain into which you can place the new learning.

Second, doing so will speed your note taking. Imposing structure on your notes as you take them, rather than simply recording what is said in class, requires you make an effort to process the material as you are hearing it which strengthens memory and increases the likelihood of later recall. Developing some basic structure in advance of class helps with imposing that structure during class.

The task is much less daunting than one might imagine. If you read like an expert and you review your professors' syllabi, the table of contents of your texts, the table of contents of supplemental texts, the questions after the cases and information in the supplemental texts, you will already have a structure for the material. Together, these resources are very likely to result in a list of major topics, sub-topics and sub-sub-topics. Reviewing this material not only makes it easier to understand the cases but also will help you plan the major topics and headings you will need for your class notes.

One caveat is important. Instructors are unlikely to follow the exact structure you develop on your own. Consequently, it is better to develop the structure on a separate sheet of paper from which you easily can copy as you take notes.

In planning their notes, expert learners also have a system for organizing notes for each course and class session. While there are a variety of note-taking formats in existence, most of them have a number of features in common. First, virtually all note-taking formats assign a separate notebook (or computer folder) for each course and a separate page (or computer "document") for each class session and suggest that students use full-sized (8½ by 11 inch) sheets of paper. These simple strategies ensure that students readily can find all the notes for each course easily, can identify the beginning and ending of their notes for each particular class session and have plenty of room to take their notes.

Expert law students use a note-taking format that will result in a set of notes that are useable during future review and study. Expert learners never use the entire sheet of paper or computer screen for their class notes; rather, they divide their paper or screen (or use more than one screen), reserving approximately one-third of the page for writing questions they have as they are taking notes, for identifying key terms and key concepts, for commenting on what they are learning, for reflecting on their understanding of the discussion, and for labeling the likely instructional purpose of the matters addressed in the notes. In any given class session, an instructor may be teaching students the rules of law, case reading and briefing, applying and distinguishing, legal ethics, etc. By determining and indicating the instructional goal to which the notes relate, the student makes his or her future use of those notes much easier.

Adopting this note-taking format is a crucial skill. It not only helps law students do better in law school, but also it helps lawyers do better in law practice. Experienced trial lawyers take notes as they listen to witnesses testify (both in depositions and in court) using a very similar format. On the larger side of the page or screen (the left two-thirds), they record what the witness said. On the smaller side (the right one-third), they note the names of additional witnesses they must depose or call, questions they should ask future witnesses, documentary and other evidence they will need to subpoena, legal research the witness' statements necessitate, and the relationship between the witness' testimony and the elements of the claims and defenses at issue in the case. In other words, they take notes in much the same way expert law students take notes, using two-thirds of the space for recording what they are hearing and one-third for expressing their reflections on the implications of what they are hearing.

The best way to understand this approach is by imagining a class discussion that reflected the above and below materials in this text (on note taking) and then considering the fictional excerpt from a student's notes about those materials as shown below:

| | |
|---|---|
| Date<br><br><u>Before Class prep</u><br>  **Taking Notes**<br>• Plan structure—use syllabi, pre-reading, etc., plan to adapt to class structure<br>• Focus on goals not just recording<br>• Set up—sep folder for each course; sep doc for each session<br>• Format—leave space for thoughts, quest. etc.<br>• Need shorthand/abbrev. | <br><br><br><br><br>*Helps with memory!*<br><br><br><br>*Would it work to use 2 diff screens?*<br>*Is there some shorthand everyone uses?*<br>*(P and D?)* |

Finally, expert law students develop a set of abbreviations and a shorthand technique that allows for rapid note taking. Expert students recognize that note-taking speed can be helpful. Consequently, they develop abbreviations and shorthand techniques. For example, many law students, lawyers and law professors use the $\prod$ symbol or the letter P for plaintiff, the symbol or the letter D for defendant and the letters ct for court. Other abbreviations used by almost all note-takers include: w/ (with), w/o (without), = (is), & (and), b/c (because). Similarly, many students leave out articles (a, an, the) and otherwise write in a form that may be termed, "caveman talk." Instead of writing, "The court held that a plaintiff in a suit for negligence must prove the defendant owed a duty of care to the plaintiff," they write "P claiming negl. must prove D owed duty to P." Of course, students develop these abbreviations and shorthand over time through usage, and, most abbreviations and shorthand techniques are idiosyncratic because each student must be able to recall what he or she means by each abbreviation. Nevertheless, smart note-takers plan their abbreviations for each subject area. For example, a student about to study the parol evidence rule in contracts might decide to use PER to refer to the rule, and a student about to study the tort of intentional infliction of emotional distress might decide to use IIED to refer to that tort. If you look at the note example above, you will see several abbreviated words.

In the next chapter, we will return to the subject of note-taking, and examine how expert learners take notes during class.

# Step Five: Develop Questions

Expert classroom learners develop lists of questions they expect to be answered by the class discussion, and questions they have about the material. Your questions should address aspects of the reading assignments that have confused you and areas you expect your professor to address in the classroom discussion. By developing these questions, expert students not only make sure that they understand what they need to understand about the materials in the course, but also make sure they are actively paying attention to the classroom discussion, listening for answers to the questions they have developed.

> **PAUSE. THINK. ACT.** Why do students who use the strategies detailed in this section get better grades than those who do not? Why will they have an easier time succeeding as lawyers?

# Allocating Your Time Wisely

As you learned in Chapter two, law school requires a significant expenditure of time and effort to succeed, which is why expert law students are experts at managing their time wisely. As you see in this chapter, and as you will learn in the next few chapters, preparation for class, and preparation for examinations do not involve the same tasks. After reading this chapter, and spending some time in law school, you might assume that case reading and briefing are more critical than other skills. While they are important skills to learn, if you spend so much time on these skills that you are unable to engage in the tasks that will prepare you for your examinations, you will likely not perform well on those examinations. So be sure to evaluate each of your tasks in light of your goals (which likely include succeeding in law school, and on exams) — the more likely the task is to help you reach your goal, the more time and energy you should likely invest in that task.

# Chapter 6

# Thinking and Acting Like a Lawyer: What to Do *During* Class

Expert law students recognize that they will learn little in class if they simply show up unprepared, hoping to be enlightened. Like any other learning experience, classroom learning is ultimately a matter of the taking control over one's own learning. Such control starts long before the scheduled start time for the class. Thus, when expert law students arrive to class they have:

1) read and briefed all of their assigned cases;
2) identified areas of confusion so they know what to focus on during class;
3) reviewed and synthesized their notes from the previous class;
4) planned a structure for their class notes;
5) selected strategies for how they will focus their attention during class; and
6) prepared questions they expect to be answered by the class discussion.

These strategies are covered in Chapters 5 and 7, because they happen outside of class. This chapter is devoted to the strategies for learning during class. It is important to understand, however, that learning in law school happens before, during *and* after class. Expert learners understand the relationship between these three areas. Expert learners understand that they must adequately prepare *before* class, take steps to cement their learning *after* class, and actively participate *during* class if they are to succeed in law school. In fact, your preparation for class helps you take in your new learning, because students retain new learning better when they have connected it to prior learning.

## Learning in the Law School Classroom

Most law school instruction occurs within the classroom context. For many law students, in fact, classroom instruction is their only contact with their professor, their only opportunity to practice the skills they need to be developing, the only place they obtain feedback on their progress, and their only chance to resolve confusion and ask questions. Consequently, expert law students are experts at learning what they need to learn from their classroom instruction and in recording that learning in a form they can later use. This begins with understanding the teaching methods and goals of law school instruction.

First-year law school instruction is most commonly described as "Socratic" in technique.[1] Law professors who use this method ask their students many, many questions. Professors select one student (or, occasionally, two or three) and typically engage in a one-on-one dialogue with a selected student, asking the student to explain an assigned statute or court opinion, to dissect the court's reasoning, the public policy underlying the statute or holding and to identify and analyze the issues in a hypothetical. For court opinions, many professors require the selected student to identify the relevant facts, the court's holding and the policy underlying it. For rules, many professors require the selected student to break the rule down into a set of sub-requirements and articulate the policy underlying the rule. The professor then focuses on the application of the holding or rule by asking the selected student to apply the rule or holding to a hypothetical or series of hypotheticals (aka "hypos"). Professors ask students in class to analyze hypos as a way of testing the students' understanding of the court opinions they have read and as a way of helping the students practice the skills which students' law school exams will test, by exploring how that case might be applied in the future. They also sometimes use hypos to help the students identify flaws in a court's reasoning, to test students' understanding of the doctrine, or to help students discern the underlying policy implications of a court's decisions.

> **PAUSE. THINK. ACT.** How might you use the techniques in chapter 5 to help prepare you for learning from this teaching methodology? How is this method different from other teaching methods?

Expert law students typically have in mind three core goals in learning from their classroom interaction: (1) understanding how the classroom instruction relates to their law school examination; (2) confirming understanding of the subject matter and resolving areas of confusion; and (3) recording what they have learned in a form that allows for easy use in organizing their course materials when studying for examinations.

## 1. Expert Learners Understand How Classroom Instruction Relates to Law School Examinations

Most professors will tell you that one of the primary goals of law school is to teach you to "think like a lawyer." Part of thinking like a lawyer means being able to apply what you learn from the cases (and statutes and other materials) you read to new situations to predict how a court will rule on that new situation. For this reason, some portion of most of your classes will include grappling with hypothetical fact situations

---

1. There is evidence that upper division law school courses are more often taught using lecture methodologies.

(aka "hypos"). A hypo is a statement of a set of facts that gives rise to one or more legal disputes. These hypos are usually stated verbally and usually relate directly to the court opinions or rules on which the class is working.

Hypos vary in length and degree of difficulty; a hypo may be as short as a sentence or as long as three pages. It may involve multiple parties or just two. Law professors create hypos (and exams) by using court opinions not assigned to the students (usually with some modifications), by changing key facts in the court opinions assigned to the students, by adapting newspaper stories to raise issues the students have studied, by using facts from actual cases they have litigated, or by simply coming up with a story from scratch.

While there are some differences in format, examination questions are really just longer hypos; you'll use the same thinking process you practice in class to answer your exam questions. The key differences are: the "hypos" on your exams will likely be multi-issue and more complex; your professor will not be there to guide you through the reasoning process; and your answers will be in writing. In the next chapter you will learn how to use your class preparation and in-class instruction to prepare for writing your exams. For now, it is important to understand how classroom instruction and the hypos posed during class help you to do the type of thinking required for law school exams and for the practice of law. It is therefore important to understand how hypos teach you to do legal analysis.

### Learning Legal Analysis by Responding to Hypos

The student's tasks in responding to a hypo are to:

1) identify the legal questions raised;
2) articulate all of the potentially applicable law (i.e., the relevant rules or case holdings);
3) identify each fact that is relevant to the resolution of each legal question raised;
4) explain how lawyers representing each of the parties would use the facts and law to argue for a result favoring their respective clients;
5) explain why a court would select one of the arguments over the other; and
6) predict how a court would decide the matter.

This type of response requires law students to use the IRAC method—a method you might have heard about and which will be discussed in the next chapter, because it is the method most commonly employed by law students as the writing method on law school examinations. Look back at the steps. Step one—to identify the legal question is really the task of spotting the legal issue, the "I" in IRAC. Step two—articulating the applicable law is the task of stating the "rule" that should be applied to resolve the issue—the "R" of IRAC. Parts three, four and five, where the student articulates the parties' arguments—using the facts and law—and explains why the court would rule for one of the parties over the other, are the "A" of IRAC, the legal analysis. Legal analysis will, by far, be the primary focus during your first year of law school—it is usually what is meant by the phrase "thinking like a lawyer." The final step is to state the likely conclusion the court would adopt—the "C" in IRAC.

While students must know the rules and case holdings and be able to identify the legal questions, they are ultimately evaluated as law students and lawyers by how well they perform legal analysis. This is where the bulk of the points are typically awarded on law school exams and bar exams. But as you can see, without understanding the rules, and how the issues are raised, it is difficult to do the required analysis. Law school exams and bar exams test students' ability to perform each of the skills described above and students' possession of the knowledge necessary to perform those skills (such as the knowledge of the rules and holdings). This makes it critical for you to master this process.

In this section, we will cover the part of the process you engage in during class—the thinking process. In a subsequent chapter in this book we will cover the part of the process you engage in when writing exams, legal writing papers and, most importantly, the documents you will draft as a lawyer, such as motions and briefs—the writing process. It is important to understand that you will be assessed (graded) almost exclusively on your written work, but the feedback you receive will be almost entirely on your (and your classmates') spoken work (answers you and your classmates give to the hypos posed by the professor)—and there are important differences between how you think (and speak) about a subject and how you write about a subject.

To help you understand these differences, we will address the thinking process in this chapter, and the writing process in the next chapter, using the same illustration. This illustration will also help you understand how to use what you are learning in the classroom to prepare for and write a law school exam answer.

### *Legal Analysis — The Thinking Process*

The thinking process involves the application of relevant law to a set of facts. For this reason, our illustration begins with the law. Although the law can come from different sources, e.g., statutes, cases, or administrative regulations, in most or even all of your first year courses, you will learn the law from cases, which is what we will be using for this illustration.

Imagine that before class you were assigned <u>Parker v. Twentieth Century Fox</u> (the case you've read and briefed as part of the exercises in Chapter 5) which appears in Appendix B. We know from Chapter 5 that the case is about the circumstances under which an employee is precluded from recovering damages for breach of an employment contract if she refuses to accept an alternative offer of employment, because the employee has a duty to mitigate her damages. Its a good idea to review <u>Parker</u> and the brief you created in Chapter 5 before you read on.

Now imagine that during class discussion of the case, the professor elicits the following rule from a student: An employee need not mitigate their damages from a breach of contract by accepting an offer of alternative employment that is different or inferior from the original offer.

Satisfied with the rule she has elicited, the professor then poses the following hypothetical:

Jack Nickels was a famous dramatic actor who lived in San Francisco. Nickels entered into a contract with GMG to star in a new, one-hour comedy television series set in a hospital. The shows were to be filed in a Los Angeles studio. Nickels was set to play the role of an emergency room doctor. Under the terms of Nickels' contract with GMG, Nickels was to be paid two million dollars for the first season of the show. GMF had the right to renew the show for each of the next two years, and to pay Nickels three million dollars for season two, and four million dollars for season four. Nickels had the right to direct two episodes per season and write one episode each season in the second and third seasons. Before filming started, GMG canceled the series. GMG offered Nickels the lead role also playing an emergency room doctor, in an already existing successful series, also set in a hospital. The lead actor in the series had already decided to leave the show. The show was a "dramedy" (a dramatic series with regular comedic scenes). Nickels would receive the same compensation, but because the show had an established team of writers, he would not have the right to write any episodes. He was instead offered the right to direct three episodes per season. The show is filmed in New York City.

Imagine that after presenting this hypothetical, the following dialogue between the professor and a student occurs:

Professor: If Nickels rejects this offer, and sues for breach of contract, will his right to recover damages be reduced?

Student 1: Yes, because the offer was different and inferior.

P. How was it different or inferior?

S1. In <u>Parker</u>, the first offer was for a musical, where she would dance and act, and it was to be filmed in Los Angeles.

P. Who is she?

S1. The actress ... the plaintiff

P. Why did it matter that the first offer was for a musical?

S1. Because the second offer was for a dramatic Western, so she was not able to show off her dancing skills.

P. And how did that make the offer for the Western an inferior offer?

S1. Because it was in Australia, and she lived in Los Angeles. And she didn't get to approve the director or the screenplay.

P. And how does that make the offer for the Western an inferior offer?

S1. Los Angeles is where movies were made—in Hollywood

P. And how does that make the Western inferior to the Musical? Do you like Westerns?

S1. Not particularly.

P. I see. So your bias against Westerns is clouding your judgment. Couldn't you argue that a Western was superior to a Musical?

S1.   I suppose you could, but even so, she was limited in her ability to pursue other opportunities, especially since this was 1966 and most deals were likely done face to face, or over the telephone—but certainly not via things like Skype or Facetime, or even email. The distance would have changed her access to studios, directors and projects.

P.    So it isn't that it is a Western or Musical—are you abandoning that position?

S1.   I guess its that the distance was more important.

P.    Important to whom?

S1.   To the court in this case. She—I mean the plaintiff—might have other opportunities while she was filming. If she was in Australia, far away from where movies were made, and movie deals were discussed, it would impair her creative interests. She was losing creative control. And that would be important to an actress. And that's the same for approving the director and the script—when she didn't get those she lost creative control over how she would be portrayed.

P.    And so your argument is that her loss of creative control is what makes the offer inferior?

S1.   Yes. And that is also why it matters that it was a Western—because that is a different type of movie, so she isn't getting creative control there either.

P.    How does the choice of genre deprive her of creative control?

S1.   Well, she might be really great at dancing, and really terrible at dramatic acting, so she might only pick a project where she could show off what she is good at—and those choices are her creative process.

P.    I take it you've never heard of the actress in this case—Ms. McClaine?

S1.   No.

P.    She was a pretty decent dramatic actress as well.

S1.   Even so—as an actress it would be important to get to pick the type of movie you do—either because you want to stretch your abilities—or because you want to keep your fans happy by doing what they want. Either way—when they change the type of movie, they take away your creative choices, which seem like a huge part of what actresses might care about.

P.    So your analysis is limited to actresses then?

S1.   Maybe to anyone who has a job where creative interests matter—like other artists.

P.    Lucky for Mr. Nickels he fits that bill. How would you apply Parker to Mr. Nickels' situation?

S1.   Nickels is the same—he signed up for a comedy, and since he is a famous dramatic actor he probably wanted to show that he could do something else—to expand his acting skills. The new show doesn't let him do that, because it is mostly drama. He also doesn't get to expand his creative interests by writing—which is what the first offer let him do. And if he writes the episodes and directs them he has creative control over how he is portrayed. He loses that with the second offer, and since the second offer does not allow him to expand his creative interests—which is critical for someone in show business, it's an inferior offer.

P.  Student 2, what do you think about that?

By eliciting this information from the student, the professor (and the student) have created a linking explanation between the case and the hypothetical and demonstrated the following components of the thinking process:

- Identifying the reasons for the outcome in the precedent case
- Identifying the similarities between the precedent case and the hypo
- Identifying how those things from the precedent case which are similar to the hypo were important to the outcome in the precedent case
- Identifying how the reasons for the outcome in the precedent case also exist in the hypo, which necessarily requires the same result (outcome) for the hypo

The linking explanation requires identifying a "proposed premise" which ties the facts from the precedent case to the facts in the hypo and forms the basis for a finding that the hypo should have the same outcome. This process is what is known as "applying" legal authority. This thinking process typically happens in a non-linear manner, which can be visually represented like this:

## Applying Cases—Thinking Process Mind Map

If we fill in the components from the Professor and student dialogue above, it would look like this:

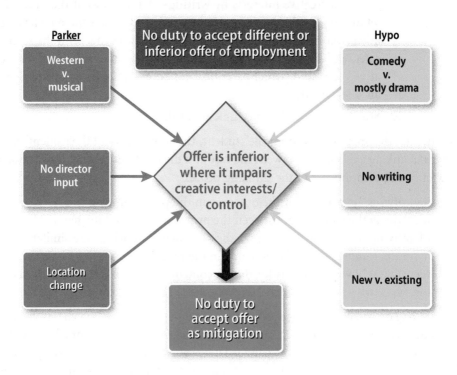

The dark gray box, which appears above the Thinking Process Mind Map, is the rule. Sometimes students attempt to use the rule as a substitute for the proposed premise. Doing so results in a lack of understanding of how and why the rule applies. You may want to try this tactic—of separately stating the rule first—so that you do not use it as a substitute for explaining how and why the application of that rule resulted in the case outcome. You'll notice that the student in the dialogue above attempted to use the rule as an explanation for the court's decision—and the professor pressed the student to explain why the court reached the outcome it did, until the student articulated a proposed premise. Go back and identify where this happened. Be on the lookout for these moments in the classroom.

In a Socratic dialogue, like the one above, information reveals itself in bits and pieces, as responses to questions from the professor; these questions are designed to guide the student through the reasoning process, helping students to discover potential "answers" (usually a variety of arguments) rather than telling students what the answers might be. This can take a significant amount of time and requires students in the course to listen carefully to each question and answer, and to ultimately assemble from that discussion an understanding of the components of the applying and distinguishing thinking process illustrated in the charts printed throughout this section.

This can be difficult, especially at first, because professors usually do not highlight or label the components—and students who are not listening carefully, or who do not understand what they are looking for, can easily miss them.

One final thing to note is that there is no magic number of supporting items or connections that must be made. Although there are three purple boxes and three orange boxes in this diagram, you do not need to create three things if only two exist, and you do not need to limit yourself to three, if four or more exist. Also, you do not need matched pairs of supporting information. You might have three things you wish to use from the case, and four from the hypo, and vice versa.

---

**PAUSE. THINK. ACT.** Review the professor student dialogue set out above.
1. Use highlighters corresponding to the colors in the "Applying Precedent Thinking Process Mind Map" above to identify each of the pieces listed in the mind map. In other words, find the student's proposed premise and highlight it in blue, find the facts from the precedent case and highlight them in purple, etc. Notice that some parts of the mind map may appear more than once.
2. Students routinely make the mistake of thinking that the rule from the case is the proposed premise, sometimes because the rule is easier to spot, and the proposed premise might be inferred from the case, rather than explicitly stated. Students also make the mistake of comparing facts from the precedent case with facts from the hypo, without any explanation of why the facts from the precedent case were significant to the case outcome. Can you locate these two errors in the student's responses?

---

Now imagine another student makes a different argument, explaining their answer this way:

Student 2:  I disagree.

Professor:  What is the basis for your disagreement?

S2:  In <u>Parker</u>, it was a total change in the kind of movie she was making—from musical to Western, and she lost all control when she lost director and screenplay approval. She also moved from the lead, starring role to a secondary role

P:  So you agree with Student 1's statement—that accepting the second offer would have impaired Ms. McClaine's—the actress in <u>Parker</u>—interests?

S2:  Yes, it totally robbed her of any creative control.

P:  So then why do you disagree?

S2: Because Nickels' creative interests aren't impaired. Both of Nickels' offers are to play an ER doctor on a TV show—both of which have comedy. He still gets to direct, so he has creative control, and he is moving to another location that also has a ton of creative opportunities—like Broadway. Plenty of shows already film in New York, so he isn't cut off from career networking—he could go on the tonight show, or Broadway. And this isn't the '60s—bicoastal meetings can easily be done by things like Skype.

P: And why does it matter that he can attend meetings via Skype?

S2: I guess it doesn't.

P: Why do you guess that it doesn't?

S2: I guess because it doesn't have anything to do with him having creative control. But I think it does matter that the first offer was for a new show—which might never make it, since shows get cancelled all the time.

P: Why do you think that would matter?

S2: Because he might never have gotten a chance to do any of those things in the second and third season—because the show would be cancelled, but this other show is already popular, and probably already has a lot of people who watch it, so he has a better chance of people seeing his work, including his directorial work, which is a new creative avenue for him.

This student has distinguished, rather than applied, the precedent, and in so doing, has demonstrated the following components of the thinking process:

- Identifying the reasons for the outcome in the precedent case
- Identifying the differences between the precedent case and the hypo
- Identifying how those things from the precedent case which are different from the hypo were important to the outcome in the precedent case
- Identifying how the reasons for the outcome in the precedent case do not exist in the hypo, which necessarily requires a different result (outcome) for the hypo

It is important to note that although this student has distinguished the precedent, they have nonetheless "accepted" the proposed premise suggested by the first student. The student then "flipped" the premise during her analysis and explanation, because her goal was to demonstrate that the opposite of the proposed premise is true for the hypothetical. She does this by identifying the differences between the hypothetical facts from the precedent case and explaining why those differences are meaningful enough to warrant a different (opposite) outcome. Notice she uses the "flipped" premise to prove the differences are meaningful. This part of the thinking process can be visually represented like this:

## Distinguishing Cases — Thinking Process Mind Map

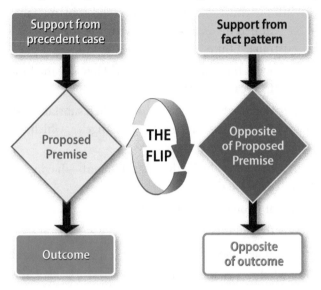

If we fill in the components from the student's statement above, it would look like this:

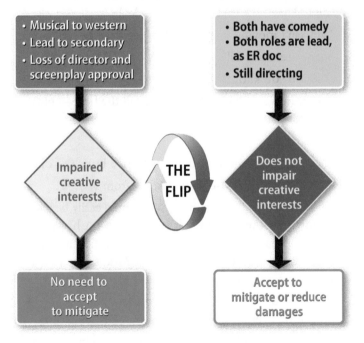

Now imagine that a third student makes yet another argument, explaining their answer this way:

Professor:  Student 3 do you agree?

Student 3:  I think the court in <u>Parker</u> was persuaded by the fact that the second offer required the plaintiff to move from Los Angeles to an opal mine in Australia. I think that was important.

P:  Why do you think it was important? How did the location impair the plaintiff's creative interests?

S3:  I think the move would have resulted in a substantial inconvenience to the plaintiff because she lived in Los Angeles, which would have meant being away from her home base.

P:  Is that enough to make the offer different—having to live away from home for some time?

S3:  Isn't that enough? It makes it different.

P:  And is that all that is required?

S3:  I guess it also has to be inferior.

P:  And what makes the offer inferior?

S3:  Maybe because it—the first offer—was in the movie capital of the world—really because movie studios didn't exist anywhere else in 1966—so she would have had to fly home, probably on a full day flight, from a time zone where it's a different day—and there wasn't Skype or texting or email. That's just different from this situation, where moving to New York isn't that big of a deal.

P:  Why isn't moving to New York a "big deal"?

S3:  There are tons of flights from LAX to JFK, non-stop, everyday.

P:  How do you know that?

S3:  I'm from New York and I fly home all the time—plus you could find it on Kayak.

P:  Kayak?

S3:  It's an app that shows you flights from a bunch of different airlines.

P:  Alright—so what else do you know from Kayak?

S3:  The flights take about 6 hours, so he could easily be back to Los Angeles at any time. And he doesn't even live in LA like the <u>Parker</u> plaintiff did—probably because it's no big deal to hop a flight from where he lives in San Francisco to LA or New York. Or he can send an email or a text, or, as Student 2 said, he can Skype—its' just a big difference from being out in the middle of Australia in the 1960's.

P:  So is it that she wasn't living at home? Or living in Los Angeles?

S3:  For Parker—it's both, the inconvenience of living away from her own home, which also happened to be a place that was important for her particular career of being an actress, because LA was where all the deals were going down, and she needed to be in town to make them happen.

That combination made the second offer much different—but here the change in location just doesn't. There isn't really any inconvenience, or it's minimal, so I think it's not an inferior offer.

This third student is also distinguishing the case. However, she has taken a different tactic—proposing an alternative premise, rather than accepting the premise offered by the student applying the case. After proposing the alternative premise, she then "flips" that premise and explains how the hypo demonstrates the opposite of the alternative premise. This is another method for distinguishing a case. This part of the thinking process involves two steps: First, the student proposes a new premise, and explains how the precedent case supports that premise. This part of the process can be visually represented like this:

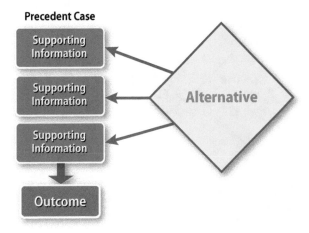

If we were to fill in the chart with the student's responses it would look like this:

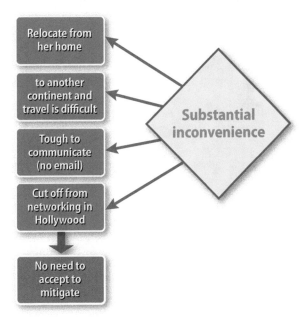

Next, rather than highlighting the similarities with that proposed premise and the hypo, as the student who was applying the case might have done, this student follows the distinguishing thinking process, by "flipping" the newly proposed premise to prove that the opposite is actually true for the hypo, such that it warrants a different (opposite) outcome. Like Student 2, she does this by identifying the differences between the hypothetical facts and facts from the precedent case and using the "flipped" premise to prove the differences are meaningful. This process, which you have already encountered, looks like this:

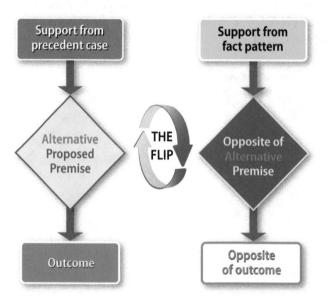

See if you can fill in this blank version of the Distinguishing Precedent Thinking Process Mind Map using the statements from the third student.

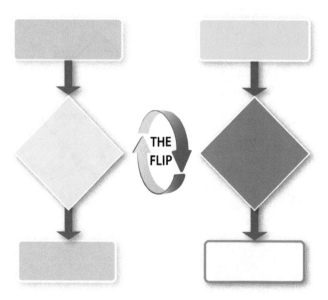

This method of distinguishing cases—offering an alternative premise, and then "flipping" that premise to prove the opposite outcome is warranted—can be used either when the original proposed premise is difficult to counter, or when proposing a new premise allows for a stronger argument for distinguishing a case.

There is one final point to be understood about distinguishing cases. Sometimes a student (or lawyer) must distinguish a case that no one has yet asked the court (or professor or grader) to apply. In such cases, the student must first offer a premise and build connections to support that premise—in exactly the same manner as the student would propose and support an alternate premise. It sometimes seems strange, because the student offers the premise for the purpose of "flipping" it, to demonstrate an opposite outcome from the precedent case is warranted. Nonetheless, no matter how a student begins the distinguishing process—whether by accepting a premise, proposing an alternative premise, or proposing an original premise—the final step is always to "flip" the premise, identify the differences between the hypothetical and the precedent case, and use the "flipped" premise to prove the differences are meaningful enough to warrant a different (opposite) outcome from the precedent case.

Once you understand and are able to identify the components in the thinking process for applying and distinguishing cases, you will be better able to construct a written analysis of a legal problem. You will also be better able to understand the importance of what is said during your class discussions, which will help you record the important points in your class notes.

### Identifying or Creating a Proposed Premise

Sometimes a court will explicitly state an idea which you can adopt as your proposed premise. However, sometimes you will have to infer it from the court's application of the law to the facts (the way we did with <u>Parker</u> in this section) or from what you know about the social policy concerns which underlie legal decision making. It might seem scary to you at first—because you will sometimes be uncertain about whether the professor (or, when you are a lawyer, the court) will accept your proposed premise. Try to remember that this is probably one of the reasons you came to law school. It is one of the most creative parts of lawyering—the part that requires advocacy, and potentially thinking beyond the words in the text. It involves risk—sometimes the court (or your professor) will accept your premise, and sometimes they won't—but also reward; being able to convince a court to stretch or expand precedent to a new situation can be hugely satisfying. Think of laws that have changed, maybe even in your lifetime; much of the time those changes are the result of creative, and persuasive, lawyering.

A significant amount of the time, your proposed premise will be derived from policy. In the most general sense, a public policy or social policy can be described as a statement about what the speaker (the judge, a lawyer or a legal commentator) believes is good for society. For example, encouraging people to drive their cars carefully is a statement of public policy; that policy is reflected in hundreds of traffic laws, such as speed limits, restrictions on passing, and signaling requirements. Lawyers, judges and law professors use the term public policy more specifically as a way of describing the social good served by a rule of law or by a precedent. For example, the rule making people liable for the injuries they cause by driving their cars carelessly can be said to serve the social good described in the above policy statement. Similarly, the rule requiring contracts for the sale of land to be in a signed writing serves the social good of encouraging people to act cautiously and carefully when they make contracts for the sale of land.

Sometimes, courts and legislatures explicitly state the policy reasons underlying their decisions; many times, however, courts and legislatures are not so explicit. Students therefore must learn to derive the underlying policies by reasoning out the social good the court or legislature must have had in mind.

> **PAUSE. THINK. ACT.** Review the brief you created for Parker. Given what you've read in this section, decide whether the information in your brief would have allowed you to participate effectively in the class discussion. Why or why not? Do you need to do change your strategies? What will you do differently?

## 2. Expert Learners Use Class to Confirm Understanding and Resolve Confusion

Successful law students are particularly vigilant in class. They know that professors assume students will learn all they need to learn by watching during class, and then studying on their own or in groups. In most instances, professors also do not tell the students how to identify legal issues or how to perform legal analysis, leaving it to the students to figure these things out for themselves. Also, law professors seldom tell students the relationships among the concepts studied in the course, expecting students to identify those relationships on their own. In fact, the most traditional practitioners of the Socratic Method refuse to answer student questions, believing students should figure out the answers on their own. Most significantly, in more than half of all law school classes, students' first feedback on their development of law school skills is their grades on their midterms and finals. Consequently, law students, perhaps even more than their peers in other educational settings, must self-teach and self-assess their learning. Each law student is the only person in a position to assess whether the student actually has learned what she needs to learn.

Expert law students know they must evaluate their own understanding during class, and confirm whether they: accurately identified the rules from their reading; correctly translated or paraphrased their reading (of the cases, rules, etc.); and were able to apply what they learned from their reading. To do this expert law students must:

a) listen effectively,
b) identify the purpose of the professor's questions,
c) interact silently,
d) study the instructor for cues,

   e)  stay "tuned in" during the entire session, and

   f)  manage their reactions

### (a) Listen Effectively

Effective listening involves making sense of what you are hearing. Effective listeners are active listeners who constantly strive to restate what they hear into their own words. Rather than simply recording the exact words your instructor uses, record your understanding of the meaning of what the instructor is saying. Of course, in law school, sometimes the specific words do matter. For example, law students often must know the exact phrasing of a rule statement, the name of a concept (e.g., the parol evidence rule, fee simple absolute, *res ipsa loquitur*) or a definition. In such instances, however, the precise term is almost always readily available from a court opinion, secondary source or Restatement, making the effort to record the exact words during lecture a poor use of limited note-taking time. Consequently, expert students record where in their course materials they can find the requisite specific words (e.g., the page number where it is located) and use note-taking time to translate the concepts into their own words.

Effective listening has several components. The first component is preparation. Formulating questions, planning the structure of notes and even reading and briefing the assigned cases will increase the likelihood that you will be able to listen effectively during class. Expert classroom learners develop lists of questions they expect to be answered by the class discussion; they follow class discussion looking for those answers; and they ask questions to clarify their understanding. By developing these questions, expert students make sure they understand what they need to understand about the materials in the course. They also give themselves incentive to actively pay attention to the classroom discussion, because they are listening for answers to the questions they have developed.

The second component of effective listening involves mental and physical readiness. Mental readiness includes removing distractions; avoiding hasty judgments and jumping to conclusions; and resisting boredom, frustration and other emotional reactions. Physical readiness includes making sure you are not too hungry, too thirsty, or too tired to focus your attention for the entire class session.

The third component of effective listening is monitoring for comprehension. In other words, you should be determining whether you understand what the instructor is trying to teach, evaluating whether your class preparation was effective, and making sure you do not lose your focus.

### (b) Identify the Purpose of the Professor's Questions

Law professors ask a wide variety of questions yet seldom identify the purposes underlying their questions. Instead, law professors rapidly transition among a wide variety of goals, which include helping students build their doctrinal knowledge (knowledge of the rules of law); developing skills in any or all of the following areas: case reading and briefing, synthesis, issue-spotting, factual analysis, legal reasoning and problem-solving; and developing professional values, such as sensitivity to facts, clients and client differences, legal ethics, thoroughness, carefulness, honesty and integrity. To be able to follow the discussion and produce notes you will be able to use later, you need to be deciding, throughout the class session, what your professors are asking and to what goal they are teaching. The next exercise will help you practice this skill.

Match the example or type of question below with the professor's objective (more than one objective may apply):

| Question: | Potential Objective: |
|---|---|
| ____ State the [facts, holding, issue, policy, reasoning] in [name of case]. | (a) Case reading |
| ____ A hypothetical for which the student must apply and/or distinguish a case or set of cases. | (b) Synthesis |
| | (c) Issue-spotting |
| ____ What did the dissent say about that issue? | (d) Legal analysis |
| ____ Do you [agree, disagree] with the [court, majority or dissent]? Why? | (e) Problem-solving |
| | (f) Fact sensitivity |
| ____ How can you reconcile [name of case] with this case? | (g) Identifying/using policy |
| ____ What does [word in case not relevant to court's reasoning or resolution of the case] mean? | (h) Thoroughness |
| | (i) Carefulness |
| ____ How does this case relate to [name of case]? | (j) Case briefing |
| ____ What other case have we read where the court did ____? | (k) Developing legal vocabulary |
| ____ Why did the two courts reach [a different result, the same result] on this point? | |
| ____ A hypothetical to which the student must apply a rule. | |
| ____ Is the court right or wrong? Why? | |
| ____ A question about an insignificant detail in an opinion. | |

When you are finished with this exercise, you may want to return to the sample professor-student dialogues in the previous section, and identify the purpose of the questions posed to the students.

### (c) Interact Silently

The Socratic Method requires students to learn vicariously because, while the selected student is being questioned, all the rest of the students in the class are not directly involved. Each of your law professors *assumes* that all the students in the class are playing along, answering the questions in their heads and learning from the selected student's answers to the questions and the professor's responses to the student's answers. The non-selected students, therefore, must learn what they need to learn from this vicarious experience of watching the professor question one of their peers. They must practice by trying to answer the professor's questions in their heads and apply the professor's feedback and corrections to their answers. When the instructor communicates dissatisfaction with a student response, each student must think about how they would have answered the question differently, and whether and why that might have produced a different result.

The vicarious nature of the experience means that the demand on students to self-evaluate their performance and regulate their own learning is particularly high; it is very unlikely your professors will have any idea whether you (or any of your peers, for that matter) have learned the material until they grade your examinations.

### (d) Study the Instructor for Cues

Most law professors expect their students to demonstrate the same set of skills on examinations, and most define excellence in very similar ways. Consequently, it is possible to write a book like this one and describe the expectations and testing methodologies of law professors. At the same time, expert students in all learning contexts know that instructors vary in their expectations — their subject matters vary, their political views vary, their interests and goals vary, and their perceptions of students vary. In other words, expert law students recognize the commonalities among their professors and also make sure they know what each individual professor expects from students.

In the law school context, this task is challenging. The dominant law school teaching method seldom involves explicit communication of expectations. This striking uniformity of teaching methodology might lead one to assume professors also test in the same way. There is greater variance in testing, however, than you would expect. As detailed in the next chapter, while there clearly is a most prevalent approach to designing law school examinations, law school exams can and do take one of several different forms, all of which can and do overlap. In fact, even professors who administer similar examinations in terms of style may be evaluating different things from their students.

In the broadest terms, law school exams almost always involve hypothetical factual stories that the students must "analyze." Analyze involves identifying issues, applying rules to facts, applying and distinguishing cases and performing policy analysis. The variation, therefore, comes in part from the mix of these expectations, in how much weight each instructor assigns to each task, both in terms of constructing the exam (e.g., how many issues, how much depth of analysis) and in terms of grading the exam (i.e., how much demonstration of each of the skills bears on the students' grades on the examination). Exams can test in all of the areas, in some of the areas, or in only one area. Moreover, some law professors expect their students to be able to integrate discussions of policy in their legal analysis or to be able to use their knowledge and skills in the context of lawyering tasks other than applying rules to facts or applying and distinguishing cases, such as creating client letters, constructing documents that might be submitted in court or drafting other legal documents.

This variation makes teacher study an important skill. Sometimes, the task is an easy one; some instructors are explicit. They tell their students whether the students are expected to apply and distinguish cases, whether they should be integrating public policy in their analyses, and whether their exams will test lawyering skills other than applying and distinguishing or application of rules to facts. Most law professors, however, are much less forthcoming. Many, however, give multiple hints about their examinations, both in terms of the testing topics they are likely to test and in terms of the relative weight assigned to each topic. These hints take the form of course and topic-by-topic objectives, classroom and office hour discussions and the availability of practice (and past) examinations. The widespread absence of explicitly stated expectations makes such teacher study a crucial skill.

Thus, expert students who are watching a peer be questioned by their instructor focus on discerning what reasoning techniques appear to produce instructor approval. While these expert law students are listening in class, they ask themselves questions such as:

- What types of student classroom responses elicit positive comments from the instructor? What types of responses elicit criticism?
- Which court opinions does the professor believe to be well reasoned? Which does the instructor believe to be poorly reasoned?
- What skills does the professor focus on (law to fact application, policy based reasoning, applying and distinguishing, etc.)?

---

**PAUSE. THINK. ACT.** Review the sample professor-student dialogues in the previous section. Can you identify where and how the professor corrected students, or expressed dissatisfaction with student responses? Can you identify which responses elicited a positive reaction? What signals does the professor give? What skills appear to be important to the professor?

---

### (e) Stay "Tuned in" During the Entire Session

Expert Law students know how to refocus their attention when they lose focus. On the one hand, attending to law school lectures is often quite easy for most students. At any given moment, there is a risk the professor will call on the student to recite information, a process that tends to keep most students focused at all times. On the other hand, most students find some aspects of the law more interesting than others. For example, a student who is planning to practice business law may not find a criminal law class particularly stimulating. Moreover, in every class, there are times when members of the class ask questions to which the student already knows the answer or a professor belabors a point the student already has mastered. For these reasons, expert law students plan techniques for focusing their attention when it lags. Those techniques might include writing answers to each of the professor's questions, rather than just playing along in their head; volunteering an answer or raising their hand (sometimes knowing you will be called on keeps you engaged); and self-talk ("Yes, that's a key point" or "Do my notes reflect what is going on?"). You may have other techniques you developed during your undergraduate education; you should try any that would apply in the law school setting.

---

**PAUSE. THINK. ACT.** What techniques do you use to focus your attention when your mind is wandering? Are they effective? Should you use them in law school?

---

### (f) Manage Reactions

Law students, law professors, practicing lawyers and judges all have commented on the stress and anxiety law school instruction produces in new law students. This type of instruction places significant demands on students in terms of preparation. Professors assume students will come to class having carefully read and briefed all the assigned court opinions. Some professors have even been known to simply walk out of class and leave the students to fend for themselves if the professor deems the students unprepared for class. Part of law school stress likely stems from the differences between college and law school, the competitiveness of many law students, the high cost of law school, and because learning any new skill, particularly an intellectual one like legal reasoning, is very stressful. Chapter 10 identifies some of the common causes of law school anxiety and offers some strategies for dealing with that anxiety. Some additional strategies are listed below.

#### (i) Acknowledge Your Reactions

Expert law students notice and acknowledge their reactions, even when their reactions cannot be expressed during classroom discussion. Many law students experience significant outrage at the many injustices still extant within our society and our legal system. Know that such frustration is normal and will be a useful tool to you as a future lawyer. Great lawyers operate from a place of passion for the needs of their clients. While law school discussions tend to focus on dispassionate dissection of arguments, statutes, and court opinions, law practice involves harnessing those skills in the service of your clients. Thus, even if a professor or peer does not appreciate your sense of outrage at the real issues in our society, you should know that your ability to feel that passion will serve you well in the long run. The key is to be vigilant about noticing how you are feeling, to reflect on your learning process as it's happening, and to find people with whom you comfortably can share your concerns.

#### (ii) Accept Instructional and Personal Quirks

Expert law students do not let themselves be distracted by the instructional and personal quirks of their professors. Law professors, like all human beings, run a wide spectrum of personality types, teaching styles and political values, all of which influence the professors' interactions with their students. Over the course of their law school careers, many law students encounter an instructor whose approach is intimidating, aggravating or, at least, off-putting. Many more encounter law professors with whom they frequently disagree. For novice learners, such issues can be distracting or even can interfere with learning. Expert law students, however, by remaining focused on their short-term and long-term goals, are better able to ignore such matters, and know that, after they graduate from law school, their professional success will depend, in part, on their ability to deal with employers, judges and opposing counsel who are equally difficult to deal with on a personal level.

### (iii) Put Performance Anxiety in Perspective

There is a performance aspect to law school classroom experiences because students are called on individually and must speak and think while their peers and their instructor are listening. This performance aspect can be intimidating and may be anxiety provoking. The most important thing for students to do is put this experience in perspective. Your performance in this context has very little, if any, bearing on your grades or your opportunities for extracurricular experiences, such as moot court and law review; it also says virtually nothing about what kind of lawyer you will be. There is certainly no evidence that the students who say "smart" (or just many) things in class get the better grades or become better lawyers. Consequently, students should never sacrifice necessary learning activities, such as listening in class, doing all the work for all their classes, studying for examinations and timely completing their papers, simply to appear "smart" to their peers and their professors when called on in class.

On the other hand, the performance aspect is not meaningless. By speaking in class, you are actively engaging in your own learning, and it is well established that active learners outperform passive ones on every measure of success. Moreover, when you speak in class, you give yourself an opportunity to practice your new skills and get professorial feedback on your efforts. One telling characteristic of all expert law students is that they seek and obtain as much practice and feedback as possible—and in many law school classes, this oral feedback is all you get, other than your results on your examinations. When you participate in class you are gaining information about your level of understanding and your approach to learning the material. Finally, for some students, articulating their understandings out loud is an essential part of their learning process (if you are such a person, frequent participation in class may be necessary).

### (iv) Agree to Disagree

Expert law students expect to disagree with some of what is said during class discussion. Most students will not agree with everything their instructors and peers have to say. Legal issues have significant political implications. For example, rules of law that award relief where one person has caused emotional, but no physical harm, to another person often invoke spirited debate about the best use of societal resources. Expert law students assume such disagreements will occur and do not allow those disagreements to interfere with their acquisition of the knowledge and skills they need to succeed in law school.

## 3. Expert Law Students Record What They Have Learned in a Form That Allows for Easy Use in Organizing Their Course Materials and Studying for Examinations

Successful students absorb the lecture, using note taking to help make connections, highlight any confusion and record important points. Note taking serves as a tool to record their learning, rather than as a place to transcribe what the professor and other students are saying during class. As successful students draw connections they use their notes to begin to organize concepts in preparation for examinations. Successful students also separate their learning of the subject matter from other information, such as exam tips, background information and even their own confusion. To do these things, successful students do the following:

### (a) Follow Instructor Cues

One of the keys to effective note taking is being able to distinguish the important points from the not-so-important points. Novice learners, eager to avoid missing anything, and unable to distinguish the important points from the trivial matters, often try to record every word their instructor says. This is one of the worst things a law student can do. In law school, writing down every word spoken is not useful; students in law school classes speak as much as one-half or two-thirds of the time and some of what they say is incorrect. Consequently, law students who aspire to record every spoken word record some matters that are inaccurate. Also, in trying to record every word, novice learners deprive themselves of the benefits of listening for understanding—because they do not have time to process and make sense of what they are hearing.

It is equally misguided to decide to simply listen and rely on memory and secondary sources such as hornbooks and commercial outlines to make sense of the course material. Students who record information themselves, as they are hearing it in class, retain it much better than those who simply listen. Thus, expert law students record no more and no less than the important points. This task is less daunting than it might appear at first glance—because expert law students know that instructors provide considerable guidance in this task.

Successful students attend to and follow the *cues* provided by their instructors. Instructors provide numerous cues about what is important in their lectures. These cues include:

1. the things they write on the board,
2. any outlines or other study guides they provide,
3. the things they repeat or restate in different words,

4. the things they summarize, and

5. the things they review at the beginning or the end of their lecture.

Instructors use these cues to help students identify the key points in their lectures. Successful students take these cues and make sure to include such matters in their notes.

### (b) Correct Confusion Regarding Rules and Holdings

Expert law students also use class discussions to correct their case briefs and rule statements. In many instances, instructors communicate correct statements of rules and holdings, either directly or by accepting students' rule statements or holdings. Expert law students use these statements as opportunities to correct any errors they may have made. At the same time, a crucial indicator of understanding is the ability to restate or paraphrase a rule or holding using your own words, but still maintaining the exact meaning of the original. Consequently, expert law students use lectures both to check the accuracy of their rule statements and holdings and to develop statements in their own words of those rules and holdings.

### (c) Organize While Writing

Perhaps the most important difference between novice and expert note takers is that expert note takers force themselves to organize the material as they take notes. In part, this effort can be made much easier by developing an outline of the key topics (major topics and sub headings) in advance of class, as described in the previous chapter. Even with such an outline, however, students learn more and learn it better by forcing themselves to think about and recognize the hierarchical relationships among the concepts they are studying. By forcing the materials into their natural structures, students assist themselves in storing the materials in their long-term memory.

Look at the two sets of notes on the next page. Both are notes from the section you've just been reading. The set of notes on the left depicts a set of notes that lacks structure; the set on the right possesses structure.

---

**PAUSE. THINK. ACT.** Compare each phrase/item from the "notes" on the left with the corresponding phrase/item in the notes on the right. How is the organization different? Why might it matter? Which is more useful? Why?

---

Note how much clearer the relationships among the concepts appear even with these relatively simple materials. Note also that the structured notes do not include numbers or letters; if necessary (e.g., for a learner with a strong read-write preference), students can add those later when they create their exam approaches; while taking notes, there is minimal, if any, gain from forcing oneself to follow perfect outlining numbering.

| | |
|---|---|
| Goal of notes = Help org. materials later/study for exams<br>make connections<br>highlight confusion<br>rec. impt points<br>sep. subj matter from other info<br>Instructor Cues — it's impt. If: on the board, any outlines/study guides, repeat or restate, summarize, rev'w @ beg. or end<br>Correct Confusion re: Rules/Holdings; check briefs + rule stmnts, look for accuracy/paraprhase<br>Organize While Writing | **Goal of notes** = Help org. materials later/study for exams<br><br>**What to record:**<br>  Impt points only<br>  Instructor Cues — it's impt. If:<br>    on the board,<br>    any outlines/study guides<br>    repeat or restate<br>    summarize<br>    rev'w @ beg. or end<br>  Highlight confusion<br>  Correct confusion re: Rules/Holdings<br>  Paraphrase<br><br>**Organize While Writing**<br>  make connections<br>  sep. subj matter from other info<br><br>**check briefs + rule stmnts**<br>  look for accuracy |

### (d) Follow an Effective Format

In addition to the formatting techniques described in the previous chapter, expert law students also:

### 1. Use Visual Cues

Many expert students also incorporate color or highlighting in their note taking. For example, it may be very productive to highlight all the rules or to use different colors of ink for different information (e.g., one color for rule statements, another for hypos, another for test advice, etc.). You might also choose to use different fonts or font sizes if you are typing your notes — or use bold, italics and underline to help differentiate sections or major topic headings. Also, whether writing or typing, you can underline, draw boxes around, or place stars next to key points to highlight critical information.

### 2. Leave Space

Students tend to fill the space they allocate to their notes, and students who leave themselves plenty of space tend to record more of the information they need than those who limit their writing space in any way. Accordingly, while expert students plan the structure of their notes, as noted above, they do not restrict the notes they will be taking by trying to contain them within a certain number of pages or within a pre-planned outline that does not end up tracking the classroom discussion.

### 3. Annotate Briefs

Many successful students choose to include case briefs in their note structure or choose to print case briefs and bring them to class. As they change or confirm rules or other information gleaned from class discussion about the cases, they annotate their case briefs to reflect whether the information is correct or should be altered.

The following websites provide more information about note-taking techniques:

http://www.sas.calpoly.edu/asc/ssl/notetakingsystems.html
http://www.dartmouth.edu/~acskills/success/notes.html
http://www.d.umn.edu/student/loon/acad/strat/ss_notetaking.html

---

**PAUSE. THINK. ACT.** Look at the characteristics set out below. Which set of characteristics most resembles your classroom experience? Which traits do you need to develop to become an expert law student? How will you develop those traits?

---

| Experts | Novices |
|---|---|
| • set concrete goals | • do not set concrete goals |
| • thoroughly prepare for class | • do not fully prepare for each class |
| • remain focused throughout each class | • have difficulty remaining focused |
| • are mentally and physically ready | • are not mentally or physically ready |
| • are in control of their own learning | • do not control their own learning |
| • write down what is important, summarizing and paraphrasing rather than transcribing | • try to write down everything their instructor says, often creating a transcript of class discussion |
| • stay engaged during class | • disengage during class discussions |
| • ask questions | • ask few or no questions |
| • volunteer answers | • rarely or never volunteer answers |
| • take clear, succinct, well-organized notes | • make little effort to organize their notes |
| • confirm their understanding and resolve their confusion | • do not recognize or correct their confusion |
| • paraphrase/restate their understanding in their own words | • do not state ideas in their own words — transcribe what they hear |
| • notice and acknowledge their feelings | • are unaware of or ignore their feelings |
| • manage their anxiety/stress | • ignore stress/anxiety or use poor coping strategies to deal with stress/anxiety |

# Chapter 7

# Preparing for Exams:
# What to Do *After* Class

The title for this chapter is somewhat misleading, because it implies that what you have been doing up to now does not involve exam preparation. However, pre-class preparation and engaging during class are prerequisites for everything covered in this chapter. If you have not prepared for and participated in class, as described in chapters five and six, it will be difficult, or even impossible, to complete the tasks described in this chapter. On the other hand, if you only do those things described in chapters five and six, you are not likely to succeed on your exams, because although those tasks lay the groundwork for the tasks described in this chapter, they will not, by themselves, prepare you for your exams. It is also important to understand that even though the activities in this chapter are described as "after class" activities, you will be doing them before your next class and incorporating what you learn into your pre-class preparation for the next class session. It helps to think about the tasks and skills described in chapters 5 through 7 as interrelated tasks and skills.

Expert learners know how to use what they have learned to prepare for examinations. Specifically, expert law students know how to use their class notes and materials, as well as self-directed practice and self-assessment, to create an exam approach that will help them succeed. Expert law students: (1) review their class performance, including their notes; (2) calibrate their learning through practice and self-testing; (3) synthesize what they have learned; (4) create exam approaches which reflect how they will be tested; and (5) consistently reflect on their performance and make adjustments based on their self-assessment. Expert learners engage in each of these tasks, on an ongoing basis, until they have developed a successful approach to each topic, and to the overall course, and have learned to deploy those approaches effectively in the context in which they will be tested.

## Step One: Review and Reflect

Expert students recognize that the first few hours after class are a crucial time period with respect to their learning from classroom experiences. At that time, the material is much fresher and more easily remembered. Students' areas of confusion are more readily identified, and their abbreviations and shorthand more quickly recalled. Students who wait days or even weeks to review their notes often struggle to recall anything specific about the class session the notes reflect, to remember what they understood and what confused them and to understand what they intended their notes actually to communicate. Consequently, expert students force themselves to review and revise their notes as soon as possible after the class session has ended. This effort actually involves reviewing for comprehension and legibility and reflecting on the student's experience of the class and on the effectiveness of the student's note-taking strategies.

## Review Notes for Comprehension and Legibility

Expert learners make sure they review their notes as soon as possible for comprehension and legibility. Expert students know that, in the rush to record what was said in class, students do not write or type as neatly or accurately as they could. By reviewing immediately after class, expert students ensure they can recall what they were trying to communicate.

This activity allows you to identify a need for any assistance from your peers or instructor and therefore to avoid becoming completely confused as the class progresses. In this sense, law school learning is like a rapidly growing tree. Trees require regular pruning because, otherwise, they grow in ways that are either unattractive or unproductive; accordingly, knowledgeable gardeners trim unsightly branches before those branches have grown too large and become unmanageable. Confusion in one's law school learning is like an unsightly branch. Trimmed early on, confusion is no problem at all; if you quickly resolve your confusion, it will have no effect on the rest of your learning. If, however, you allow your confusion to persist, it becomes more widespread and therefore much more difficult to resolve. Such confusion, in fact, is likely to produce additional confusion, much like an unsightly branch, not trimmed, will produce sub-branches as it grows. Expert students know when to seek help. They seek help from trusted classmates or study groups to help fill in any gaps or missing information. They make sure they understand everything they wrote down and, where necessary, either make appointments with their instructors for assistance or send their instructors questions by e-mail.

You should also recognize that instructors appreciate students who are eager to understand and seek help as they go. Before midterms and final examinations, instructors receive dozens of requests for assistance. Those students who seek help as they need it, therefore, are more likely to get their needs met and to inspire willingness on their instructors' parts to provide last minute help when it is needed.

## Reflect on Your Experience of the Class — And Plan How to Adapt

Of course, for every learning experience, expert learners include time for reflection. As part of your review, you need to determine the extent to which you understood what occurred in the class session and evaluate the success of the learning strategies you used in preparing for and participating in that class session. This information helps you prepare for the next class and to make any necessary changes to ensure the next class will be even more successful than the last.

In the context of taking lecture notes, expert learners reflect on the success or failure of their efforts to take notes and the cause(s) of the success or failure. (Did they plan their notes? Were they able to focus attention throughout the lecture? Did they prepare for class sufficiently by reading and briefing the cases? Did they review the previous class session's notes before the class started? Did they take proper notes?) Expert learners attribute successes to personal effort and failures to strategy selection, and then adapt their techniques accordingly. Expert learners also take time to notice any feelings of pride, anxiety, or even outrage; they know that suppressing feelings doesn't make them go away, and might even be harmful to their learning and well-being.

# Step Two: Calibration and Practice

Expert students recognize that it is much easier to be able to follow a class discussion during that discussion than it is to be able to understand the concepts and use the concepts on an examination. Expert students hold themselves accountable for their learning, by testing themselves on what they have learned. Expert students do not wait until they think they understand material to test themselves. Instead, they use testing as an opportunity to learn material and to develop a rich, deep understanding of how the material applies and can be used in the future. Expert law students do this on at least a weekly basis, because they know that repeated, spaced review of topics increases the speed and accuracy of later efforts to recall the learning, which is important, because law school exams are almost always drafted to ensure that students will have difficulty finishing within the time constraints (to simulate the time constraints lawyers regularly face). In short, expert law students find early and frequent opportunities for practice and self-testing— and they do not allow class preparation tasks to prevent them from finding time to do so.

## Accountability

Expert law students know they must hold themselves accountable for what they know and don't know. Expert law students calibrate their learning; calibration is an objective assessment of what you know. To objectively assess what you know, you have to hold yourself accountable. For this reason, experts commit to a specific answer before they review the correct answer or explanation, and then honestly assess whether they followed each step, and thought about each piece of the required analysis. Many expert law students hold themselves accountable by stating their answers to their peers (in study groups) or writing an answer to problems before reviewing sample answers or explanations.

## Spaced and Interleaved Study

In addition, spaced study (studying several different times over a long period of time) and interleaved study (study which varies the subjects and types of practice) results in students remembering more and remembering better than single event studying (also known as cramming), or even multiple event studying when sessions are very close together and focused on a single subject. Consequently, expert law students space their study throughout the semester rather than trying to learn the material the week, or even the day before an examination, and vary their study—alternating subjects and types of practice and review.

## Checking for Comprehension

The primary purpose of studying is to check for comprehension. Expert law students check for comprehension in four ways. First, they make sure they understand the words of the rules and holdings they are including. Second, they make sure they can paraphrase the rules and holdings in their own words. This usually involves elaboration, an excellent learning and memorization tool, which is described more thoroughly in the memorization section of this chapter. Third, they make sure they understand the reasons for the rules. Finally, they make sure they are able to apply the rules and holdings to new situations and accurately explain the possible results. To do each of these things they find, and generate their own, practice materials.

### Finding Practice Materials

There are a variety of supplemental sources law students use for checking their understanding of the law; these include online exercises like CALI, as well as a number of popular series such as Examples and Explanations, Q and A, and Law in a Flash. Your professor, the academic support faculty at your law school or successful upper level students can be good sources for recommendations about specific materials to use for this practice. A brief description of some of these sources—as well as some guidance as to how to use them—is provided in Chapter 8.

Although taking almost any practice test helps, expert law students devote some care to the selection of appropriate questions. The two best sources of exam questions are the student's professor and any collection of past exams given by that professor. In fact, as noted above in the discussion of teacher study, expert law students review every past exam question authored by their professors they can find. Many professors post their own practice materials or past exams on course websites, or make them available in the law library. Where professors provide such materials, you should be sure to use them.

### Generating Practice Materials

Expert students also create their own practice materials. They create examples and non-examples of each individual concept, as described later in this chapter in the elaboration section. They also create their own practice exam questions. This task involves thinking broadly about the course material, because exam questions combine concepts, almost always in ways the student has never seen them combined before. To draft exam questions, students must not merely understand each concept individually but also must understand the relationships among all the concepts in the course. The thinking needed to create a good exam-like hypothetical prepares a student for the challenges of responding to such questions.

In fact, as explained in Chapter 9, the correct answer on law school exams is, at best, a prediction of how a court would rule and, often, even a moderate degree of certainty as to how a court would actually resolve all the issues on the exam is impossible. Law school exams test students' ability to develop and evaluate the arguments reasonable lawyers might make in response to hypothetical fact patterns; consequently, the exams provide sufficient information for good students to develop persuasive arguments on behalf of all parties involved in the fact pattern. This aspect of law school exams, which law professors call "testing on the line," "creating debatable issues," or making students "argue both sides" requires a higher level of understanding and therefore is a particularly effective examination preparation tool. To create a good exam question, students must understand the concepts, must see where the line is located between a set of facts for which there is a clear answer and one about which reasonable lawyers would argue, and must be able to add or eliminate facts as needed to achieve a proper position along the line. This difficult mental task is, in fact, more mentally tasking than answering the actual exam question will be. Consequently, it both makes the exam-taking process easier and helps students develop sensitivity to small factual differences, a crucial skill on law school exams.

For these reasons, creating exam questions is both extraordinarily difficult and extraordinarily important. Many students find it helpful to approach the task in one of the several ways their professors do it; those ways are described below. Regardless of which of these approaches you take, your learning experience is likely to be a rich one.

A few caveats about writing exam questions apply to the design of all questions and are worth noting at the outset. First, a crucial component of the learning process is planning a model answer while you are drafting the question. Most law professors have discovered, at one time in their teaching careers, that, if they do not plan an answer as they write, they discover, either after a lot of work or, worse yet, while grading the students' answers, that a question that sounded great actually was a poor question. This approach is particularly important to law students because the purpose of the process is to create a representative question and to learn from the process of creating one. Second, the learning goal for this task is always the following: creating an exam question that accurately reflects how the student will be tested on the examination. Consequently, students need to pay careful attention to how they are likely to be tested (see the above discussions of teacher study and the professor-student dialogues and accompanying materials in Chapter 6). Third, most law professors reflect on the question and whether it tests the issues they hope to test, and revise their questions several times; students who wish to draft an effective question should do the same. Finally, many professors have a peer review the question. Expert students do something similar—they have a peer answer the question.

To create an exam you should also understand three approaches law professors use to create essay exam questions. One way professors create essay exam questions is to start by selecting the areas in which they would like to test the students. After selecting a topic, the professor brainstorms a story that gives rise to issues the professor wishes to test. Many professors initially just try to get a story from any source (newspaper articles, current events, subjects relevant to law students) from which they can work. The professor then starts editing the story to make sure the story includes issues about which reasonable lawyers could argue on behalf of the fictional parties in the exam hypothetical. The professor adds and deletes facts to give the students information they need to build arguments, to clarify the story or to otherwise make the test as fair as possible.

A second approach involves starting from the cases the students have read over the course of the semester. In fact, if the instructor has emphasized applying and distinguishing skills during the course, this approach is likely one their instructor will adopt. After selecting a case, a set of cases, multiple cases or multiple sets of cases as a starting point, the instructor will begin combining the issues while altering the facts to make the exam question sufficiently unique. Much like professors pose difficult hypotheticals in class that require students to apply or distinguish cases the class has discussed, a professor using this method to create an exam question will alter the facts of the case(s) in ways that make the "correct" answer difficult and open up possibilities for arguments on behalf of all the parties described in the hypothetical. Almost always, by the time the professor has finished changing the facts, the exam question looks only a little like the case(s) from which the instructor started.

A third approach involves performing legal research. The professor decides what areas of law she might be interested in testing and then performs searches in those areas to find recently-decided cases, older, interesting cases, or even news stories that the instructor can use as a starting point for creating the exam. What the professor finds becomes the starting point for the creation of an exam question. Once again, the professor alters the facts of what she finds to add issues the professor is interested in testing and to make the exam question more challenging, more interesting, or otherwise more appropriate.

Any student who adopts any or all of these approaches is likely to be engaging in a learning process that will help prepare the student for the exam. In fact, if a student can create appropriate essay exam questions, there is no doubt that she has mastered the material. Nevertheless, all other things being equal, the approach in which the student starts by finding a case is probably the most helpful because it has an added benefit; the approach causes the student to read additional cases relating to the topics on which the student will be tested. These additional examples may increase the student's understanding of the subject area.

## Converting Thinking to Writing

Expert law students know that they are tested in writing, so their practice always includes written work. Through this writing practice expert law students learn how to reorganize information—to convert thinking to writing. Expert law students understand that the thinking process they engage in during class differs in some key respects from the writing process they must engage in during examinations. In other words, expert law students understand that articulating thoughts verbally, in class, is different from articulating thoughts in writing, during an examination, and so expert law students prepare for the way they will be tested. Remember the thinking process from Chapter 6—which looks like this:

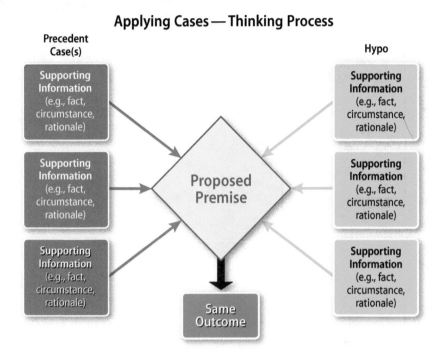

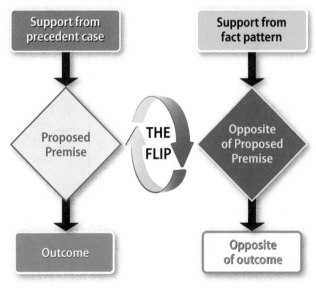

Here is a representation of what that thinking looks like when it is converted to writing:

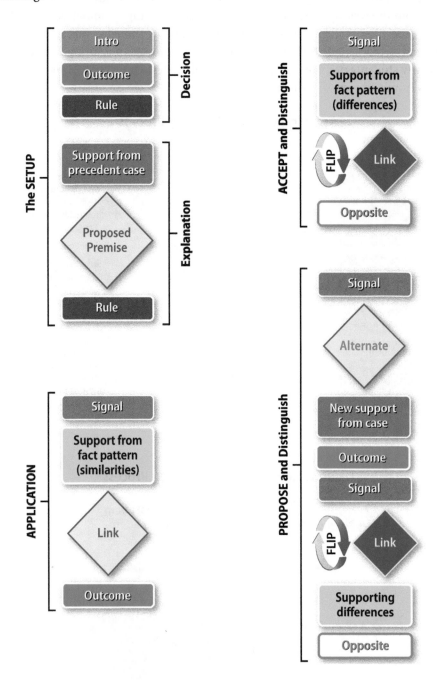

As you can see, there are some similarities and some differences. To help you understand these similarities and differences, this section will review the writing process, using the same hypothetical from the sample class dialogue in Chapter 6 which we used to illustrate the thinking process. Here is the hypothetical:

Jack Nickels was a famous dramatic actor who lived in San Francisco. Nickels entered into a contract with GMG to star in a new, one-hour comedy television series set in a hospital. The shows were to be filmed in a Los Angeles studio. Nickels was set to play the role of an emergency room doctor. Under the terms of Nickels' contract with GMG, Nickels was to be paid two million dollars for the first season of the show. GMG had the right to renew the show for each of the next two years, and to pay Nickels three million dollars for season two, and four million dollars for season four. Nickels had the right to direct two episodes per season and write one episode each season in the second and third seasons. Before filming started, GMG canceled the series. GMG offered Nickels the lead role also playing an emergency room doctor, in an already existing successful series, also set in a hospital. The lead actor in the series had already decided to leave the show. The show was a "dramedy" (a dramatic series with regular comedic scenes). Nickels would receive the same compensation, but because the show had an established team of writers, he would not have the right to write any episodes. He was instead offered the right to direct three episodes per season. The show is filmed in New York City.

You should note that law school examinations look much like this hypothetical. They vary in length and complexity, but generally speaking they are simply a story, like the one above. To write an answer to the hypothetical, a student would need to reorganize the information from the thinking process, using some variation of the format set out above. First we will examine the pieces in detail—and then explore the different possible variations.

## Applying Cases — The Writing Process

The party who desires the same outcome as the precedent case will argue that a case applies to the client's situation, and that the case is sufficiently similar to warrant the same outcome. In law school, much of the writing you do will be objective—meaning you will argue both sides—explaining the arguments for each party. For this reason, there are many instances where you will both apply and distinguish the same case. In law practice, this is seldom, if ever, the case. You will argue that a case either applies—because you desire the same outcome for your client, or that it is distinguishable—because you desire a different outcome. Thus, some of what you will learn about the writing process for law school will be different from what you do in law practice. Some of those adaptations are addressed in the final section of this discussion of the writing process.

### The Setup

When you apply a case to a hypothetical set of facts (or to a client's case, when you are a lawyer), you must explain the decision to the reader (your professor or the court). This means you first need to convey the key pieces of the decision—the specific outcome in the precedent case, and the aspect of the rule the court applied.

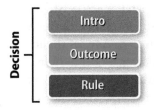

In <u>Parker</u>, the court found that an actress did not have to mitigate her damages for a movie studio's breach of her employment contract by accepting an offer of employment because the new offer was different or inferior.

Notice that you first identify the case by name (and, in a court document or legal writing paper, by proper citation). Next, you must describe the outcome with a fair amount of precision. Notice that the outcome is not stated in general terms (e.g., the plaintiff was entitled to damages, or the defendant breached the contract). Instead, it precisely describes the legal issue resolved by the court—and it ties that issue to the rule the court (or perhaps the professor) articulated.

The next step in the setup is to "pitch" your idea to the professor (or the court). You must explain and support your proposed premise. Even if the premise is one articulated by the professor, during class discussion, you must still provide support for it, from the precedent case.

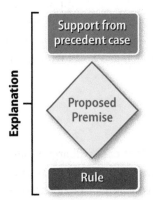

The plaintiff was an actress who was originally offered the lead role in a musical where she was to dance and act. She was also given the right to approve the film's director and the screenplay. The proposed replacement offer was to star in a supporting role in a Western, which required dramatic acting, and no dancing—and which did not include director or screenplay approval. The second offer impaired plaintiff's creative interests—by depriving her of creative control over the director, screen play and even genre, and so, the court found the second offer was different and inferior to the first offer.

It is important to understand that the three pieces of the explanation do not need to appear in any particular order—but they must all be present. Here are some additional examples of the how this paragraph might be written. Try to identify each of the three pieces (you may even want to highlight each piece in a different color, using the above as your guide):

*Example 2:* The offer was different and inferior because it impaired the plaintiff's creative interests—by depriving her of creative control over the director, screen play and even genre. Plaintiff, an actress, was originally offered the lead role in a musical where she was to dance and act and she was given the right to approve the film's director and the screenplay, while the proposed replacement offer was to star in a supporting role in a Western, which required dramatic acting, and no dancing—and which did not include director or screenplay approval.

*Example 3:* The new offer impaired plaintiff's creative interests — by depriving her of creative control because the new offer was for a supporting role in a Western, with no control over the director or screenplay, while the first offer included approval of both director and screenplay, and was the lead role in a musical where she was to dance and act. Thus, the court found the second offer was different and inferior to the first offer.

Once you have described the decision and explained the reason for the outcome, you are ready to move to the next step — applying the precedent case to the hypothetical.

### The Application

In the application section, you signal to the reader that you are applying the precedent case to the hypothetical or client's facts — and then explain how the hypothetical facts are linked to the proposed premise, thus requiring the same outcome as the precedent case.

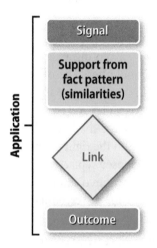

Similarly, here Nickels' is a famous dramatic actor, so acting in a comedy, which was the original offer, would have allowed him to expand his acting skills. **Since** the new offer is for a drama it impairs his creative interests by preventing him from expanding his repertoire. **Also, the second offer** deprives him of creative control over how he is portrayed **since, unlike the first offer, it** does not allow him to write episodes. **Since the second offer** impairs his creative interests — which is critical for his job as an actor, it is a different or inferior offer, which he does not have to accept to mitigate his damages.

While the application section should begin with a signal, and end with the outcome, the supporting information from the fact pattern and explanation linking that information to the proposed premise does not need to appear in any particular order. Below are some additional examples of the how this paragraph might be written. Try to identify each of the pieces (you may even want to highlight each piece in a different color, using the above as your guide).

*Example 2:* Like the replacement offer in <u>Parker</u>, the offer here is different and inferior because it similarly impairs Nickels' creative interests. Nickels is a famous dramatic actor, so acting in a comedy, which was the original offer, would have allowed him to expand his acting skills. Since the new offer is for a drama, it prevents him from expanding his range and potentially reach a new audience. Also, the second offer deprives him of creative control over how he is portrayed since, unlike the first offer, it does not allow him to write episodes. Since the second offer impairs his creative interests and is therefore different and inferior, he does not have to mitigate his damages by accepting it.

*Example 3:* GMG's second offer to Nickels deprives him of creative control and impairs his creative interests, just like the inferior offer to the plaintiff in Parker. Nickels is a famous dramatic actor, so acting in a comedy, which was the original offer, would have allowed him to expand his acting skills. Since the new offer is for a drama it prevents him from taking that creative risk and potentially developing a new audience. Also, the second offer does not allow him to write episodes, something that was included in the first offer. Writing would have allowed him another creative outlet, and another chance to expand his skills; it also would have given him control over how his character was portrayed. Since the second offer impairs his creative interests and deprives him of creative control, it is a different or inferior offer, which Nickels is not required to accept to mitigate his damages from GMG's breach of contract.

These components—the Setup and the Application—form the basis for an answer applying a case to a hypothetical. Here is an example of what a written answer, which follows this format, would look like:

In Parker, the court held an actress did not have to mitigate her damages for a movie studio's breach of her employment contract by accepting an offer of employment that was different or inferior to the original offer. The offer was different and inferior because it impaired the plaintiff's creative interests— by depriving her of creative control over the director and screen play and changing the movie genre. Plaintiff, an actress, was originally offered the lead role in a musical where she was to dance and act and she was given the right to approve the film's director and the screenplay, while the proposed replacement offer was to star in a supporting role in a Western, which required dramatic acting, and no dancing—and which did not include director or screenplay approval.

GMG's second offer to Nickels' similarly deprives him of creative control and impairs his creative interests, just like the inferior offer to the plaintiff in Parker. Nickels is a famous dramatic actor, so acting in a comedy, which was the original offer, would have allowed him to expand his acting skills. Since the new offer is for a drama it prevents him from taking that creative risk and potentially developing a new audience. Also, the second offer does not allow him to write episodes, something that was included in the first offer. Writing would have allowed him another creative outlet, and another chance to expand his skills; it also would have given him control over how his character was portrayed. Since the second offer impairs his creative interests and deprives him of creative control, it is a different or inferior offer, which Nickels is not required to accept to mitigate his damages from GMG's breach of contract.

If you were a lawyer wanting the court to apply Parker to your client's case, you would need to go no further. As a law student, however, who often must argue both positions, the next step would be to distinguish the precedent case.

# Distinguishing Cases — The Writing Process

The party who desires a different outcome from the precedent case will argue that a case is different from the client's situation, and that those differences are sufficiently significant to warrant a different outcome. This is what is known as distinguishing a case. Lawyers distinguish cases for a variety of reasons — and understanding those reasons can help you understand why the writing process for distinguishing cases has greater variation than the writing process for applying cases.

First, lawyers often must distinguish cases cited by opposing counsel in motions, briefs and other legal documents. If opposing counsel argues that a precedent case requires an outcome you find undesirable (usually because your client would lose), you must find a way to demonstrate to the court that the precedent does not require the same outcome. In such cases, you can respond to opposing counsel's portrayal of the case in one of two ways — by accepting or rejecting opposing counsel's characterization of the case, i.e., their proposed premise.

## Accepting a Proposed Premise

First, you might "accept" the proposed premise offered by opposing counsel — and demonstrate that your client's case does not "fit" the proposed premise offered by opposing counsel. Here is an example of accepting the premise proposed in the previous section, and then distinguishing the case, by proving the "flip" side of the premise — i.e., the opposite of that proposed premise is true for the client's case:

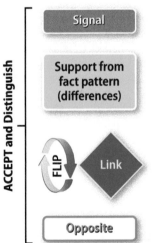

Nickels' claim is distinguishable from <u>Parker</u> because Nickels' creative interests aren't impaired in the same way.

Both of Nickels' offers are to play an ER doctor on a TV show, and both offers allow him to do comedic scenes — which is not the same as a shift from a musical to a western. His role is the same — a TV lead, whereas the Parker actress had her role reduced from the lead role to a supporting character. Although the second offer does not give him the power to write episodes, under the first offer he could not write until the second season, which, with a new show, might never have happened; also, because the second offer gives him the right to direct even more episodes, on a highly successful show, he has greater creative control. This is a stark contrast to the complete loss of creative control in <u>Parker</u>, where the actor lost the right to approve the director and screenplay. Because Nickels' creative interests are not similarly impaired, the second offer is not sufficiently different or inferior, and Nickels damages must be reduced accordingly if he refuses to accept the offer.

## Rejecting a Proposed Premise

A second way a lawyer might distinguish a case is to "reject" the proposed premise put forward by opposing counsel, and to offer her own. A lawyer might choose to take this route where the lawyer believes she can propose a premise which better highlights the differences between the precedent case and the client's case. In such cases, your first task is to convince the court that your proposed premise is actually a better explanation for the case outcome. The writing process for this section might feel familiar to you, because it is nearly identical to the Setup section of the "Applying Cases Writing Process." Here is an example:

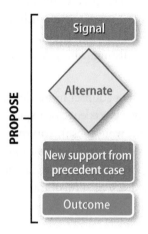

In Parker, the court found **the offer was different or inferior because of the** substantial inconvenience **imposed on the actress.** The first film was to be shot in Los Angeles — which was where most, if not all, movie studios were located. The replacement offer was to be filmed in an Australian opal mine. The actress would have been required to relocate, to travel thousands of miles away, at a time when most industry deals would be made in the Los Angeles area, probably in person, and she would have been accessible only via a long intercontinental flight or international long distance telephone calls. **This** substantial inconvenience rendered the second offer different and inferior, which is why the actress was not required to accept it to mitigate her damages.

The next step is the same process as the "Accept and Distinguish" process—essentially because you are "accepting" your own proposed premise and then demonstrating how your client's case is different from that proposed premise. Here is an example:

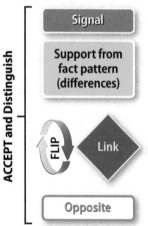

However, in the present case accepting the replacement offer would not cause any inconvenience. Nickels was already relocating for the initial offer — so the second offer did not impose an additional burden on him. He also would relocate to New York, not to a remote area, **like an Australian opal mine,** and he can be in LA (for work) or San Francisco (for home) on the same day if he chooses, via a direct five or six hour flight, which is far different from the long intercontinental flight home in Parker. Unlike Parker, he would still be able to network and further his career, since New York provides ample creative opportunities for actors. **Also,** communication has changed, making it far easier to network and stay connected (via Skype, email, etc.) than it was when Parker was decided, making it more convenient to work in other places. Because Nickels would not be substantially inconvenienced, the second offer is not inferior and so if Nickels chooses not to accept it, his damages should be reduced accordingly.

## Putting It All Together: Distinguishing Cases

You are not limited to choosing one or the other of these paths. A lawyer, (or law student taking an examination) might want to do both—accept a proposed premise and show how it is distinguishable, and then also reject the premise and show that the case is distinguishable for other reasons. By putting all of the "pieces" from this section together, you have an example of how to do that on an examination. Here is what a sample answer looks like, using the "pieces" from this section to explain how the Parker case can be distinguished from Nickels' situation:

Nickels' claim is distinguishable from <u>Parker</u> because Nickels' creative interests aren't impaired in the same way. Both of Nickels' offers are to play an ER doctor on a TV show, and both offers allow him to do comedic scenes—which is not the same as a shift from a musical to a western. His role is the same—a TV lead, whereas the <u>Parker</u> actress had her role reduced from the lead to supporting character. Although the second offer does not give him the power to write episodes, under the first offer he could not write until the second season, which, with a new show, might never have happened. Also, because the second offer gives him the right to direct even more episodes, on a highly successful show, he has greater creative control. This is a stark contrast to the complete loss of creative control in <u>Parker</u> where the actor lost the right to approve the director and screenplay. Because Nickels' creative interests are not similarly impaired, the second offer is not sufficiently different or inferior, and Nickels' damages must be reduced accordingly if he refuses to accept the offer.

Moreover, in <u>Parker</u>, the court found the offer was different or inferior because of the substantial inconvenience imposed on the actress. The first film was to be shot in Los Angeles—which was where most, if not all, movie studios were located. The replacement offer was to be filmed in an Australian opal mine. The actress would have been required to travel thousands of miles away from her planned location of Los Angeles, at a time when most industry deals would be made in the Los Angeles area, probably in person, because social media, skype, etc. did not exist, and she would have been accessible only via a long intercontinental flight or international long distance telephone calls. This substantial inconvenience rendered the second offer different and inferior, which is why the actress was not required to accept it to mitigate her damages.

However, in the present case, accepting the replacement offer would not cause any inconvenience. Nickels was already relocating for the initial offer—so the second offer did not impose an additional burden on him. He also would relocate to New York, not to a remote area, like an Australian opal mine, and he can be in LA (for work) or San Francisco (for home) on the same day if he chooses, via a direct five or six hour flight, which is far different from the long intercontinental flight home in <u>Parker</u>. Unlike <u>Parker</u>, he would still be able to network and further his career, since New York provides ample creative opportunities for actors. Also, communication has changed, making it far easier to network and stay connected (via Skype, email, etc.) than it was when <u>Parker</u> was decided. Because Nickels would not be substantially inconvenienced, the second offer is not inferior and so if Nickels chooses not to accept it, his damages should be reduced accordingly.

## A Third Tactic: Proposing a Premise to Distinguish

A third way a lawyer might distinguish a case is to raise and distinguish a case that has not yet been raised by opposing counsel. Lawyers may not ignore precedent in hopes that the court will not find it. A lawyer is obligated to bring applicable precedent to the court's attention. Sometimes there are cases which every lawyer in the field will know—these are sometimes called seminal cases. A lawyer whose case is potentially governed by such a case would have to raise such a case, even if it wasn't in her client's favor—because the lawyer knows the court will be thinking about the case and the lawyer would want the opportunity to help the court "see" the case from the lawyer's client's perspective.

In such situations, the lawyer must first propose a premise and then distinguish the premise. This process looks exactly like the "reject and distinguish" process, because the lawyer must first set out and explain the proposed premise and then "flip" the premise and demonstrate the opposite.

## Some Final Thoughts

As you can see, although all of the "pieces" of the thinking process are utilized in the writing process, the writing and thinking processes follow a different structure. Also, the writing process contains some additional "pieces." Understanding these differences will help you convert your thinking to writing.

### Variations

You should also know that there are a number of variations you may use to adapt this writing structure to the preferences of your faculty, and to the specifics of your examination. For example, sometimes professors will craft an exam which explores the differences between two cases, intending for you to apply one case, and distinguish another. In your legal writing class, you may have to begin with a discussion of the facts of the case, because you are learning to write to judges and lawyers who may not have read the case you are utilizing (whereas your contracts professor will have read and discussed the contracts cases).

There are also other writing variations for examinations which are described in Chapter 9, for use on examinations which do not require you to specifically apply or distinguish cases. For now, you should know that you must practice writing your thoughts to become proficient at this skill. Understanding the material and being able to talk about the material in class does not necessarily translate to good grades in law school. Almost every professor can tell you about students who performed well in class, but who earned low grades, and about students who did not perform well in class, but who earned high grades; usually this is the result of the disconnect between how law school teaches students thinking skills in the classroom, evaluates students on the basis of speaking skills and then grades students based on writing skills. This is why expert law students practice writing their answers—and get feedback on their practice from each of their professors, or, where that is not available, from other sources, such as peer help and self assessment, as described in Chapter 8, so they are sure they can translate their understanding of the material into the format that is used to assess their learning, and award grades.

### Using a Proposed Premise to Synthesize Cases

You also should know that you can create a proposed premise which explains the outcome in multiple cases—this is sometimes what professors are referring to when they ask you to synthesize cases. Sophisticated students, and lawyers, are able to use a single proposed premise to explain many case outcomes—those that are for and those that are against the client. This is particularly effective, because courts generally favor arguments that reconcile seemingly contradictory or disparate authority.

## Step Three: Creating an Exam Approach

Each law school course requires students to know and understand large amounts of information. For this reason, law students typically create highly structured summaries of course materials. Nearly all law students do this by creating documents they call their "course outlines," mostly because it so common for law professors, "how to" books and upper division law students to recommend outlining. The fact that not all students succeed in law school or succeed at as high a level as they would like to succeed suggests, however, that not all course outlines are created equally. Law student outlines vary greatly in quality, quantity, depth and effectiveness.

The two most common errors made by novice law students in outlining their course material are (1) failing to understand the purpose of a law school outline and thus failing to create a tool that is useful for that purpose; and (2) failing to start early and work continuously on their outlines.

## Strategy and Structure: Understanding the Goal of Outlining

Remember from the previous chapter that law professors seldom tell students the relationships among the concepts studied in the course, expecting students to identify those relationships on their own. For this reason, it is particularly important for you to understand what this task entails. If the goal of rule deconstruction, which you learned in Chapter 5, is to break rules into their constituent parts, the goal of outlines is to construct an organization of how the rules work in relation to each other, and, most importantly, in relation to how they will be raised and tested on a law school examination. Expert law students understand this second piece, and their law school outlines reflect an understanding of how they will use what they have learned during an examination. The following example should help you understand this critical difference.

Imagine that you needed go to the grocery store to pick up the following items:

| Carrots | Cottage Cheese | Orange Juice |
| Frozen potatoes | Almond Milk | Roast beef |
| Cold Medicine | Tomatoes | Lettuce |
| Grapes | Crackers | Salad dressing |
| Napkins | Potato chips | Bread |
| Ice cream | Ginger Ale | Mustard |
| Bagels | | Toilet Paper |

Take a minute to try to memorize this list. Cover up the list and try to recall the items from memory.

If you attempted this exercise, you probably tried to "chunk" and "cluster" the information—to create categories of related items to help you remember the items. For example, you might have grouped the items something like this:

- Salad
  - Carrots
  - Tomatoes
  - Lettuce
  - Salad Dressing

- Sandwiches
  - Bread
  - Roast beef
  - Mustard

- Breakfast
  - Bagels
  - Cottage cheese
  - Frozen potatoes
  - Almond Milk
  - Orange juice

- Paper products
  - Napkins
  - Toilet paper

- Snacks
  - Potato chips
  - Grapes
  - Crackers
  - Ice cream

- Stuff for sick kid
  - Ginger Ale
  - Cold Medicine

You probably already instinctively know that it is easier to learn and remember a large body of information in smaller sub-groups of information than it is to learn and remember all the information in a single grouping. Rather than having to remember all the information at once, you remember a series of groups and then remember the items in each group. This activity of reorganizing a large amount of information into groups so it can be memorized is known as chunking. Clustering is a particularized form of chunking that involves organizing information into meaningful categories. In other words, the learner classifies the information into groups based on some set of criteria, such as their common features or the concepts that underlie them. Textbook authors, including the authors of law school textbooks, cluster information in this way; they categorize topics by grouping them together with other related topics. Professors sometimes also group concepts this way when they teach a course.

The list above is "chunked" or "clustered" (organized) by the reasons someone might need the items or how someone might use the items (e.g., to make a sandwich). Your list is probably clustered by some criteria which is meaningful to you. You are able to cluster these items because you probably know something about them—you have some idea about what they are used for—and your prior knowledge about these items helps you organize and then store the list in your memory.

To understand how prior knowledge impacts your ability to organize information, try this exercise. Look at the list below and try to memorize as many of the items as you can, in two minutes:

|  |  |  |
|---|---|---|
| remate | chic chac | pelota |
| zaguero | dejada | rebote |
| picada | fronton | cortada |
| faja | chula | costada |
| arrimada | cancha | cesta |
| buzzball | carom | cinta |
| contracancha |  | delantero |

Cover up the terms, and try to recall them. Now think about the difference between this exercise and your earlier attempt to memorize the grocery list. If you found this list more difficult to organize—if your "clusters" of information were more difficult to create, and to remember—it is likely because you are not familiar with the context for this set of terms—jai alai.

Your brain stores information by organizing it into structures called schemata. These structures work something like folders you might create on your computer to store and organize information. You might have a folder for each class you take, stored under a folder by the name of the school you attend. In your class folders you store your documents for that class. You might even have sub folders under your class folders for separating briefs from class notes from practice exams. This is not the only way information is stored (according to schema theory)—information can be stored similar to a database or computer program—in more than one place, using more than one criteria, etc. Your brain organizes complex structures—including the processes for performing complex skills like playing an instrument. The key point is that you can more easily store information when you organize that information in meaningful clusters, and new information is more easily stored when you have enough prior knowledge to create such meaningful clusters. If you do not yet understand how the concepts are related, it will be hard to create a structure for grouping the information. This is why it is important to develop some knowledge about the subject matter before trying to make sense of the relationships between concepts. One of the ways to do this is by reading explanatory material in a supplemental source, as described in Chapter 8.

Now imagine the purpose of studying the grocery list is not just to remember all of the items, but to remember them quickly, and for a particular purpose. Let's imagine you have a time limit on how long you can be in the grocery store—and it is a very short time limit: 5 to 7 minutes. To simulate this task, try this exercise: from memory, without going back to look at the list, try to recall the items from the list which fit into each of the following categories (give yourself 30–45 seconds for each category):

| Produce | Dairy | Bread | Frozen Foods | Deli |
|---------|-------|-------|--------------|------|

If you found it difficult to recall the items, or if you were not able to recall them quickly, it is probably because your "chunks" of stored information were different from these categories. Had you known you would have to recall information in these categories, you would probably have chosen a different method of organizing the information, since organizing the information by how to use the item when you arrived home (e.g., to make a sandwich) would not really help you accomplish your goal of getting through the grocery store quickly. In other words, organizing by how the items are related to one another (salad, breakfast, etc.), does not help the "shopper" complete the assigned task of getting through the store as quickly as possible. To be able to meet your goal of getting through the store quickly, with all of the items, the organization of the list needs to reflect the task. You might want to cluster the information according to which items are located in each section of the grocery store, and then organize by location, according to where the categories in the store are located. For example, the following list is clustered by typical sections in a grocery store:

- **Produce**
  - Carrots
  - Grapes
  - Tomato
  - Lettuce
- **Bread**
  - Bagels
- **Deli**
  - Roast beef

- **Frozen Foods**
  - Frozen dinners
  - Ice cream
  - OJ
- **Paper Products**
  - Napkins
  - Toilet-paper

- **Pharmacy**
  - Cold medicine
- **Dairy**
  - Cottage cheese
  - Almond Milk
- **Snack foods**
  - Crackers
  - Potato chips
  - Ginger Ale
- **Condiments**
  - Salad dressing
  - Mustard

You would next want to order the categories according to the order you will encounter them in the grocery store. For example, how would you organize your list if the store was laid out this way:

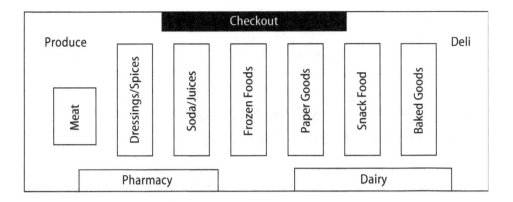

How might your list be different if your store was laid out this way:

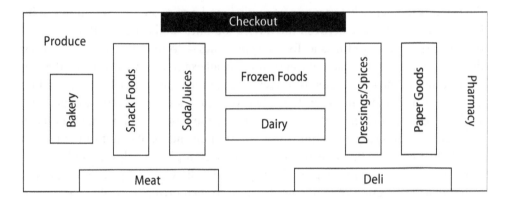

You might even change your list depending on where the entrance is located—your list might look different if you knew you would enter through the pharmacy vs. the produce section. The point is that your list is most effective when you draft it with the purpose of the list in mind and with a clear idea of how that list will be used.

This task, of clustering and organizing for the task, rather than just for the relationships between concepts, is the same process you must engage in to reorganize the concepts you have studied in your law school classes into an approach which will help you get through your law school exams. The process of creating your "outline" is similar to the process of reorganizing a grocery list to be able to find things in the grocery store quickly and efficiently. A law school professor generally covers a list of topics or concepts that the student has to organize (the grocery list), and the student must figure out how the concepts fit together so that they can be used to spot issues and construct an exam answer in the time allotted (get through the store without missing any items).

Like the grocery list, law school "outlining" is much more effective if you think about why you are organizing the material and how you will need to use it. If you understand the goal or purpose for your outline (getting through a law school exam in an organized manner, within the time limits, without missing any issues), your organizational system will usually start to take shape and make more sense—because it will be created to help you perform the assigned task. Conversely, if you organize material without giving some thought to why you are doing it and how you will use the material (i.e., how you will be tested, what the fact patterns will look like, etc.), your outline will not be an effective learning or study tool.

## Creating Effective Law School Outlines: Converting "Lists" to Exam Approaches

Novice law school learners often give up on the difficult task of creating meaningful structure and therefore create "outlines" that are really just lists of information chunked together by how the topics relate to one another, like the first organized grocery store list. The absence of meaningful structure—tied to how the material will be used—makes their outlines much less valuable as tools for writing an examination. This is the primary difference between expert outlines and novice outlines. From this point forward, to differentiate between the novice "outlines" and expert outlines, we will refer to these expert outlines as Exam Approaches—to reflect that the expert has thought about how the material will be used on an exam, and has organized the material to reflect the critical step of understanding how the material will be used on an exam. Understand, however, that when your professor or successful upper level students refer to "outlines", they are referring to the type of outline that reflects an approach to answering an examination question on the topic—not to the type of outline that merely reflects the relationship between topics. It helps to think of your exam approach as the list of procedures you will follow during your examination, rather than a collection of materials you need to memorize. To create an exam approach, try the following steps:

### 1. Make a List

First, you'll need to make a list of "items" (i.e., all of the issues you've studied). To make your list, look at:

- your course syllabus
- the table of contents in your casebook (all of the sections covered by your reading assignments)
- your class notes
- your case briefs

### 2. Plan Your Strategy

This second step requires you to identify and organize the "items" in light of how you will need to approach the subject during the examination. If this seems daunting, it is probably because you do not yet understand how the material will be tested. Imagine how difficult the task of organizing the grocery list (for the purpose of getting all of the items quickly while in the store) would be if you had never been to or seen a grocery store. How would you even begin to understand how to organize?

Unfortunately, many novice law students try to create outlines without having taken practice exams—the equivalent (for this analogy) of never having seen or been to a grocery store. Additionally, if you've only seen one exam, or very few, there is a good chance your actual exam will be something you haven't practiced—which is like being dropped into a store you've never been to, one where you are not familiar with the layout. You might have had this experience, if you have ever been to a store in a different neighborhood and found the store was laid out differently from the store you were used to shopping in. In such cases, it feels strange, disorienting even, and usually takes you longer to find what you need. You're slower at your task. The same thing is true for exams—if you are unfamiliar with the different ways issues can be raised—with the different patterns your professor follows—it will take you time to reorient yourself and get through the exam. The more stores you've been into (i.e., the more exams you've practiced), the easier it is to adapt your plan, quickly and effectively, when you are in an unfamiliar store (i.e., a new exam). For this reason, preparing for exams and creating an effective exam approach necessarily involves reviewing many practice exams, trying to write answers to those exams, and reflecting on how and why your approach is or is not working. As you begin this process, of organizing the topics, consider:

- What will the exam look like? How will the issues come up?

- Is there a specific order that is necessary? Do all sample answers follow the same order? Why or why not?

- Did your professor lay out an order of topics for you to use on an essay?

To better understand the difference between an outline of information and an outline which serves as an essay approach, compare the following excerpts from two different student outlines on the same topic—the Parol Evidence Rule:[1]

---

1. These sample excerpts are intended to help you understand how to create an effective outline. They are not model approaches to the Parol Evidence Rule for all Contracts professors. Professors vary widely in what they emphasize, how they interpret the law, and what objectives they hope to achieve. For this reason, it is never wise to use an outline created for a class with a different professor. Moreover, if you do not create your own approach, you are less likely to internalize and understand the material, making it more difficult for you to retrieve the information you need during an exam in a timely manner—and you will be less likely to retain the information long term—for the bar exam and for practice.

**Outline Version One:**

I. PAROL EVIDENCE RULE (PER)

  a. Intro

    i. Sometimes circumstances surrounding a contract can reveal the meaning of ambiguous terms—this is called extrinsic evidence. Extrinsic evidence can clarify what the parties contemplated by language in the written memorial of the agreement.

    ii. Problem with extrinsic evidence = sometimes it suggests an interpretation that is not readily apparent from the writing.

    iii. PER Policy—when parties record their agreement in writing, they often intend the writing to incorporate the final and complete version of what they agreed and to supersede terms that they may have discussed or even agreed to in prior or contemporaneous negotiations. Any evidence of the parties' expectations that is not reflected in the written agreement (parol or extrinsic evidence) may be suspect.

  b. Application of PER

    i. Ambiguity of written agreement

      1. If the judge finds the written agreement to be ambiguous, that fact finder may consider the evidence but the party tendering the evidence has to persuade the fact finder that the evidence is credible and the parties in fact agreed to the alleged term.

      2. If the judge finds the written agreement to be unambiguous, the PER bars consideration of the evidence and its exclusion may result in the collapse of the claim or defense;

    ii. when one party argues that the true expectations of the parties either contradict or supplement the terms of the written agreement PER bars admission of evidence on these issues.

    iii. Integration

      1. Type of integration

        a. fully integrated (expresses the final agreement of the parties as to the matters discussed in that writing) or

        b. partially integrated (the writing is not reasonably intended to be comprehensive)

        c. Although an integration clause is a strong indication that the parties intended complete integration of a written agreement, a boilerplate clause will not be given effect if it appears that the provision is factually false. When material extrinsic evidence shows that outside agreements were relied upon, those parole agreements should be given effect rather than allowing boilerplate "to vitiate the manifest understanding of the parties."

      2. Test applied

        a. Older cases use "Four Corners" test: court refuses to go beyond the written document

        b. Plain meaning approach: meaning of the actual words used by the parties

        c. Modern Approach: Where there is a binding agreement, either completely or partially integrated, evidence of prior or contemporaneous agreements or negotiations is not admissible in evidence to contradict a term of the writing.

        d. Evidence of oral collateral agreements should be excluded only when the fact finder is likely to be misled

        e. When determining that a collateral agreement is such that it might naturally be made as a separate agreement, the court must look to the actual experience and dealings between the parties as they view the status of such a collateral agreement.

**Outline Version Two:**

**PAROL EVIDENCE RULE (rules in italics)**

I. *Does the PER apply?* (Determine what evidence is being offered and if the PER is at issue)

*Rule: Generally, the parol evidence rule bars extrinsic evidence of prior written or oral agreements or simultaneous oral agreements for which there is no separate consideration*

A. Is this evidence about a <u>prior</u> <u>written</u> agreement? (PER in issue)

B. Is this evidence about an oral agreement made <u>before or</u> <u>at the same time as</u> making of the writing (difference between oral and written) (PER in issue)

C. Is there <u>separate consideration</u> for this agreement?

1. If YES, Treat as separate K, and PER does not apply

2. If, NO, continue, PER in issue

II. *DETERMINE WHETHER THE NEXT ISSUE TO DISCUSS IS EXCEPTIONS OR INTEGRATION* (where there is a clear exception that resolves the issue, it is better to discuss that first)

A. *Determine the degree of integration and effect of that determination*

1. First, determine <u>what court will consider</u> to determine level of integration:

a. Look for an <u>Integration/Merger Clause</u>: These often explain that there are no terms not stated in the writing that should be treated as part of the parties' agreement (although these clauses are not dispositive)

b. <u>Corbin</u> Jurisdiction (Majority of courts): *All evidence and surrounding circumstances will be analyzed to verify whether the parties intended an agreement to be integrated*

c. Older cases use "<u>Four Corners</u>" test: court looks only at the written document to determine whether it is fully or partially integrated (whether writing was intended to be a comprehensive statement of the parties' agreement)

2. Based on that evidence/information/agreement, what is <u>degree of integration</u>:

a. Is it <u>completely</u> integrated?

*A K is completely integrated if it is a final and complete writing that says everything to which the parties have agreed, and contains no ambiguity*

b. Is it <u>not at all</u> integrated?

*A K is not integrated if there is nothing that the parties have agreed to finally and completely.* (note that there may be some things the parties have agreed to, but for which they do not have a final agreement)

c. Is it <u>partially</u> integrated?

*A K is partially integrated if it is final with respect to some terms actually included in the writing, but is silent or incomplete with regard to other terms*

3. Determine the <u>effect</u> of the degree to which it is integrated

*If an agreement is completely integrated, the PER applies and no evidence is admissible to add to, vary, or contradict the terms of the writing (no additional terms). If an agreement is only partially integrated, evidence of consistent additional terms is admissible (additional terms are ok).*

a. Completely integrated = <u>no</u> extrinsic evidence is admissible, even it consistent

b. Not integrated = <u>All</u> parol evidence is admissible

(*Continued*)

    c. Partially integrated = evidence of <u>consistent</u> additional terms is admissible, but no evidence of contradictory terms

      • Consistent if: "reasonable harmony" with the overall substance of the writing

**B. *Does an exception apply?*** *(*evidence that falls under these exceptions is admissible, but for the limited purpose reflected in the exception, not for the purpose of adding a new term to the K)

    1. Is it evidence of a <u>contract defense</u>? (e.g., fraud, mistake, duress)

    2. Is it evidence of an <u>oral condition precedent</u>?

    3. Is it evidence that helps to <u>explain an ambiguity</u>? (something that is "reasonably susceptible to different interpretations")

---

**PAUSE. THINK. ACT.** Answer the following questions in the space below. (1) What differences do you see between version one and version two? (2) Why are those differences important? (3) What makes version two a better outline for succeeding at the task of writing a law school examination answer?

---

# Understanding Key Differences Between Outlines of Information and Exam Approaches

"Outline version one" is a collection of information the student has learned about the topic. "Outline version two" is a list of the procedures a student should follow to evaluate an examination problem. Version two is most effective for helping the student reach her goal—of spotting and covering each tested issue in the time allotted on an exam, because it is reorganized according to the task, so the student doesn't have to spend time trying to reorganize concepts during the actual exam—and waste valuable and limited time.

This process—of reorganizing the information from version one into version two—increases the likelihood of spotting issues on an examination—because by reorganizing learning, students can identify connections among the subject areas that are not apparent when the student first reviews the material. These connections will suggest to the student different ways professors can combine topics on examinations. In other words, students can anticipate possible combinations of topics that professors might choose to test. Reorganization also helps students better understand how to use information by helping students think about places where decisions will lead in different directions. Finally, when students reorganize material to see how each rule is a part of an overall approach to solving a problem, they better understand the purpose for each individual rule.

### 3. Add the Important Details

Once you have the framework for your approach, you can add other important details—including examples, explanations and information from cases. You should also be certain you have rules for each testable issue, element, factor, etc. It's a good idea to go back through your class notes, case briefs and deconstructed rules—to find information that will be useful to you—but be very careful about what you choose to put in your approach.

Novice law students, who are focused on creating an "outline" (like version one, above) are often confused about what they should include. Part of this problem stems from the multiple objectives that law professors have in mind when they are teaching, as explained in Chapter 6. Remember that in any given class session, law professors provide instruction in case reading, synthesis, legal analysis, fact analysis and investigation, issue spotting and the doctrinal subject matter, i.e., torts, contracts, criminal law. Law professors almost never signpost their transitions among these instructional topics, and often are teaching to multiple objectives at the same time. For example, in the course of discussing the doctrine addressed in a particular case, an instructor might both teach students how to apply the particular rule or holding and might also focus on the procedural posture of the case, but as well as teach students new terminology by focusing on terms that are present in the case, but which may not have any bearing on the meaning of the case. An exam approach would only include those things the student will need during their examination—in this case, the points the student learned about how to apply the particular holding of the case. This might include the case holding, social policy and other rationale for the doctrine and holdings, especially when that information helps explain how and why to apply the rule in a particular way, or helps to create a "proposed premise" to apply law to new situations, like exam fact patterns.

Also, know that that some rules, cases and other information you learn can legitimately go into more than one place in your exam approach—the same way items from the grocery list can be in more than one place. For example, ice cream could be classified as dairy or frozen foods. This is also true of legal concepts. Intent is a component of all intentional torts; in evidence, we balance the probative value of evidence against any prejudicial effect of admitting that evidence in a variety of circumstances. Putting things into multiple categories ensures that you know the different ways that the issue (concept) can be raised—so you don't have to limit items to a single location in your approach.

Finally, know that some items might be difficult to categorize until you have more information. Although sometimes concepts should be listed in different or multiple places in an outline, sometimes they only belong in one place, and you may need more information about the topic before you truly understand where. Don't be afraid to move something in your approach when additional information—in the form of class discussion or calibration or practice—clarifies where it should go.

### 4. Check for Accuracy and Comprehension

Expert law students check the accuracy of what they are including in their exam approaches. Perfect recollection of an incorrect rule or holding is, of course, useless. Expert law students check for accuracy by comparing their work with their peers, the cases and materials they have read, and their case briefs and class notes. Expert law students check for accuracy with their instructors by asking questions about any rule or holding about which they have doubt.

Expert law students also know the only way they can ensure their exam approach is working is to use the approach to take practice exams, to reflect on their performance, and to revise their approach to respond to what they have learned from taking practice exams.

### 5. Timing

Many novice learners, perhaps even recognizing that a course outline is a tool for preparing for examinations, choose to delay most of the work on outlines until their examinations are imminent. At this late juncture, however, students have less time to think through the organization of the material—resulting in the creation of outlines of material, rather than exam approaches. Rushing through the processes, in turn, increases the risk of omission of key material or inclusion of extraneous or erroneous information. Even more significantly, using time at the end of the semester or year to create an exam approach takes away time that could have been spent on other tasks necessary to success on examinations, including necessary practice. It also almost certainly will result in focusing on memorization via some type of repetition—the worst choice for effective storage and retrieval of information.

For some students, the press of time becomes so great that they simply choose to forego doing an outline altogether and try studying from their class notes, or memorizing another student's outline or exam approach, which creates a risk that they will fail to see the relationships among the course concepts and be unable to retain and use the materials they actually need to know for their examinations.

Finally, and most importantly, students may either fail to identify areas of confusion in the rush to finish or may be unable to obtain access to the resources (fellow students, instructors, supplemental texts) they need to resolve any confusion they do identify. For this reason, after the first semester, expert law students start working on their exam approaches within the first week or two of the semester; in the first semester students typically need at least a few weeks before they have studied enough material to warrant creating an approach. In any case, expert law students work persistently on their approaches throughout the semester, and do not wait until the final weeks to begin. Also, rather than saving their questions or not developing questions until close to exam time, they identify their need for clarification and get that clarification as the semester goes; as a result, expert students consistently get their assistance needs met. Because expert law students are working on their exam approaches throughout the semester, they avoid missing the opportunity to ask these questions because they are not competing with their peers who have procrastinated until the end of the semester. They also strive to complete an exam approach by the end of the semester so they have time to ask any final questions, and spend the time between classes ending and the start of exams to continue to practice using the material and refine their skills.

### The Importance of Spaced Study

Law school requires you to learn more and retain information longer than other types of educational experiences, including other graduate education. You will need to recall information you learn in your first semester of law school when you take the bar examination in three or four years, and even when you become a lawyer. The material covered in your classes is not something you memorize for an exam, and then forget when the exam is over. For this reason, it is important to study in a manner that improves your ability to retrieve the information long after your first year exams are over.

Spaced study—studying material multiple times over an extended period of time— results in remembering more and remembering better. Consequently, expert law students space their study and practice throughout the semester, rather than trying to learn and memorize material at the end of the semester, or the week or even the day before the examination. If you postpone study until the last few weeks or days, you will most likely be forced to choose repetition and rehearsal as your only methods— and these methods are the least effective tools for producing long term memory. And unlike undergraduate programs, where you may not need to remember what you have learned after the semester has ended, at the end of your legal education, you will need to pass a bar exam to become a lawyer, so you need to retain what you study in the first year for at least two to four additional years, and sometimes, depending upon your practice area, for much longer. Additionally, if you choose to try to learn material at the last moment, you may be studying late into the night before the examination. This decreases your ability to store the information, because the brain catalogues information you have studied while you sleep; it also decreases your ability to retrieve what you know because your brain works less efficiently when it has been deprived of sleep.

## 6. Format

The only essential rule for formatting is for you to adopt a format that works for you, and for the task. It is a good idea to let go of the notion that a law school outline must look like a traditional linear outline, since this type of outline may not be the best choice for the task, or for you. For example, take a look at the information contained in "Outline version two," above regarding degree of integration, and effect of that determination. That information might be easier for you to understand and remember if it were expressed in a chart like this:

| Degree of Integration | Effect |
| --- | --- |
| Completely integrated | <u>No</u> extrinsic evidence is admissible, even it is consistent |
| Not at all integrated | <u>All</u> parol evidence is admissible |
| Partially integrated | Evidence of <u>consistent</u> additional terms is admissible, evidence of contradictory terms is not |

In some cases, and for some students, visual depictions—like timelines and flow charts—are a better method for expressing the information. For example, the graphic organizer on the following page  is a different way of expressing the Parol Evidence exam approach.

The key to creating an exam approach is to understand (1) information can be represented in many different ways; (2) the format you select should help you achieve your goal—being able to use and remember the information during your examination. Sometimes one type of format works better than another. Expert law students consider multiple ways of organizing the material and know why they have selected one method over another. The next section describes some of the methods you might select.

### Using Timelines

Timelines are extremely useful for organizing a sequence of events or a progression of information that follows a particular order. Timelines are sometimes helpful in making sense of a line of cases treating the same issue differently if those differences are the result of an evolution in the law over time. To create a timeline, draw a line and mark the earliest possible starting point at one end and the latest possible event at the other end. It is helpful to then mark a few intermediate points in time. Then, plot each event along the timeline, identifying both the date of the event and the nature of the event, making sure that the events are correctly sequenced along the timeline. A timeline can be drawn vertically or horizontally.

There are some important limitations to timelines. First, timelines are very limited in the quantity of information they can depict. Students can communicate only small

## An Approach to the Common Law Parol Evidence Rule in Flowchart Form

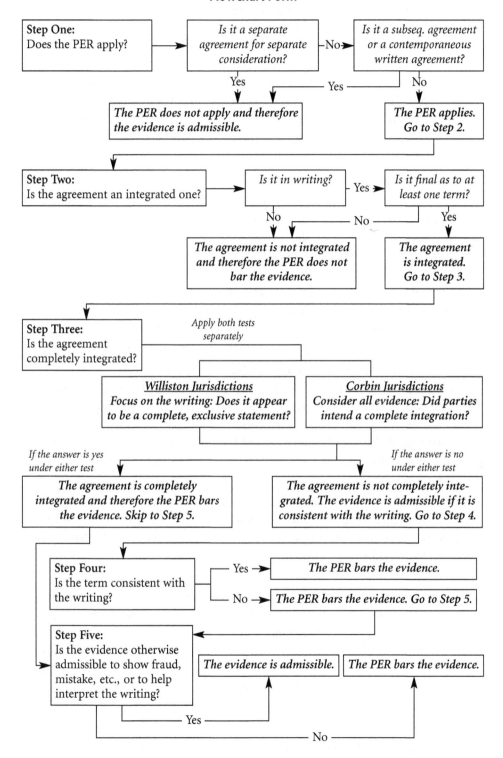

bits of information at any given location along a timeline. For complicated matters, timelines can oversimplify necessary complexity. Second, students cannot readily use timelines to depict events that overlap or are of long duration. Moreover, students using timelines sometimes force events into a sequence that does not reflect what really transpired. In many, if not most, human interactions, events progress in an order that does not necessarily follow a straight line. In other words, events can cause immediate responses but also can have longer-term effects, or may not result in an immediate effect but may later produce such an effect or may produce a result that really was a cumulative result of several events. For these reasons, students should use timelines only in situations where linear sequence is important and needs to be clarified.

### Using Comparison Charts

Comparison charts allow you to depict the similarities and differences among concepts or ideas. The items to be compared are listed down the left hand side of the table and the bases of comparison are shown across the top. Comparison charts help identify similarities and differences between and among like things. They are particularly helpful tools for synthesizing cases and for helping to apply or distinguish a precedent because they can help you identify and think through the similarities and differences between/ among cases They are also helpful for preparing students to spot issues, because they allow students to identify the similarities and differences among like concepts and therefore assist students in identifying which one(s) would apply in a particular context.

To create a comparison chart, create a table in which you list the items to be compared along the left side (e.g., the names of the cases that will be compared) and, across the top, list the characteristics on which you will be comparing the items. In the context of a case comparison chart, these characteristics will depend on the facts the courts regarded as significant in each of the cases. After you have completed the lists of cases and characteristics you wish to compare, fill in the open boxes with the relevant information.

The comparison chart on the following page depicts a group of cases that all address the same legal issue but which reach slightly different conclusions. In each of these cases, the courts have applied the rule that a party may be liable for damages sustained by the other party only if those damages were "foreseeable" at the time the contract was made.

By organizing the five cases together, students can gain insights into how to apply the rule and how they might apply and distinguish the five cases. For example, by looking at this chart, a student wishing to argue that a particular loss was not foreseeable would immediately be able to see that the student would have to apply the *Hadley* and *Lamkins* cases and distinguish *Victoria Laundry*, *The Heron II* and *Hector Martinez & Co.* Students could add a column for listing potential reasons for the decision which could be used to create a proposed premise during an exam.

Comparison charts, while helpful for certain tasks, such as applying and distinguishing cases, have only limited application to other tasks. Because the student must

## A Comparison Chart Depicting the Application of the Forseeability Rule

| Case | Result | Holding |
|------|--------|---------|
| *Hadley v. Baxendale* | Not foreseeable | Loss of profits from inability to use mill stemming from defendant's failure to deliver broken shaft to repairperson held not foreseeable because defendant only knew the shaft was broken and not that mill could not operate until it was repaired. |
| *Lamkins v. International Harvester Co.* | Not foreseeable | Loss of crop profits stemming from inability to use plaintiff's tractor at night stemming from defendant's failure to deliver lighting equipment on time not recoverable because huge difference between cost of lights and loss suffered by plaintiff suggests defendant could not foresee the loss. |
| *Victoria Laundry, Ltd. v. Newman Industries, Ltd.* | Foreseeable | Loss of profits from inability to use new boiler caused by seller's delay in delivering a functioning boiler to laundering and dying business recoverable where seller knew business would be using boiler for doing laundering and dying. |
| *The Heron II* | Foreseeable | Loss caused by dip in value of plaintiff's sugar caused by defendant's delay in delivering sugar deemed foreseeable where defendant knew plaintiff was planning on selling the sugar. |
| *Hector Martinez & Co. v. Southern Pacific Transport Co.* | Foreseeable | Reasonable cost of renting equipment to use while awaiting delayed delivery by defendant delivery company of mining equipment foreseeable where bill of lading described equipment as used mining equipment and the equipment required multiple train cars to ship. |

fit all information in a comparison chart into pre-defined categories, the student may exclude important information simply because it cannot be classified into one of the categories. In addition, comparison charts can only depict a small amount of information and only in a limited way; more complex relationships among ideas often do not fit comparison charts. Nevertheless, comparison charts are useful tools for law students to include in their arsenal.

### Using Hierarchy Charts and Flow Charts

Hierarchy charts depict the relationships among the materials to be learned in a top-to-bottom or broadest-to-narrowest structure. The items at the top represent the broadest or highest level concepts, the items at the next level represent the next broadest or highest level concepts and so on.

These charts are helpful in a variety of circumstances, but are particularly helpful when the student needs to learn not only the concepts but also the relationships among those concepts. Hierarchy charts depict those relationships visually. Because, as explained above, expert law students always choose to ascertain the relationships among the concepts they are studying, hierarchy charts are a useful tool. Hierarchy charts also may be a useful tool for issue spotting because, by knowing the relationships among concepts, students are better able to identify likely links among issues and to recognize situations where the raising of a higher-level issue necessarily (or at least usually) implicates a lower-level issue.

To create a hierarchy chart, start with the highest-level concept. Draw that concept near the top and in the center of the page. Next, draw all of the sub-concepts for that highest-level concept. All the items on the same level need to be the same height. Draw lines from the highest-level concept to these second level concepts. Then, look at each of the second level concepts individually, and determine what sub-concepts are on the level below that second level. Draw all of these items on this third level and then draw lines from the second level item from which each third level concept emanates to the new third level items you have drawn. Repeat this process for each of the other third level concepts. Continue until you have fleshed out all underlying concepts.

You can draw out your charts on whiteboards, and photograph them for later use. You can use large poster boards to create charts with large amounts of information. You can create charts using most word processing programs, and there are even "apps" that allow you to create interactive charts—where you can "click" a box to display the information organized within that topic—and carry them with you on your smartphone or tablet.

Hierarchy charts, however, can only depict relationships between concepts. Flow charts, which often look a little like hierarchy charts differ from them in crucial ways; flow charts show procedures—the order in which to proceed on a task. Flow charts allow students to show both simple and very complex processes, including places in the processes where decisions would lead in different directions. They also allow students to think through how they would work their way through particular types of problems. Note that flowcharts can sometimes restrict student thinking, if students fail to see complexities in a rule's application—choosing, for example, to proceed down just one path when it's not clear which path to take—or fail to see arguments that will take them out of the process altogether.

To create a flow chart, you first need to determine all the steps involved in the particular process and the order in which those steps should be carried out. Once you have determined the steps, you can use arrows to show the relationships among the steps. Be sure to indicate places where a particular result on a step will take you out of the process or allow you to skip a step of the process. Outline version three, above, is a flowchart which depicts an approach to analyzing application of the parol evidence rule.

Like hierarchy charts, you can draw flow charts on whiteboards, and photograph them for later use. You can use large poster boards to create charts with large amounts of information. You can create charts using computer programs, and there are even "apps" that allow you to create interactive charts—where you can "click" a box to display the information organized within that topic—and carry them with you on your smartphone or tablet.

### Using Mind Maps

Mind maps, which are sometimes referred to as "spider maps," are very helpful tools for learning. A mind map is like a hierarchy chart in that a mind map shows the relationships among the concepts that the student is learning. The differences are that the connections and relationships need not be hierarchical. You can connect anything you want to know about the core concept or sub-concepts, regardless of hierarchy. Consequently, the process of creating a mind map is more free-flowing than the process of creating a hierarchy chart and will allow you the freedom to create your own connections and structure, to make sense of the material for yourself. Mind maps also help students avoid creating artificial hierarchies because they need not force concepts into lower and higher categories. Because mind maps are more free-flowing, however, they are less helpful for showing real hierarchies and for creating a process or structure for answering an examination question.

There are several steps to creating a mind map. Start with the central concept on which you are working. Then draw a line connecting the main idea to each category or concept that relates to that main idea (e.g., the elements, the policy and the key cases applying the central concept). Then, draw a line connecting each of the categories or concepts to its sub-idea(s) or sub-concepts (e.g., each element connected to a circle labeled "the elements"). This task is completed for each category or concept. Then, draw lines connecting each sub-idea to each of its sub-sub-ideas (e.g., each element's definition connected to the name of that element). Continue until you have completed your depiction of the central concept.

Like hierarchy charts, and flow charts, you can draw mind maps on whiteboards, and photograph them for later use. You can use large poster boards to create maps with a vast number of ideas. You can create mind maps using computer programs, and there are even "apps" that allow you to create interactive mind maps—where you can "click" a box to open up new sub ideas—and carry them with you on your smartphone or tablet.

## Step Four: Internalize Your Learning

Although expert law students will have memorized all of the information needed for their examinations, expert law students spend very little time engaged in the task of memorization as that term is commonly understood (the practice of repeating information—out loud, in writing, via self testing methods like flashcards, etc.—until it is committed to memory). Expert law students do not need to spend significant amounts of time "memorizing" in the traditional sense, because they have done all of the work described in the prior chapters. For example, creating an exam approach will improve your retention and recall of material—and result in spending less time actually trying to memorize the subject matter—leaving you time for critical exam practice. If you have prepared for class as described in Chapter 5, engaged during class as described in Chapter 6, and done the things described in this chapter, your brain will already have stored most of the information you need.

First, the act of creating an organizational device of any type facilitates recall. The mental effort needed to organize material in a meaningful way, and then depict it on paper or on a computer screen, constitutes a type of mental exercise that, for many students, will itself store the new learning in their long-term memories. When you create structure, you essentially create a mental location in which to store the new learning. In this sense, by creating an exam approach, you are building a storage facility for what you are learning, much like one might create a file drawer and set of folders to store new documents. In fact, the richness of the connections among the topics in an exam approach, and the quality of its organization, often determines whether a student succeeds in recalling knowledge when she needs it.

Second, when expert law students struggle to understand how the material will be used on an examination, by practicing with the material to calibrate their learning, and to reorder the concepts in their exam approach to reflect that learning, it requires a type of deep mental processing that creates the strong memory traces that make recollection, during the stress of examinations, much more likely. Expert learners make sure they create their own understandings, recognizing that the effort to do so is, itself, crucial to their learning.

Third, by engaging in regular and repeated practice, over the course of the semester, expert law students give themselves time to forget information, which helps them accurately assess what they do and don't know. Moreover, contrary to what many students believe, struggling to retrieve information is a good thing—when you have to struggle to remember (and retrieve) information, it results in stronger, deeper memories that will be easier to retrieve in the future.

## Fine Tuning Your Memorization

If you follow the suggestions in this book, and spend each semester working on your exam approach, working on practice problems, reflecting on your strengths and weaknesses, using what you learn to revise your approach and repeating this cycle, you will likely need to expend little time and effort memorizing information for your exams. One of the first things you can do to check your learning is to try to recall your approach from memory (before you actively try to memorize it). Either handwrite or type it from memory, or recite it out loud, to yourself or to a friend. Once you have finished, compare your exam approach with what you have written, typed or spoken, and highlight the things you missed. This will help you identify the things you have not yet committed to memory. Review and study only the highlighted items. Repeat this process until you don't miss anything. Also, one of the best things you can do is take a practice exam on the topic or create your own hypothetical fact pattern that tests these topics. You may also wish to use some of the techniques in the next section to help you.

Before you take your law school exams, your goal should be to overlearn the material so that you develop automaticity with your exam approach, including every rule and sub-rule. Automaticity means your recall of the information requires such little brain power that it happens almost without you realizing you've made any effort at all. Most adults have experienced this with respect to driving home from school or work—arriving with the strange sensation of not being able to recall any part of the drive, because they had driven home on "auto pilot." Most adults have also over-learned the steps required for reading—no longer needing to sound out words or stop and think about their meaning. This level of automatic recall happens when we repeatedly and consistently use information.

## Memorization Techniques

### Elaboration

Elaboration, which most expert learners automatically do, involves adding to new information to make sense of it. The learner rephrases the information in words that make sense to the learner, fills in gaps, makes inferences and imagines examples to process the new learning in her mind. Elaboration is an excellent learning and memorization tool for law school, because it can result in both understanding and memorization. From an understanding perspective, elaboration is the way learners make sense of new information; they attach their own independent meaning to the learning to reconcile the new learning with what they already know and understand. From a memorization perspective, elaboration facilitates recall by connecting the new learning to the learner's prior knowledge. The deeper processing produced through elaboration, which involves more of the brain, and greater mental effort, than merely memorizing information, also facilitates recall.

In the law school context, there are two particularly effective approaches to elaboration. The first technique involves **paraphrasing**. Paraphrasing is an excellent learning tool because a learner must possess an accurate understanding of a principle to be able to accurately paraphrase it. To paraphrase, the student translates the words of the rule into his or her own words. Thus, for example, a student learning the three tasks involved in the performance phase of the SRL cycle (attention-focusing, implementation and self-monitoring) might rephrase the tasks as (1) zeroing in on the learning, (2) doing the learning, and (3) making sure you are understanding what you are supposed to be learning.

The two crucial aspects of this technique are: (1) accuracy (which requires the student not only to study the words in the rule but also to study the cases that have applied the rule) and (2) using one's own words (rather than someone else's). Accuracy is crucial, because a paraphrase is useless if it is wrong. Thus, expert law students may develop tentative paraphrases which they then test (and usually revise) as they read the cases that have applied the rule. Using one's own words (rather than adopting someone else's paraphrase) is crucial, because the struggle to create the paraphrase is a large part of what creates the memory trace.

The second technique involves generating **examples and non-examples** of each of the concepts the student must learn. An example of a legal concept is a hypothetical situation that includes each attribute required by the rule defining that concept, and a non-example is a hypothetical situation that includes every non-critical attribute of the example but not all the critical attributes. For example, imagine you are a law student in a criminal law class learning that a burglary requires "breaking and entering," and a breaking is "the application of force, however slight." You might generate the following example and non-example:

> *Example:*  B kicks down the closed door to A's home, walks into A's house because he's planning to steal A's $5,000 stereo system, and he does so.

> *Non-example:*  B walks in through a wide open door to A's house because he's planning to steal A's $5,000 stereo system, and he does so.

Notice the example includes the critical attributes of the breaking element; B applies force (in the form of a kick). Notice the non-example possesses all the non-critical attributes of the example, same parties (A and B), the same plan of action (stealing A's stereo), the same additional actions (walking in and taking A's stereo). The difference, of course, is that the non-example omits any application of force; it is unnecessary because the door is already "wide open." The non-example accurately depicts a situation where there has been no breaking.

The effort to generate examples and non-examples is a powerful tool for learning; to be able to generate an example of a concept and a non-example of that concept (a situation similar to the example, except as to the aspect critical to the concept), learners need to understand the concept well. Moreover, the example and non-example serve as additional paths to the words of the definition, thereby increasing the likelihood of recall. For this reason, this approach is a technique commonly used by successful law students to memorize their materials.

### Associational Techniques

Associational techniques are similar to connecting new learning to prior learning. The difference is that the student creates the associations somewhat artificially and arbitrarily for the purpose of memorization, rather than as a means to facilitate understanding. There are three types of associational techniques, **imagery**, **analogies** and **mnemonics**.

#### Imagery

Imagery is a technique whereby students create their own images to remember the essence of concepts they wish to remember. The student matches up the concept they wish to remember with an image that captures the key aspect of that concept. For example, a student wishing to remember the memorization concept "clustering" may imagine a star cluster. A star cluster is a group of stars from among the millions in the sky that appear to have been organized together into a particular pattern; this image helps the student remember that "clustering" is a learning technique that involves grouping information into categories based on their particular patterns or attributes. A law student can remember the parol evidence rule, a rule that prohibits the jury from hearing about contract terms not contained in the parties' written agreement, by imagining a wall between the jury and the terms not contained in the writing. This image is particularly apt, because there are many ways to get somewhere that appears, at first glance, to be protected by a wall. A person can go over, around or even through the wall, and similarly, there are many ways to avoid having evidence barred by the parol evidence rule. An image of keeping the evidence in a jail cell based on the similarity of the word "parol" to the word criminal law word "parole" would be an alternative powerful way of remembering the concept.

Particularly for visually-oriented students, color is a useful tool for making large-scale discriminations among topics. For example, a contract law student may choose to write the portion of her outline dealing with the measure of damages for breach of contract in green ink or on green paper, hoping to trigger recollections based on the association of green with money. She might choose red for contract defenses, such as misrepresentation and illegality, because contract defenses stop the enforcement of contracts. Finally, she might choose a soft blue color for contract formation because blues are associated with serenity and, when parties are forming contracts, everything is calm between them.

Images are excellent tools for remembering because they involve parts of the brain that students seldom use to remember what they need to learn. Thus, by creating a very different type of connection to the material they are memorizing, students strengthen their memory traces and ability to recall the material.

### Analogies

The use of analogies as a memorization tool is effective because it connects the new learning to prior knowledge. An analogy is a comparison to something which is similar; analogies are used to explain or clarify understanding of new skills or information. A good example of an analogy is the section in this chapter which uses the example of a grocery list to teach outlining. Analogies are effective because, if you connect a new skill or new learning to something you already understand or know how to do, it makes it easier to understand and remember what you have learned.

### Mnemonics

Mnemonic devices are, for the most part, best used as a last resort. Students only should use mnemonics when they cannot develop more meaningful associations. There are four types of mnemonic techniques: (1) the single-use coding method, (2) the pegword method, (3) the method of loci, and (4) the keyword technique. Generally, the selection among these methodologies depends on each student's preference. Mnemonics work best when a student generates personal mnemonics rather than using mnemonics developed by professors or by law school peers or predecessors.

*Single-use coding.* The first technique, single-use coding, probably is the only one with which you may be familiar. In its most common form, students first identify the first letter in a list of words or a list of sentences that they wish to remember.

They then recombine the letters to create a new word or to create a sentence that uses words that begin with each of those letters. For example, many music students learned the order of notes on the lines on a music staff by the sentence "Every good boy does fine," which represents the notes E-G-B-D-F.

This technique is helpful for remembering the key words in a list of elements. For example, property law students must learn the elements of a concept called adverse possession, a property law concept that allows a non-landowner to acquire title to property if the real owner ignores her property for many years while the non-landowner openly uses and improves that property. The non-landowner's use must be for the time period specified in the applicable state statute and must be (1) *h*ostile, meaning without permission, (2) *e*xclusive, meaning exclusive of the owner's use, (3) *o*pen and notorious, meaning it would be visible if the true owner cared enough about the property to look, (4) *c*ontinuous, meaning without interruption and (5) *a*ctual, meaning the use must involve the whole area claimed. These five elements can be remembered by the following sentence: *H*is *e*nergy *o*nly *c*auses *a*nguish. Note that the first letter of each word references one of the above elements.

Single-use coding is also the term associated with the creation of rhymes, stories and jingles to help the learner remember something. The internet is filled with such examples, by creative law students across the country who have done everything from rewriting and recording popular music lyrics to producing animated videos.

*The pegword method.* The pegword technique is a tool for memorizing items in an ordered list. It involves two phases. In Phase I, the student creates and memorizes with a high level of automaticity an arbitrary, rhyming association with each of the numbers within the sequence the student wishes to memorize. This phase produces a permanent set of associations that the student will use over and over again. Then, the student associates each item on the list she wishes to remember with the rhyming association (the pegword).

*The method of loci.* The third technique, the method of loci (or the place method), requires the learner to imagine a room with which she is extremely familiar, such as her living room, her bedroom or her classroom. Each has its advantages, although, if the student is readily familiar with the room in which she will be taking her examinations, that choice is probably optimal. (Of course, there may be some risk the student would be accused of cheating if her instructor sees her looking around the classroom at her fellow students or their desks.) The learner then slowly scans in her mind from one side of the room to the other, noting each thing (piece of furniture or decoration) in the room and associating each item in her list of things to remember with something in the room. It is helpful to think of scanning the room like a movie camera might scan from one corner of the room all the way around the room. In addition, try to imagine focusing on each thing as you create your associations, much like a movie camera might zoom in on something important in the room. This approach allows you to organize your associations in a defined order and to create focused associations. For example, a student who wishes to learn the eight parts of speech: nouns, pronouns, verbs, adjectives, adverbs, prepositions, conjunctions and interjections, might imagine her classroom and start with the door to the classroom in her imagination.

- The first thing she imagines seeing is the classroom coat rack. She knows that coat racks are for hanging things and recalls that interjections (such as "Ouch!" or "Hey") are what writers use to hang emotions in their sentences.

- She then moves in her mind towards the student cubbyholes and recalls that cubbyholes are where the students place things like their backpacks and lunch boxes and recalls that nouns are persons (students), places (cubbyholes) and things (backpacks and lunch boxes).

- From the cubbyholes, her mind moves to the front of the classroom, where most of the action in the class takes place and associates that action place with verbs, which are the action words in a sentence.

- Next, her mind moves to a bulletin board on which her teacher places students' best work. She imagines the comments from the teacher on those student papers, such as "excellent" "good" "wonderful," all of which describe the papers and therefore are adjectives.

- Her mind then moves to the clock, which she recalls looking at frequently on days that are moving slowly, and she recalls that adverbs describe how actions are being performed. "Frequently" and "slowly" describe how often she is looking and how the clock is moving and therefore are adverbs.

- She then notices the candy box that her substitute teacher brought to class one day and left there, and recalls that pronouns, such as he, she and it, are substitute words used to represent previously used nouns.

- She then sees that the flag in the classroom is over the candy box and under the clock, and recalls that prepositions locate things in their place or time, just as she has located the flag over the candy box and under the clock in her imagination.

- Finally, she comes back to the front door of the classroom, which links the class-room to the rest of the school building, just as the conjunctions—and, or, but—link words and phrases.

This approach is equally effective for remembering legal rules. For example, a student who wishes to memorize the four requirements to accept an offer of a contract may use his bedroom as his focus location.

- Starting to the left of the door to his room, he first notices his dresser and recalls how he once brought a friend to his room and discovered, to his great embarrassment, that he had failed to put his clean laundry away. He may then recall his promise to himself that he would always put his laundry in the drawers as soon as he does it so that never again does a surprise visitor embarrass him. He can then associate that promise with the requirement that an acceptance must express commitment.

- He then notices the poster for his favorite rock group and recalls that he was unable to get a ticket to the group's most recent concert and that only people who had a connection were able to get tickets. Similarly, the only one who can accept an offer is the person to whom the offer was made.

- Next, the student imagines seeing his bed and recalls that he had to buy the bed "on terms" because he could not afford the full price outright. He connects this recollection to the requirement that the offeree agree to all the terms specified in the offer.

- Finally, he scans towards the bedroom window. He recalls that the window often sticks closed and can only be opened if he finesses and jiggles it in just the right way. Similarly, an offer can be accepted only in a proper manner, a manner expressly required by the offer or reasonable under the circumstances.

This method works, as the above examples demonstrate, because the associations are personal to each student, have a visual component, and are easily created and easily recalled. It is, therefore, a very effective tool. In fact, the loci method was created by an Ancient Greek sect known for their ability to remember vast quantities of information.

*The keyword technique.* The final technique is known as the **keyword technique.** To use this method, a learner who is trying to learn a series of matched items, such as a list of elements and their definitions, associates keywords in each item of each matched set by imagining a bizarre image that combines each item in the associated pair. The student searches her brain for things that either sound like or look like each of the items in the matched set. The keys to effectiveness of this technique are the time spent on the task, the closeness of the matches between the images and the items being memorized, and the vividness and uniqueness of the images.

For example, imagine that a student wishes to remember the three activities in the performance phase of the SRL cycle. By identifying similar-sounding phrases, the student creates memory traces. Thus, the student associates "perfume" with "performance phase," associates an "elf-wandering" with "self-monitoring" and "attentive locusts singing" with "attention-focusing." She then puts it all together by imagining a perfumed elf wandering into a hive of attentive locusts that are singing.

The keyword technique, while helpful in certain circumstances, requires considerable effort to adapt to the complicated definitions common to legal usage and therefore may not always be a fruitful memorization tool for law students. Of course, the effort to use the technique almost always pays off because quantity of effort itself correlates with successful retention. The more you struggle to learn, retrieve and store information, the more likely you are to be able to recall that information in the future. In any event, the other mnemonics described above can be readily used in most legal contexts.

### Rehearsal

By far, the most commonly used memorization technique in all learning contexts, including law school, is rehearsal. Rehearsal refers, in simplest terms, to practicing. The learner attempts, repeatedly, to speak out loud or write out the information he or she is seeking to memorize. While rehearsal is the one strategy nearly all students know and use, it is almost never the best choice as a stand-alone strategy. Rather, expert students use rehearsal in tandem with other memorization strategies as described above, and only use rehearsal alone if other strategies are unavailing.

While rehearsal is not often the best strategy, it is nevertheless worthwhile knowing how to engage in productive rehearsal. Rehearsal, particularly in the law school context, can take many forms, and, in fact, there are best practices for using rehearsal. Actually, it is more accurate to state that there are worst practices for engaging in rehearsal. Rehearsal in the form of reading and re-reading one's class notes or textbook is extraordinarily inefficient and non-productive. More productive rehearsal techniques include: (1) the Gradually Shrinking Outline Technique, (2) the Course Summary Sheet Method, and (3) the Flashcard Method. Each of these techniques can be attempted by the student on his or her own or may be very successfully assisted by a family member or other loved one (friends and loved ones actually may appreciate the opportunity for interaction with the busy law student in their lives). What all productive rehearsal strategies have in common is that the student is practicing and actively testing herself as to whether she can do what she needs to be able to do during examinations — recall on command what she needs to be able to recall.

*The Gradually Shrinking Exam Approach.* Of the three rehearsal techniques, this method probably is the most effective because it combines self-testing with respect to the organization of the course material with self-testing of the details the student must know. To use this technique, the student must first complete her exam approach (or, at least a complete section of her exam approach ). The student starts this technique by going point-by-point through her approach to see if she can derive each of the rules from seeing the name of the concept or element. In other words, she covers up the definitions of each of the concepts with a piece of paper, book or even a hand and tests herself by speaking aloud the portion she has covered. She repeats this exercise until she can accurately recite all the rules.

The student then reduces her exam approach in half by only including things at a certain level of hierarchy, such as removing the elements and their definitions. She then tests her recall by speaking aloud the portion not reflected in the reduced version of her approach. Once she can do so, she reduces her approach to no more than five pages and again makes sure that she can recite the entire approach from looking at the five pages. Finally, she reduces the approach to one page and self-tests whether she can recite the entire approach from that one page.

*The Course Summary Sheet Method.* This approach is a variation on the gradually shrinking exam approach technique. At least twice during the semester (and, ideally, much more often), the student forces herself to summarize the entire course (her entire exam approach) on one page. She then tests herself to see if she can speak aloud the entire approach based on that summary sheet.

*The Flashcard Method.* Many students have used flashcards at some point in their educational careers, perhaps to memorize dates for a history test or to learn words in a foreign language. Flashcards have the advantages of being easy to create and easy to use for self-testing. On the other hand, flashcards really cannot depict the organization of a body of law.

There are two keys to successful use of flashcards. First, the student should create the flashcards for herself and not use commercially-produced flashcards or flashcards created by another (or former) student. The act of creating the flashcards itself produces significant memorization (often students have memorized one-half or more of the material simply through the process of creating the cards). Recalling the material on the cards also triggers a memory of the episode of creating the card; this episodic memory is an additional memory trace. Moreover, only the creator of a set of flashcards can fully understand how the cards were intended to work and how they are organized. For example, every student leaves things out of their flashcards because they feel they already know those things, but the portion left out varies tremendously.

The second key to successfully using flashcards focuses on how the student uses the cards for self-testing. Expert learners recognize that they need to develop automaticity to ensure rapid and easy recall during examinations. The easier it is for the student to recall her learning, the more brainpower the student can devote to the thinking demands created by the examination. This effort is crucial, because law school examinations test analytical skills that require memorization of the knowledge but do not directly test the knowledge itself. In other words, memorization is a prerequisite for success but does not at all insure success on law school examinations. Consequently, freeing up brainpower to focus on analytic efforts is crucial to success, and students need to develop automaticity with respect to the knowledge. This goal requires thus students to test themselves with flashcards until their recall is rapid and automatic with respect to every piece of knowledge they will need for the examination.

## Selecting Memorization Strategies

Ultimately, the selection of memorization strategies is task and individual specific. Each student needs to be an expert in his or learning preferences and make selections most likely to help the student achieve her mastery memorization goal. It is also critical to memorize not only the law, but the specific steps or procedures the student will take to apply the law. In other words the student must memorize both the exam approach framework, as well as the details contained within that framework.

# Chapter 8

# Why, When and How to Get Help

Expert learners recognize their need for help. They know when to seek help, they have strategies for getting help, and—most importantly—they unflinchingly seek such help. There really are three steps in the help-seeking process: (1) recognizing the need for assistance; (2) obtaining assistance; and (3) continuing to seek assistance until the issue is adequately addressed.

Expert law students are able to recognize their need for assistance because they seek out opportunities for practice and feedback, and they are honest and accurate in evaluating their own performance. They identify the causes of their failures to learn and revise their learning process accordingly. This frequent self-reflection and self-assessment helps expert law students obtain the help they need before their lack of comprehension causes them serious learning or educational problems. Novice learners either simply accept their failure to learn or fail to seek help from appropriate resources. In contrast, expert learners recognize that help-seeking is simply another of the strategies they should employ to be a successful learner.

Expert law students are also expert in the help resources available to them. The materials below describe some of the most common supplemental resources, their strengths and weaknesses and their appropriate uses. This chapter also describes how and when to use self-help, peer help and instructor help.

## Self-Help

There are several reasons why self-help is usually the first choice for resolving law school learning problems. First, you are, by far, the best gauge of your own learning issues and how best to resolve those issues. Not only do you know when you do not understand, but also, you are in the best position to know the particular aspect of the material that confuses you. And students are best able to recall, understand and use learning they have figured out for themselves. Accordingly, expert learners begin obtaining assistance by looking to themselves.

One of the most empowering experiences a law student can have is to resolve his or her own confusion. Novice learners, believing that their failure to learn reflects a defect in intellect, either seek help from others too soon, or too often, or simply ignore their problems. Expert learners, who know that failures to learn are a matter of strategy selection and time on task, take control over their own learning and try to resolve their confusion by changing their learning strategies and cycling through the SRL process again.

While expert law students are able to look to themselves for help, they also know when to use self-help and when to seek outside assistance. For example, expert law students would seek outside help immediately for those matters that could be quickly clarified by checking with a peer or asking for a clarification from the instructor. Also, in instances where the confusion is great, continuing to rely exclusively on self-help, without at least some guidance from an outside source, may be futile.

Once of the ways expert law students help themselves is by using supplemental resources. Expert law students know the types of resources that are available and how to best use those resources to achieve their current goals.

## Selecting and Using Supplemental Resources Like an Expert

There are an enormous number of resources designed to assist law students with their self-help efforts. Legal publishers have produced a wide variety of print and electronic resources designed to help law students learn their course material better. Moreover, law professors, eager to help students develop their learning and law school skills have created course web pages and supplemental materials. Consequently, law students have ready access to a wide variety of resources to facilitate their learning.

On the other hand, the ready availability of such resources does not benefit all law students equally or sometimes at all. Law students, particularly novice legal learners, are eager, perhaps overeager, consumers of such materials. The large market, in other words, is a response to student insecurity; novice law students' insecurity about their ability to learn what they need to learn makes them a ready market for materials promising law school success. In fact, novice legal learners often spend hundreds of dollars on supplemental resources materials, some, or even many, of which they never actually use.

> The key to using these resources effectively is to understand why and how you might use each resource—by understanding what each resource is designed to provide—so you are able to select the appropriate resource for a particular task.

The first thing you should recognize is that supplemental sources are generally used for two distinct purposes: (1) as explanatory material—to provide background information, or orient you to the main concepts, or elaborate on a particular concept; and (2) as a means of calibrating your learning—to help you accurately assess your understanding of the material, and how it applies. Expert law students understand these two distinct purposes, and select sources accordingly.

There are so many secondary sources available to law students that a complete catalog of these resources is beyond the scope of this text. Instead, this text focuses on a list of commonly used resources, explaining how and when to use them, and which resources you may want to avoid.

## Using Supplemental Sources as Explanatory Material

The goal of some supplemental resources is to explain the law. Some sources do this by providing background, historical context and discussions of policy reasons for the choices made by courts deciding particular cases. Others provide brief summaries of legal doctrine, and many provide discussions of the main points of key cases students are likely to encounter in their casebooks. These sources may (1) help explain the reason(s) the author included a particular case in the textbook; (2) identify the key facts and reasoning in an opinion—making it easier to see which facts will be manipulated during class discussion or on an exam; and (3) identify when there is a disagreement among the courts regarding a particular point of law and explain the rules the differing courts have adopted.

These types of sources rarely, if ever, provide practice problems or questions, and are not intended to help students assess their own knowledge. For this reason, such sources are valuable for developing the background knowledge which is helpful to you for reading cases. Remember that new information can be stored in the brain through connections to prior knowledge. By gaining knowledge about a topic, you create a schema for taking in the new learning. Also, knowing something about what you are about to read makes the reading easier to understand and recall.

In short, these sources can help make your case reading more effective and efficient because they:

- Aid you in understanding what is important in your reading
- Preview what you are supposed to "get" out of assigned cases
- Provide context for your reading

For these reasons, these types of supplemental sources should generally be used **before** you read and brief cases, and are particularly useful when your casebook does not provide context for your reading. In some cases, such sources might aid your understanding of a particularly difficult topic by providing further explanatory detail. However, other supplemental sources, such as those described in the next section, which require more active learning (via application practice), are usually better for achieving mastery.

The following supplemental sources provide explanatory material:

*Hornbooks.* A hornbook is a lengthy, exhaustive recitation of the law within a given field. Often as long as 1,000 pages, these supplemental texts are characterized by completeness, thoroughness and, for the most part, accuracy. These books are excellent resources for long descriptions and explanations of current law and trends in the law and for cross-references to court opinions and important law review articles in the field. For law students, they provide much more detail than law students either can recall or are expected to recall for law school examinations. In fact, all law school courses involve a set of choices by the instructor as to what not to include. Students who rely exclusively on a hornbook, therefore, actually make greater demands on themselves than their instructors have made. However, hornbooks are useful for developing background knowledge about topics you are about to study, and for explaining the main point of key cases—some of which may be found in your textbook.

*Other Summaries of the Law.* In addition to traditional hornbooks, there are many other, shorter summaries of the law. These books usually contain explanations of the key points of law in a topic area, and descriptions of some of the most frequently used casebook cases. Almost every legal publisher has such a series. You can often find one written by your casebook author or recommended by your professor. Faculty in your law school's academic support department usually have great insights about which of these sources are most helpful for your particular professor and course.

## Using Supplemental Sources to Assess and Calibrate Your Learning

Supplemental sources can also be used to evaluate how well you understand a topic. By testing yourself and accurately evaluating your response, you can use these sources to determine the extent and accuracy of your knowledge, fill in missing details or gaps in your knowledge, and identify missing analytical steps in your exam approach. These sources can also help you gain insight into the relationships between the topics and sub-topics, which helps to develop schema (and your approach). By using these sources as a source of practice you can learn how potential issues are raised and tested. These type of supplemental sources have one thing in common, they each contain problems and answers to those problems, and require you to practice applying what you know (or think you know).

To benefit from using these sources, you have to actually answer the problems and hold yourself accountable. You may have had the experience of reading a problem, thinking of an answer in your head and then reading the actual answer, and giving yourself "credit" for missing information, because you "knew it" even if you didn't actually include that information in the "answer" in your head. Expert law students know this is dangerous to do when evaluating whether they understand how to accurately apply legal concepts—because it can cause them to gloss over what they don't actually know. For this reason, expert law students frequently choose to write out their answers to problems and they are honest with themselves about what their answer actually contains, and whether it was accurate.

*Examples and Explanations.* These books usually contain a brief summary of the key doctrinal principles, followed by problems and model answers with explanations.

*Law in a Flash.* These flashcards, which are also available as an "app" for your smartphone, consist of hypothetical problems on one side with an answer on the reverse. The first cards in each section usually prompt you to recall the rules for the particular topic.

*CALI exercises.* The Center for Computer-Assisted Legal Instruction, also known as CALI, provides computer-based, interactive tutorials that cover narrow topics of law. Students at member lawschools have free access to CALI Lessons through the CALI website. Many faculty also select particular CALI exercises and provide links through course webpages.

*Other On Line Practice Problems and Sample Examinations.* Many faculty post their own practice materials—past exams and rubrics, sample answers, quiz problems, etc. If your professor is one such person, you should use these materials. Additionally, there are thousands of faculty created practice materials posted by students and faculty at law schools across the country. If you choose to use these exercises, pay close attention to whether they cover the same skills, materials and issues covered by your professor— since there is wide variety among law school faculty as to course goals and content.

## Using Supplemental Sources to Help Structure Your Exam Approach

There are a wide variety of commercially produced outlines, flow charts and hierarchy charts. Recent versions are even available electronically. The outlines and hierarchy charts can be a helpful tool for suggesting one possible organizational structure for the course material and can be tools for clarifying certain areas of confusion. However, they are not always accurate, very likely do not contain the exact information you have studied, and may not be organized effectively for writing an exam for your professor. Therefore, you should use them with caution. These commercially-created versions of law school outlines can be very attractive to law students pressed for time, but if you use them as a substitute for creating your own exam approach, you cheat yourself out of a crucial learning experience—the critical task of understanding how the material should be raised and employed during an exam. You also risk adopting a product that likely does not reflect your instructor's particular course design choices.

## Supplemental Sources to Avoid

Some supplemental sources may lure you in with the promise of doing your work for you. Expert law students do not rely on use these sources to substitute for doing their own work. They recognize that such sources are frequently inaccurate and that such sources do not help them understand how to apply what they have learned, or understand how to approach material during an examination. They also understand that struggling to learn and understand material produces the best learning. Figuring out a confounding problem on one's own not only builds self-efficacy but also creates a much stronger memory trace then resolving a question through the use of a secondary source. Accordingly, a modest amount of time trying to work through a problem is a worthwhile investment.

*Canned Briefs.* Canned briefs are simply briefs of the court opinions contained in a casebook. Of all the tools designed to facilitate student learning, canned briefs are the ones most despised by law professors and for good reason. Canned briefs cheat law students of their ability to learn how to read court opinions, with little gain to the student, particularly because they often are inaccurate.

*Student-Produced "Outlines."* Nearly every law student, at some point in his or her career, is handed a student-produced outline that someone claims came from a student who received an "A" in the class. On the one hand, these resources have the benefit of, perhaps, having been created specifically for the class the student is taking. On the other hand, the recipient has no way to evaluate the truth of any of the claims about the outline, including claims about its completeness and accuracy. In fact, instructors and law schools change their course coverage from semester to semester in large and small ways so that, even if the outline had been sufficient for the session for which it was created, it may no longer reflect course content. Moreover, the recipient does not know whether the "A" student was simply lucky, actually good, or maybe both. Finally, using someone else's outline cheats the student of the learning that can come only from creating one's own organization of the course material. Consequently, expert legal learners do not rely on such outlines.

## Using Supplemental Resources Strategically

The keys to effectively using supplemental resources lie entirely within your control. First, you need to develop the ability to accurately and honestly monitor your comprehension and skill development (and not simply wait for the results of examinations). By actively seeking opportunities for practice and feedback and constantly self-assessing their own learning, expert learners almost always are aware not only when they are learning and when they are not, but also what they are learning and what they are not learning and the causes of both their successes and failures. This optimal mix of feedback seeking, self-monitoring and assessment of learning allows students to determine both the need for a supplemental resource and the likely cause of each learning problem.

Second, select a resource tailored to your particular learning issues. Know whether you need to use a source as explanatory material—to provide background information, or orient you to the main concepts, or elaborate on a particular concept, or whether you need to use a source to accurately assess your understanding of the material, and how it applies.

Finally, use the resource appropriately. Use explanatory material before you read cases, to help speed up and make your reading more productive. Write out answers to problems and hold yourself accountable. Merely reading problems and answers won't help you identify weaknesses or gaps in your understanding.

# Assessing Your Own Performance Like an Expert

Much of the practice and preparation you do for law school (and for the bar examination) is not graded or evaluated, so it is essential to learn how to assess your own performance. The goal of self assessment is to identify strengths and weaknesses, to correct problems and weaknesses and improve skills. One of the means of doing this is to compare your own answers to sample answers or rubrics.

Below is a sample process you can use to assess your performance using a sample answer or rubric. You will likely want to read this section after you've completed your first practice exam. To begin, put your answer side by side with the sample answer or rubric. Go through each of the following steps. For the best results, do each step on its own—which means going through your answer several times. Each step has a particular focus, and doing the steps one at a time ensures that you "catch" the problem areas. Students who attempt to look for all of the common problems in one or two read throughs miss important points. This is especially true when a student is new to the process.

## Step 1: Issue Matching

Look at the issues in the sample answer or rubric and compare them with the issues in your own answer.

- Do you have each issue raised by the sample answer or rubric?
- Do you have each of the sub-issues?
- Did you cover the issues/sub-issues in the same order as the rubric? If not, why? Should you write issues in a different order the next time?
- If you are missing any issues:
  - Did you miss the issue because you thought it was a non-issue and therefore did not address it?
  - Do you now understand why the issue should have been addressed?
  - Is the issue in your exam approach?
  - Is the issue in your issues checklist? If not, consider adding it. If it is, try to determine why you missed it.
- Did you use headings for the issues or sub-issues (and make them easy to spot)?
- Did you address each of the issues or sub-issues listed in the rubric in a separate paragraph? Would that have made it easier for the grader?

## Step 2: Evaluate Your Headings

Headings help flag issues. The concern is not that you have more headings than the sample answer, but that you have fewer. Compare your headings with the sample answer: If you have fewer, look to see whether you've addressed that issue. If you have addressed the issue, look to see if you may have buried an argument that the sample answer highlighted with a heading. Highlighting the key issues with headings shows the grader that you know what is important in your answer, and ensures that the grader will see where you have analyzed the issue.

## Step 3: Evaluate Your Organization

Sometimes there is more than one way to organize a topic or sub-topic. There are other times where order is important and where issues and sub-issues naturally go together. For example, you would probably need to establish the existence of a contract before showing that a party breached that contract. Still other times, a professor will require or prefer a particular order. If your order is different from the sample answer or rubric, think about the following:

- Is this one of those times where order was important? Why or why not?

- Why did you do it differently?

- Did it make it more difficult to award you points (because it didn't follow the rubric order)?

- Did it make it more difficult for the grader to see that you covered the issues/ sub-issues?

- Would the order in the sample or rubric make your essay answer easier for the grader to follow?

- Do you need to make changes to the order? If so, how will you do it the next time you encounter this set of issues?

## Step 4: Review Rule Statements

Compare the rules you've written for each issue with the rules in the sample answer or points listed in the rubric. Thinking only about the rule statement and not the facts, consider:

- Is the law/rule correctly stated?

- Is the rule complete?

  ○ Are there elements, key phrases or other important information missing from the rule? (Remember: If a rule is missing key pieces, the analysis for those pieces will also be missing.)

  ○ Does the rubric list more components than you have in your rule?

- Is the length appropriate for the essay?
  - Did you list more of the rule than was necessary? (If a one sentence rule would do and you've used four, you've probably wasted valuable time writing information which was not required.)
  - Does your rule contain information not listed in the rubric?
  - Did you spend time writing information that was not needed?
- Is the rule where it should be?
  - Did you list the rule under the same issue as the sample answer or rubric?
  - Did you list the rule for a sub-issue in your general rule when it should have been listed with the sub-issue?

## Step 5: Fact Matching

Compare your answer with the sample, one issue at a time. Sometimes a rubric will list the key facts for each issue, but sometimes it will not. Where the rubric lists key facts, or when you have a sample answer, compare your answer with the rubric or sample answer, one issue at a time. Where you've used a fact in your answer and that fact appears on the rubric or in the sample answer, under the same issue, highlight that fact in the rubric or sample answer. If a fact in your answer is not in the rubric or sample answer, highlight the fact on your own answer. Continue this process for every issue until you have gone through each of the facts in the rubric and each of the facts you used in your answer. Consider the following:

Are there any facts listed on the rubric or in the sample answer that you did not use correctly in your answer? (These will be the facts on the rubric or in the sample answer that are not highlighted.) For each of these facts ask yourself:

- Why is the analysis better with those additional facts?
- Why did you not use those facts?
- How could you have used those facts to improve your analysis?
- Do you now understand why they were important and what they contributed?
- Reread the sample answer for each issue, and think about the additional facts. Do you understand the analysis better with those additional facts?

If you used facts that the rubric did not list or that were not used in the sample answer (these will be the facts that are highlighted in your own answer), consider whether those facts were necessary.

- Did they strengthen your analysis?
- Did you use those facts <u>instead of</u> the facts listed in the rubric or sample answer (for that issue) <u>or in addition to</u> the facts listed in the rubric or sample answer?
  - If you used the facts highlighted in your answer *instead of* the facts from the rubric or sample answer, you missed the facts the grader thought were critical.

    ∘ On the other hand, if you used the facts highlighted in your own answer <u>*in addition to*</u> the facts in the rubric, it is less concerning, because rubrics do not always identify every useful fact, and so use of additional facts may have been appropriate.

Review the fact pattern:

- Did you use every fact in the fact pattern? If not, where should you have used the homeless facts? Where would they have improved your analysis?

Look at each of your sentences in each analysis section.

- Did you recite facts? Are there sentences that merely restate the fact pattern? What did you need to do to explain the significance of those facts?

- Did you summarize facts where it would have been more effective to state each fact?

- Did you ignore any of the important facts listed in the fact pattern?

- Did you misread or misstate any of the facts?

## Step 6: Looking for Both Sides

Often a weaker answer is one that sees a single perspective, when there are really two. A student may see all the reasons why Dan is guilty of murder or why the landlord owed a duty to the tenant, and write a good analysis of that one perspective. The problem may be that there are *two* perspectives. Look at the rubric or sample answer to see whether any of the issues had a discussion of two perspectives—i.e., also explained why Dan was not guilty of murder or the landlord did not owe a duty to the tenant. Keep in mind that not all issues will have two sides. If there is nothing in the facts that allows you to argue for an opposing view, don't reach for something.

- Did you miss a second perspective?

- Did you write about a second perspective that wasn't in the sample? Were you "reaching" or was it worth spending time to write about?

## Step 7: Evaluate Your Conclusions

Look to see whether you have a conclusion. Your conclusion should be at the end of your analysis and it should match your analysis. They should be logically consistent.

Consider whether it was important to draw a specific conclusion. Was there only one answer that was correct? It may be that the specific conclusion you reached was not important, so long as it was well reasoned and matched your analysis—check to see whether any specific conclusions are required, and compare your answer to see if you reached that conclusion.

## Step 8: Fixing Format

Compare your answer with the sample answer to see if yours has similar:

- Organization
  - Is your answer written in the same order as the rubric?
  - Is your paragraph formation the same as the sample answer? Did you skip lines between paragraphs, and isolate each part of IRAC in its own paragraph, etc.? Would that have made it clearer and easier for the grader to read? (There is not necessarily a specific way to format paragraphs, but the sample answer can be a good guide. If you have page long paragraphs and the sample has a series of short paragraphs on the same issue, ask yourself whether the style in the sample makes it clearer and easier for the grader to read.)
- Heading presentation
  - Did the answer or rubric use the same headings in the same order?
  - Does the rubric or sample answer have long issue statements or a one word description? Do yours match the style and content of the rubric?
- Did you use the correct structure? Was IRAC required?

Finally, look to see whether there are grammar, spelling and typographical issues — these will detract from your answer, and most likely, your grade.

A worksheet, which provides a checklist for completing these steps is located in Appendix E.

# Peer Help

Throughout law school you will be asked to think about problems from different perspectives — to mirror the practice of law, which requires lawyers to think about the opposing parties' best arguments as part of accurately assessing client's cases, and being prepared to respond to such arguments. Your own perspective will be limited by your experiences; you can broaden your perspective and your thinking by discussing and solving problems with others whose perspective differs from your own. Moreover, in law school, self-help efforts will sometimes fall short, and peers can be an effective source of help. Also, students learn more, retain information better and enjoy the learning process more when they work collaboratively, including studying in small groups of peers who follow the practices described in this section.

Successful practicing lawyers also tend to be excellent at working in groups, because so much of law practice, contrary to common images of lawyering, requires working in small groups. Lawyers form working groups to handle large litigation and transactional matters and must be able to work cooperatively, even as adversaries, in the regular course of dispute resolution. These facts help explain why law professors and law school teaching experts generally recommend that law students create and regularly use study groups. Consequently, not only do expert law students seek peer help when they need it, but they do so within the context of properly structured cooperative learning groups. The sections below detail the characteristics of successful learning groups—and some of the exercises and tools you can use to ensure your group is an effective one for all members.

## Characteristics of Successful Cooperative Learning Groups

Successful groups are made up of at least three people, but no more than six. Size does matter. While groups of two can succeed, such groups generally are too small to ensure the diversity of opinions and skills typical of successful groups. Working only in a pair, students cheat themselves of the multiple sources and types of feedback available from a larger group; moreover, the smaller the group, the more likely that it is homogenous, resulting in a group in which each member has the same strengths and the same weaknesses. At the other end of the scale, groups of seven or more tend to be unwieldy and less helpful to individual students. Most of us have had the experience of attending a social function in a group of seven or more. By and large, the group subdivides into two or more separate conversations because of the difficulty of accommodating such a large group. In fact, large study groups often end up focusing on the interests of one or more small sub-groups at the expense of two critical group components—accountability and positive interdependence—which are described below.

Successful groups are not homogenous but, rather, diverse. Diversity of group membership is, first and foremost, a matter of diversity of experiences, skills, knowledge, and interests. Where possible, diversity is also a matter of gender, race and culture. Diversity within a group has been correlated with increased achievement and productivity, creative problem solving, growth in cognitive reasoning, and increased perspective-taking ability. Students in such groups gain sophistication in interacting and working with peers from a variety of cultural and ethnic backgrounds, which prepares students for interacting with their colleagues and clients, who often are different from the students in many ways.

In addition to thoughtful composition, including group size and member diversity, there are five other characteristics of excellent cooperative learning groups:

- Positive Interdependence
- Promotive Interaction
- Individual Accountability
- Reflection on Group Processes
- Interpersonal and Group Skills

Each of these characteristics is described below:

### 1. Positive Interdependence

Positive interdependence means that every member of the group invests in the learning success of every other member of the group. The idea of positive interdependence is often expressed by phrases such as "It's all for one and one for all," "We sink or swim together," and "We're all in this thing together." Positive interdependence makes learning groups more productive because it eliminates social isolation and creates a safe harbor from the normal competitiveness of education (particularly legal education) so that each student can ask for help.

Positive interdependence requires effort. It requires a commitment from each member of the group. It also is inextricably linked with the other characteristics of excellent learning groups, because absent the other characteristics, such as individual accountability for doing the group's work and honest group reflection on the progress of the group, students are often unwilling to invest in each other's success.

#### Creating Positive Interdependence

At the start of each session, set group learning goals, i.e., what each member of the group should work to get out of the session. It is also often helpful to assign a specific role to each group member for each session so that each group member contributes and learns. These roles should change for every session. Commonly assigned roles include: a recorder (a person who takes notes), a leader (a person who runs the group session), a checker (a person who makes sure everyone is contributing to the discussion), a skeptic (a person whose role involves questioning assumptions), and contributors (people who are responsible for making the most frequent, but not the only, contributions to the discussion). In addition, the group should establish ways to reward itself if the group accomplishes its goals. A reward can be going out to a movie or dinner or even going for a walk.

### 2. Promotive Interaction

Promotive interaction involves group members supporting, encouraging, challenging, teaching and otherwise helping each other learn. In other words, members of effective cooperative learning groups support each other's success. It requires each member to be trustworthy and trusting. It requires the group to maintain an atmosphere of stimulation but low pressure.

### 3. Individual Accountability

Successful groups avoid the two most common student concerns about participating in cooperative learning experiences, Dominators and Freeloaders (also known as social loafers).[1] Freeloaders let others do the group work and do little, if any, work themselves—often viewing group time as either a chance to use the efforts of others

---

1. You may want to have your group view the student created videos illustrating the behavior of the dominator and freeloader at: https://www.youtube.com/watch?v=oEK1DKBr3vU and https://www.youtube.com/watch?v=b6gOIkyax-8.

for their own gain, or as an opportunity for socializing (rather than learning). They may cause resentment and anger to build up in the group to the point where the group is unable to function. Dominators take control of the group; they may participate not as a means of facilitating group learning but, rather, as a way to demonstrate their intellect, or they may not be willing to trust other group members—resulting in taking over group tasks. While some Freeloaders like having Dominators in their group, because Dominators do all the work, most group members resent the Dominator's insistence on always being the focal point of the discussion. The solution for both problems is individual accountability.

Individual accountability requires each member of the group not only to hold himself or herself responsible for doing group work, but also to hold every other member of the group responsible for doing group work. It also means that each group member must vigilantly guard against both Dominator and Freeloader problems within the group. One way to avoid both problems is the development of clear group rules from the outset—including rules with respect to both issues—as well as clearly delineated consequences, large or small, for violating such rules. Another helpful tool is the one noted above—assignment of one student to serve as the "group checker," the group member whose job it is to assess whether everyone is fairly contributing to the group. Ultimately, however, each group member's interest in his or her own learning should encourage him or her to address Dominator and Freeloader behavior whenever it arises.

## 4. Reflection on the Group Process

During group meetings, successful groups reflect upon the extent to which the group is functioning effectively and efficiently, and the causes of that success or failure. The focus of such discussions is more on the process than on the ultimate outcome; a successful group regularly identifies and discusses which group and individual activities and behaviors are contributing to achieving the group's goals and which are not. The group discusses how to improve the process, and plans future group and individual activities and responsibilities. In other words, successful groups regularly engage in the self-monitoring step of the performance phase and the entire reflection phase of the SRL cycle. The only difference is that the monitoring and reflection are occurring on a group, rather than on an individual, level.

## 5. Interpersonal and Group Social Skills

Groups whose members have strong interpersonal and social skills actually perform better academically. The specific social skills most conducive to group success are: (1) honesty and clarity in communication, (2) acceptance and support of fellow group members, (3) trust, and (4) constructive conflict resolution.

All of these characteristics may be developed by having group members agree to and sign a group contract, in which each member promises to promote the necessary positive interdependence, promotive interactions, personal accountability, reflection on the process and communication skills. Appendix F includes a form you can use to create a group contract.

> **PAUSE. THINK. ACT.** What experiences have you had with group study in the past? Were those experiences positive? Why or why not? What have you learned from those experiences that can make you an effective member of a law school study group? How might you benefit from a law school study group?

## Some Commonly Used Cooperative Learning Exercises

Cooperative learning experts have developed some very effective techniques for fostering the six characteristics of successful groups. Below is a list of some of these techniques.

*Think-Pair-Share.* In this exercise, each student in the group thinks through, often in writing, the analysis/resolution of a hypothetical question. The students then pair off and exchange and try to understand and, to the extent possible, reconcile their analyses. Finally, the group as a whole discusses, tries to understand and, to the extent possible, reconciles the pairs' analyses.

*Reports.* Each member creates and delivers a presentation (using a poster or handouts) on a small part of a portion of the course material. The other students must ask questions and provide the presenter with feedback on the presentation.

*Drill Review Pairs.* In this exercise, students pair in sub-groups of two to analyze two short hypotheticals. For one of the two hypos, one student acts as the analyst (this person analyzes the problem) and the other as the checker (this person observes the analysis and evaluates it for thoroughness and accuracy); for the other hypo, the roles reverse. The analysts not only communicate their final analysis, but also their thinking process as they work their way through the problem. The checkers ask the analysts questions to make sure they understand the analysts' thinking processes. When all pairs have completed their answers to the hypos, the group gathers as a whole to compare and discuss thinking processes and analyses.

*Roundtable.* Students start with a hypothetical and a single blank pad of paper. Each student writes a portion of the analysis (one or two paragraphs) and then passes the pad onto the next student until the group has produced an answer. The group then reviews and evaluates the answer as a whole. This approach also can be done in smaller bites where each student writes one sentence.

*Pass the Problem.* Students break into pairs and each pair is given a hypothetical clipped to the outside of a folder. Each pair writes an analysis of the problem and then puts their analysis inside the folder and passes the folder to the next pair. The next pair, without looking at the prior pair's analysis, writes their own analysis and puts it in the folder. After each pair has analyzed each problem, the group compares the pairs' analyses and tries to reach a consensus about what would be a proper analysis.

For some students, both the exercises above and the general principles of cooperative learning groups can seem hokey; research, however, suggests that these techniques are extraordinarily effective in producing student learning. For many of these activities, study groups can make use of the supplemental sources which contain practice problems and answers—and individuals who have answered the problems on their own can quickly see the benefit of another persons' perspective, who may spot additional issues, or make better or different use of particular facts, or solve the same problems in a different way.

# Professorial Help

On the one hand, many professors are glad to meet with students, and many professors believe that those students who seek help from their professors outperform those who do not. On the other hand, law professors often teach two sections of students per semester, and the typical size of first-year law school classes is at least 50 students and often twice that number. Even if only half of an instructor's students sought 15 minutes of help per week, the instructor would have to hold at least twelve and one-half hours of office hours per week and as many as 25 hours of office hours per week to meet his or her students' needs. In fact, most law professors hold no more than six office hours per week. These facts suggest the very real scarcity of professorial help and the importance of students' acting professionally about their office hour meetings.

## Seeking Feedback

Dozens of professors have authored law review articles detailing a crucial failure within legal education: students are given almost no opportunities to practice the skills on which they will be tested and therefore receive little, if any, critical feedback on their development of legal analysis skills. Novice law students simply accept this status quo without question. Their fear of or discomfort with negative feedback and their lack of knowledge of the learning process cause them to practice their legal analysis skills only when forced to do so and to avoid, at all costs, feedback.

Expert law students know better. Critical feedback is crucial to the development of any skill. To understand this point, try to imagine an athlete who never obtained coaching, a mathematician who never received teaching, or a musician who never had a music lesson. Feedback helps students know what they are doing well and what they are doing poorly. It guides students' studying and future practice efforts. Expert students therefore ask for practice and welcome feedback from anyone who might be willing to give it, including their professors, before, during and after class.

Expert law students also do not fear or even feel uncomfortable when they receive harsh feedback because they expect it as a part of the learning process. Interestingly, law professors do not characterize such students as "pesky" or "demanding" but, rather, as "teachable" or "good learners."

Of course, because expert law students practice more often and receive more feedback, they are able to correct errors, improve their skills and minimize exam anxiety. These factors, of course, have the ultimate result of causing the expert learners to perform better on exams than their novice peers. They also enjoy the learning process more and feel better about themselves (because they do not experience any ego deflation when they receive critical feedback).

## Acting Professionally

Acting professionally means (1) the student has tried to resolve those matters he or she can resolve without professorial intervention (using self-help and peer help); (2) the student asks her questions with professional respect; (3) the student has prepared for the meeting by having specific questions (it is not wise to use office hours for general questions, such as asking the professor to re-explain class discussion); and (4) the student has remembered to bring the materials she needs for the meeting (a notebook for taking notes and the court opinion, paper, or examination question or answer the student wishes to discuss).

It is also worth noting that many professors are willing (and may even prefer) to respond to questions posted by e-mail or on a course web page. This tactic allows the instructor to address the student's concerns at the instructor's leisure and gives the student the benefit of a written product from which to study. The approach also helps the professor reach students who are too shy to ask for help on their own.

Moreover, many professors have placed supplemental materials, including things like frequently asked questions (FAQs) on their course web pages. If the student's professor has a FAQ section on his or her course web page, the student should check it out before contacting her professor for help. Students who fail to heed this advice risk annoying their professor and slowing their own learning process.

Finally, just as it is a good practice to review class notes shortly after the class session has ended, it is also a good idea to review notes of a professorial meeting shortly after the meeting has ended. Doing so allows the student to consolidate his or her understanding and makes later integration into the student's course outline easier.

> **PAUSE. THINK. ACT.** The strategies for obtaining help addressed in this chapter are offered in a conscious order—the order students should follow in seeking help. Why is this order probably the optimal one?

# Chapter 9

# Your Preparation Pays Off: What to Do *During* an Exam

In many law school classes, the final examination is the sole determinant of each student's grade in the course. In nearly all other law school classes, the midterm and final examination together determine each student's grade. In other words, excelling on law school examinations is essential to law school success. This chapter therefore identifies and explores the strategies expert law students use when taking law school exams.

## Pre-Exam Preparation

Preparing for law school examinations is a marathon, not a sprint. Unlike students in some (or, perhaps, even many) college-level courses, law students cannot excel on law school exams simply by reserving hours or even days of "cramming" time at the end of the semester. Nor does real law school studying have much in common with its media depictions, such as those in movies like *The Paper Chase* or *Legally Blonde*. There is no way to make law school easy or to reduce in any significant way the amount of work required; it is not true that smart law students either do not need to work very hard or that they avoid having to work hard in law school by dividing up the work among members of a study group. Even very talented law students must work incredibly hard, and they and their fellow study group members do not divide up the work. Expert law students start studying for their examinations right from the beginning of the semester and continue throughout, using each other as tools for acquiring the knowledge and for practicing the skills on which they will be tested. In short, the process of exam preparation in law school requires thought and self-reflection, planning, self-assessment, and lots of practice and feedback.

If you were to follow the recommendations of this text, you will already have engaged in many of the activities in which expert students engage to prepare for their law school examinations. This chapter assumes you have come to the exam having adopted these recommendations, including the following:

### 1. Mindset

Expert law students avoid, at all costs, negative feelings about themselves, negative people and negative activities. Rather than focusing on their fear of failing, they focus on showing how well they have learned. Rather than imagining the consequences of failure, they envision the pleasure of success. Rather than spending time with people who do not believe they can succeed, they choose to be with people who believe they will succeed. Rather than wearing out their bodies with unhealthy food or drink, such as sugar and alcohol, and with sleep deprivation, they focus on eating brain-strengthening food and drink, and try exercising regularly.

The reason to avoid negative feelings about oneself stems from the well-established fact that self-efficacy, a person's belief that they can and will succeed, is critical to success in educational settings. Self-efficacy is so powerful it is better correlated with success in educational settings than scores on standardized tests, such as the LSAT. Students with low self-efficacy, because they doubt whether they can ever learn, study less hard than they need to study or do not persist with their studying when they encounter the inevitable difficulties all law students encounter. They also are less likely to seek the help they need because they perceive, incorrectly, that their peers are superior students and do not need or seek such help. Similarly, they are less likely to self-assess their learning or to write practice examinations and obtain feedback on their practice efforts because they excessively fear critical feedback. Finally, students with low self-efficacy are less likely to adopt the recommendations detailed in this text because they believe their results are outside their own control and, therefore, efforts towards preparing themselves are a waste of time. The saddest part of all of these consequences is that students with low self-efficacy, because they do not engage in the behaviors most likely to prepare themselves for their examinations, usually get the grades they expect, poor ones; in fact, even when such students get good grades, they almost always attribute their success to luck or error and, as a result, miss out on the pleasure that comes from crediting themselves for their success.

It is equally negative, however, for law students to possess unrealistically high perceptions of self-efficacy. Nearly all law students enter law school having enjoyed considerable success at the high school and undergraduate levels. Hundreds, if not thousands, of law students, however, draw a poor and unreasonable inference from these past results. They assume their high school and college successes mean that their methods of studying were effective and efficient. In many instances, those methods were simply good enough, effective enough and efficient enough for them to get good grades but by no means are effective or efficient in an absolute sense. Such students therefore assume their current learning strategies do not need refinement. Unfortunately, too many law students do not discover this error until it's too late, until after they receive grades that do not reflect their capacity for success in law school. Some simply get B's when they could have had A's; others, however, risk academic dismissal.

The key, from an exam preparation perspective, is for you to possess the belief that law school will require you to work very hard, and it will probably be difficult, but if you do the work, you can learn and you can succeed. In other words, you are more likely to study appropriately and productively for your examinations if you recognize you can learn what you need to learn—*if you do the work.*

For different but related reasons, eating healthy food, consuming only low levels of alcohol, getting plenty of sleep and rest and even getting exercise all help students ready themselves for law school examinations. Law school examinations are long and therefore require stamina; most are at least three hours and some exceed four. Law school exams also require students to operate at peak mental efficiency. Eating healthy food, drinking only small amounts of (or no) alcohol, exercising and sleeping well all stimulate the brain and all allow students to perform at their best. In fact, studies in other educational disciplines show that students who are the most mentally fit in these ways do better on examinations. Unhealthy eating, alcohol abuse, or drug use, poor sleep and lack of exercise, in contrast, have been associated with higher levels of depression, muddled thinking and slower mental processing speed.

## 2. Proper Planning

Studying for examinations is no different than any other learning task. It begins with planning. The difference is that the time frame within which the students must do the planning is much lengthier. Expert law students plan their examination preparation by working backwards from the date of their examination. This planning is crucial for a number of reasons. First, students who plan their studying can take advantage of the benefits of spaced learning. Second, students who plan their studying make sure they include time for healthy eating, plenty of sleep and exercise. Third, students who plan and space out, through the semester, their learning, study and exam preparation, seek help as they discover they need it. At the end of the semester, while their peers compete for the shrinking amounts of professorial time available, the expert law students, having already had all or nearly all of their questions answered over the course of the semester, can devote themselves to more productive exam preparation activities. It might even be true that students who have sought help throughout the semester actually receive more help at the end of the semester as well because their professors, being human, respect and appreciate their semester-long diligence. Finally, students who plan their studies cope better with unplanned events, personal crises, extra assignments and other such matters.

## 3. Before, During and After Class Preparation

The preceding chapters describe the tasks which lay the groundwork for success on examinations. For example, by carefully reading and briefing the cases, you will ensure that you understand the rules and have given yourself the base level information you need to apply and distinguish those cases. Applying and distinguishing is impossible unless you understand both the results the courts reached in all the cases and the courts' reasons for reaching those results. Even in courses in which you are not expected to apply and distinguish cases (but are expected to apply rules to facts), the cases play an important role in learning and skill development. The cases provide examples of how legal experts have applied the rules and therefore either serve as models, or in those cases where they are examples of ineffective application of the rules, as opportunities to develop your ability to apply the rules by figuring out, through the class discussion and outside of class study, what an effective application might have looked like. Thus, both the excellent cases and the poor ones teach lessons about how to apply the rules.

By adopting the recommendations of this text, you also will have deconstructed the rules you have learned. Deconstructing the rules into their constituent parts prepares you to be able to isolate each aspect (i.e., element, factor) of every rule so that you are able to apply each separately. It also helps you to spot each of the issues and sub-issues, and to organize your writing.

You will also have created an exam approach, and used it to take practice exams which will have prepared you to be able to quickly recall the rules and holdings when you need them (by creating schemata for storing the learning) and to be able to spot issues (because you know and understand the relationships among the concepts you have learned). This high degree of organization allows you to more readily identify, analyze and solve problems described in law school examinations. Likewise, by memorizing your approach — and the rules and/or case holdings (depending on the expectations of your professor) in that approach, you will possess the baseline knowledge that is a necessary component of success on law school examinations.

Finally, by doing practice problems, holding yourself accountable for your learning, and revising your approach to reflect that learning, you are developing a deeper understanding of how that knowledge applies. Experts in every field are characterized not only by their skill and the organization of their knowledge but also by the depth and breadth of their knowledge; experts do know more, and they know how to do more. Expert law students, therefore, possess more knowledge and deeper understanding of that knowledge than their novice peers.

## 4. Overlearning

Many of the tasks described in the previous chapters are designed to help you overlearn the material. Law school examinations require students to apply their knowledge, not simply recite it. Moreover, law school examinations are complex and dense and therefore test not only the students' lawyering skills but also their speed. A typical one hour law school essay exam question is at least three-quarters of one page single spaced and as long as two or three pages. In the assigned one hour, students must be able to read the hypothetical facts, identify what question(s) they are being asked, discern which details are important and which are not, identify which topics, from among all the topics they have studied, are being tested by the exam, plan and organize an analysis of the exam, recall and accurately state all the relevant rules and holdings they have studied over the course of the semester and write a coherent essay in which they demonstrate the ability to apply what they have learned to this unfamiliar set of facts.

In other words, during law school examinations, students simply do not have time or mental resources to spend struggling to recall the knowledge, to think about how the concepts they have studied are related to one another, or to remember how to perform the skills they should have practiced. They need to free up as many mental resources as possible for thinking, brainstorming, analogizing, reasoning and writing. Consequently, expert law students try to master their knowledge of the rules and holdings, understand the relationships between the concepts, and become so competent at performing legal analysis that the knowledge and skills come to them automatically, without great mental effort. Just as anyone who has mastered reading does not need to "sound out" words and therefore possesses the mental resources necessary to think about the substance of what they are reading, so do successful law students strive for a level of knowledge and skill development that frees up their brain to focus on the substance of their exam task. Expert law students strive for the law school equivalent of what expert athletes call "The Zone," a mental state in which athletes are so immersed in their sport that they play without thinking consciously about what they "should" be doing.

Students who have overlearned their course material are less likely to forget what they have learned, even under the stress of the examination. They also are more confident (because they are confident that they know the material well) and, therefore, they are less likely to fear failure or to feel stress. They also are more likely to have an initial success on the examination, such as by spotting an issue or by recalling a case analogous to the hypothetical on the examination. This initial success builds their self-efficacy, causing the students to be more likely to persist, even in the face of difficulty on the examination, because they believe their persistence will pay off. And, of course, such persistence does pay off when they get their grades, which further builds their self-efficacy and willingness to persist and further reduces their examination stress (unless they have chosen not to prepare properly for the examination).

In contrast, students who fail to overlearn are more likely to feel anxious going into the examination because they recognize their vulnerability. They also are less likely to feel self-confident, to have an initial success or to persist in the face of difficulty on the examination. For these reasons, expert law students strive to overlearn their course material as part of their regular examination preparation.

This overlearning requires students to devote more effort to practice and study than they would normally need to devote. In other educational settings, expert students memorize information until they can demonstrate to themselves the ability to recall everything they need to know for their exams (such as by being able to accurately paraphrase all their flashcards). Expert law students, however, need to go further. They need to practice what they know until they can recall and rapidly recite everything from their exam approach and know how to deploy the processes in that approach. Students' efforts towards this goal are made much easier if they have already used the strategies addressed in Chapter 7.

## 5. Instructor Study

In most respects, most law professors expect their students to demonstrate the same set of skills on their examinations and define excellence in very similar ways. Consequently, it is possible to write a book like this one and describe the expectations and testing methodologies of law professors. At the same time, expert students in all learning contexts know that instructors vary in their expectations — their subject matters vary, their political views vary, their interests and goals vary, and their perceptions of students vary. In other words, expert law students both recognize the commonalities among their professors and make sure they know what each professor expects from students.

In the law school context, this task is challenging. The dominant law school teaching method seldom involves explicit communication of expectations. This striking uniformity of teaching methodology might lead one to assume professors also test in the same way. There is greater variance in testing, however, than you would expect. As detailed below, while there clearly is a most prevalent approach to designing law school examinations, law school exams can and do take one of several different forms, all of which can and do overlap. In fact, even professors who administer similar examinations in terms of style may expect different things from their students.

In the broadest terms, law school exams almost always involve hypothetical factual stories that the students must "analyze." Most professors agree this involves: identifying issues, applying rules to facts, applying and distinguishing cases and performing policy analysis. The variation, therefore, comes in part from the mix of these expectations, in how much weight each instructor assigns to each task, both in terms of constructing the exam (e.g., how many issues, how much depth of analysis) and in terms of grading the exam (i.e., how much demonstration of each of the skills bears on the students' grades on the examination). Particular exams can test in all of the areas, some of the areas, or in only one area. Moreover, some law professors expect their students to be able to use their knowledge and skills in the context of specific lawyering tasks such as creating client letters, constructing documents that might be submitted in court or drafting other legal documents.

This variation makes teacher study an important skill. Sometimes, the task is an easy one; some instructors are explicit. They tell their students whether the students are expected to apply and distinguish cases, whether they should be integrating public policy in their analyses, and whether their exams will require the drafting of legal documents. Most law professors, however, are much less forthcoming. They may, however, give multiple hints about their examinations, both in terms of the topics they are likely to test and in terms of the relative weight assigned to each topic. These hints take the form of course and topic-by-topic objectives, classroom and office hour discussions and past and practice examinations.

For these reasons, expert students use their class notes not only to record what they are learning about the subject areas and skills addressed in class but also to record their instructors' examination hints and the students' reflections and questions about their instructors' examination expectations. Thus, expert students who are watching a peer be questioned by their instructor focus on discerning what reasoning techniques appear to produce instructor approval. While these expert law students are listening in class or reading an answer to a past exam question, they ask themselves questions such as:

1. What types of student classroom responses elicit positive comments from the instructor? What types of responses elicit criticism?
2. Which court opinions does the professor believe to be well reasoned? Which does the instructor believe to be poorly reasoned?
3. If the instructor communicates dissatisfaction with a student response, how should the student have answered the question?
4. What would a written answer to this question look like? What would it include? Exclude?

In other words, expert students frequently use the 1/3 of their classroom note-taking designated for "reflection" and "questions" to record what they are learning about their professor's exam-related expectations.

Expert law students also get their hands on every exam question ever authored by each of their professors. Notwithstanding the fact that many law professors devise new questions every semester, past exams provide crucial insights. At a minimum, such review allows students to review the instructions their instructors commonly include with their exams. Moreover, in many instances, reviewing past exams provides students with insights into their instructors' formatting preferences and helps students get used to their instructors' exam writing style. The review also allows students to identify the skills and knowledge their instructors have emphasized in the past.

## Taking Essay Exams

Remember that law school essay examinations are complex and dense—testing your skills, speed, understanding, writing ability and response to stress. Expert law students understand law school essay exams require that they: (1) plan and organize an analysis of the exam before they begin writing; (2) allocate and manage their exam time; (3) write a coherent essay, in the proper format, demonstrating their ability to apply what they have learned during the course to a new situation; and (4) manage their exam stress.

### 1. Planning and Organizing Your Analysis

One of the critical mistakes novice law students make is to begin writing an answer before organizing the information from the exam question and planning what they will write. Just as you would organize or outline what you plan to say if you were giving a speech—so that you wouldn't ramble, would use your speaking time wisely, and would remember everything you wanted to say—organizing your exam before you begin writing ensures your writing is logical and easy to follow, you are able to cover all of the issues in the allotted time, you remember to discuss each of the applicable issues and sub-issues you spot, and you use every fact or other detail which supports your arguments.

During the stress of a law school exam—which is usually high stakes—it is easy to panic, and begin typing or writing everything you know. It is common for novice law students to react to a law school exam which raises many issues by frantically typing without first taking the time to plan what they will say. It is also common for novice law students to hear other students typing, or see them writing, begin to worry about falling behind, and begin typing or writing themselves, rather than completing the organization process.

Expert law students know that the time they spend organizing the material and planning what to write is time well spent. They know it will make the writing process more efficient (and effective). They also know that a well organized exam is usually a higher scoring exam. Unlike undergraduate or even other graduate exam writing, where faculty may forgive organizational problems, grammar and other errors, and award credit if the correct answer is "in there somewhere," in law school, and on the bar exam cohesiveness and clarity of thought, as well as presentation, matter. For this reason, expert law students take time to organize and plan their analysis before they start writing.

The next section provides you with tips for organizing your exam and planning your analysis before you start to write.

### a. Using the Call of the Question(s)

Most law school exams end with a question or series of questions you are expected to analyze. You will be graded, in part, by how well you respond to that call or calls. Although you may have studied a massive amount of information, it is very unlikely you will be tested on everything you have studied. One of the jobs of a lawyer is to sort through a client's "story" to determine what legal issues are raised, how the law will apply, and the likely outcome for the client. For this reason, a law school exam is a story (a set of hypothetical facts) and the law student's job is to sort through the facts of that story, identify the legal issues raised by those facts, apply the law to those facts and predict the likely outcome. Part of what you are tested on is whether you understand which portions of the material you have learned are applicable to your examination.

Perhaps more important is that you receive NO CREDIT for discussing things which are not responsive to the call of the question. In fact, some law school essay exam questions raise more issues than can possibly be addressed within the time allotted; for such questions, the call of the question tells the student what she needs to do to be able to finish the exam in the time allotted. For these reasons, expert law students read the call of the question first.

Frequently the questions at the end of an essay exam help you narrow the topics you should consider. For example, the following calls provide direction about the legal issue or group of issues you should discuss:

1. Is Dannica liable for false imprisonment? Discuss.
2. Does the court have personal jurisdiction over Steph?
3. Was Owen's letter of January 3rd a valid acceptance of Reza's offer?
4. How likely is it that the court will award specific performance of the land sale contract?
5. Does County's ordinance violate the First Amendment?

Calls can also narrow your focus in other ways. For example, these calls narrow your task by directing you to consider social policy arguments:

1. Should courts impose a duty on residential landlords to protect their tenant's from third party criminal acts?
2. Discuss the implications of legalizing marijuana for medical use.
3. Should the U.S. sanction torture by government agents?

When the call of the question provides you with such guidance, reading the call first helps you orient your thinking to the details your instructor intends for you to address. You are then in a better position to identify relevant information and more easily organize the information you are reading.

There are times when reading the call is not helpful for narrowing the issues or the task. Sometimes the only word at the end of the examination question is: Discuss. In such situations everything you have studied is "fair game," and your task is a bit more challenging. However, the following steps still apply, and will help you in your quest to organize and plan your analysis before you write.

### b. Understanding the "Big Picture"

It is easy to jump to conclusions when you don't know the whole story—and on law school exams, those types of early conclusions are often incorrect. It is important to hear the whole story before making up your mind, and it is important to read the entire exam question before you decide what is important, what is in issue, and what you will discuss.

During your first read through an exam, try not to take notes, or annotate the exam. Instead, try to absorb the "big picture," without drawing any conclusions about what is in issue and what the outcome will be. Read to gain a feel for what the exam is generally about—knowing you will read the exam again (maybe even three or four times) to find all of the important details.

### c. Mapping Out Your Writing Plan

The next step is to create a plan for what you will write. This step involves four tasks: (1) spotting the issues; (2) recalling and understanding the applicable legal standard(s) for each spotted issue; (3) identifying relevant facts or other information which helps you analyze each spotted issue; and (4) organizing all of this information into a coherent plan.

This process is recursive, meaning you will not engage in these four tasks in a linear fashion—rather the order may change, and at times you may do one or more simultaneously. For example you may spot an issue because you identify a relevant fact, which causes you to write down the issue, elements of the rule and key facts on your writing plan, and writing down the elements of a rule might trigger your knowledge of an additional rule for one of those elements, which leads to understanding why another fact is in the fact pattern, resulting in spotting additional sub-issues. It is precisely because this is a recursive process that organizing the information before you write is so important. Expert law students know they must work *carefully and systematically until they have a coherent writing plan.*

### (1) Issues, Rules and Facts — A Necessary Trio

Because law school exams test only a subset of the rules you will learn in each class, and because that subset changes every semester (because most law professors write new exams every time and most law professors try to vary what they test), law students must be able to "spot" (identify) the particular set of rules raised by their exam questions. This task requires students to know all the legal concepts they have studied, to understand the relationships among all those concepts, and to recognize which particular concepts are being tested on the particular exam question they are reading. In shorthand, this task is referred to as "issue-spotting." Spotting the issues is a prerequisite skill, because an analysis of something that is not an issue is a waste of time; it's like playing the wrong musical note perfectly on an instrument—it *sounds* good but misses the point. Spotting issues involves a number of distinct, but related, skills, which are described in this section.

#### Knowledge of Rules and Holdings

First, spotting issues requires **excellent knowledge of legal rules and case holdings**. This knowledge is indispensable, because it serves as an issue-spotting checklist. To better understand how knowledge of the rules is linked to issue spotting, read the following hypothetical fact pattern and try to spot the issues:

> Al, Bob and Carla were contestants on a television show called "Cruel World." Producers for the show obtained the secret cooperation of the contestants' employers, spouses, medical providers and others. As part of the show, each of the contestants was led to believe a variety of horrible, but untrue facts. For example, Al was led to believe he had been fired from his job, his wife was leaving him and that he had a terminal illness.
>
> Al lived in Connecticut at the time of the taping of the show. Following the show, he was so distraught over his friends' and loved ones' conduct that he moved to Texas to live with a childhood friend who had not participated in the game show ruse. Bob and Carla are lifelong residents of New York. Bob

is currently in California, where he has been living for the past eight months, trying to sell his story to a production company to turn it into a "made for TV" movie. If that happens, Bob plans to stay in California. Last month, Carla in an effort to "get away from it all," moved to her Laguna Beach, California vacation home.

Al, Bob and Carla would like to file a lawsuit against TVCorp. for Intentional Infliction of Emotional Distress. Cruel World is produced by TVCorp. TVCorp is a Delaware corporation, with its production offices in Los Angeles, California. They hope to file the suit in federal court in New York. Will the court have subject matter jurisdiction?

Unless you have studied Civil Procedure—specifically Subject Matter Jurisdiction—it will be difficult, if not impossible, for you to spot the issues in the above hypothetical. But now assume you know something about the rules. Here is a brief description of some of the rules which are in issue in this exam:[1]

Federal courts are courts of limited jurisdiction. They may hear cases involving federal questions. They may also hear cases where there is diversity between plaintiffs and defendants, and the amount in controversy is more than $75,000.00. For diversity to exist, no plaintiff may be domiciled in the same state as any defendant. An individual is domiciled in a state if they are physically present in that state, with an intent to remain. A corporation is domiciled in the state where it is incorporated and the state where it has its principal place of business.

Knowing these rules should help you begin to identify some of what is in issue—perhaps you can see that where Al, Bob, Carla and TVCorp. are domiciled might be important questions to resolve. But, as you have learned from this text, knowing the elements of the rule is only a starting point.

To spot and organize all of the issues, you will also need to **understand how the concepts are related to one another and to the big picture.** For example, here is one way you might organize the above summary of rules into the framework for an exam approach:

I. Does the court have subject matter jurisdiction?
   a. Is there federal question jurisdiction? OR
   b. Is there diversity jurisdiction?
      i. Determine the domicile for each plaintiff and each defendant:
         1. For each individual:
            a. Where are they physically present? AND

---

1. This description is intentionally oversimplified because the purpose is to illustrate how rules are used to spot issues, and not to teach you everything you need to know about Subject Matter Jurisdiction. You will likely spend several class sessions on this topic in your Civil Procedure course.

        b.  Do they intend to remain in that place?

OR

    2.  For each corporation:

        a.  Where incorporated? AND

        b.  Where is principal place of business?

  ii.  Does any plaintiff have the same domicile as any defendant? If yes, no diversity, If no, consider:

  iii.  Is the amount in controversy more than 75K?

Notice this organization reflects your task of determining whether subject matter jurisdiction should be based upon federal question or diversity. It also reflects that the question of domicile only arises if the action is based on diversity jurisdiction. You would then know to address the issue of domicile, if subject matter jurisdiction, based on diversity, is in issue, but not if subject matter jurisdiction is based on a federal question.

Many expert law students use their exam approach to develop an actual **checklist of potential issues** as part of their examination preparation. They use their checklists as a way to make sure that they mentally consider all possible issues before consciously deciding not to address particular ones. For example, here is a checklist based on the above material:

SMJ?

    Fed Q.?

    Div?

        Domicile—Ps and Ds (indiv v. corp)

        >75K

Notice that it represents the key issues a student would need to consider, and that it is written in shorthand, to save time during an exam should a student choose to write out the checklist during the exam, to help keep track of the potential issues to consider.

---

**PAUSE. THINK. ACT.** Use the above rules, exam approach and checklist to help you spot issues in the hypothetical. Write down the list of issues you would address, in the order you think you would address them.

---

While you were likely able to spot some of the issues in the hypothetical—you also likely missed a number of issues, because you do not yet possess a deep knowledge and understanding of the nuances of the law—the potential variations and exceptions for each concept. For example, although you know that domicile is established by physical presence and an intent to remain, you don't have information about what it takes to establish either of these elements. For example: When must you be physically present? Year round? At the time suit is filed? What establishes physical presence? Must you have a residence? A driver's license? A job? Can you still meet this requirement if you are visiting another state? Working in another state? Expert students know answers to these and other questions—which is why they would be able to address these issues for the above hypothetical.

Expert law students are able to recall hundreds of details about the rules and cases they have studied. They know an exam approach like the outline of information set out above is just a starting point—which must be filled in with details from lecture notes, cases and knowledge gained from practice and self-assessment.

### Pattern Recognition

One of the reasons it is important to understand each of your assigned cases is that professors often model exams on the cases you've read—and the discussions you've had about those cases. You can spot issues by **recognizing commonalties between the facts in an exam and cases you have studied** or hypotheticals raised by your professor during class discussion.

For example, imagine in your civil procedure class you read a case where a person moved from Wisconsin to Connecticut to attend college; she did not plan to return to Wisconsin, and planned to find a job upon graduation, although she was not sure that new job would be in Connecticut. In this hypothetical case, the court held that the student did not establish a new domicile in Connecticut because it was not clear whether she would find a job in the new state, and until it is clear that a person is establishing a new domicile by having a definite plan to remain, her domicile does not change. According to the court, because she did not establish a new domicile, she remained domiciled in Wisconsin. By recognizing that this case and the fact pattern above have things in common—someone moving from one state to another, without a clear plan to stay in the new state—you can spot the issue in the fact pattern by remembering the issue from the case (i.e., what it means to have in intent to remain, for purposes of establishing domicile).

Expert law students can make these types of connections because they overlearn material; they know details about the cases they have studied (facts, reasoning, holdings, etc.) so they can recall the information automatically and analogize between their exam questions and the cases.

### Fact Sensitivity

In addition to the above techniques, you can also spot issues by **attending closely to the details in the fact pattern**. On most law school examinations, almost every phrase includes facts that students must recognize as issue signals. Law professors sometimes refer to this skill as "fact sensitivity" because the skill involves paying close attention to each fact—each piece of information contained in the hypothetical. One way to understand this point is to imagine your law professor writing your exam question. Law professors, being careful people, consciously choose and discard each word in their examination questions; thus, imagine your professor sweating over each word, consciously choosing what to include, what to delete and how to phrase each sentence. In other words, the care with which your professors construct their examination questions tells you something about the care with which you should read those questions. For these reasons, expert law students always force themselves to read their examination questions slowly, carefully and multiple times.

One of the things that may help you is to examine each adjective and adverb, because these descriptive words are often signals. For example, in the exam above, there are several such signals—Bob and Carla are *lifelong* New York residents and Carla moved to her *vacation* home. Why do you think the professor drafting this question included those descriptions? How would you explain the significance of these descriptions? The answer to these questions can help you spot additional issues and arguments. For example, the fact that someone is a lifelong resident makes it more likely they plan to return, especially if they left to move to a vacation home (which is typically a temporary residence). These facts can be used to argue Carla does not intend to remain in California (one of the required elements for establishing her domicile).

This illustrates how important it is to be sure to make a conscious decision about the legal significance of each fact in the hypo. To keep track, as you plan how to use each fact in the exam question in your answer, highlight the fact in the exam using a highlighting pen. As a final review of the facts, identify and consider the "homeless" facts, i.e., those facts that are not yet highlighted. Then decide whether you can make some use of each homeless fact. You may want to go back through your issues checklist, and see if any of the issues are triggered by the homeless fact. Repeat this with every homeless fact until you find a use for the fact or you consciously decide the fact is not relevant, given the call of the question or the issues raised.

### (2) Creating a Coherent Plan

As you can see from the above discussion, before you begin writing, there is a good deal of information to think about and organize. If you try to hold this information in your head, you will overtax your working memory, and your thinking will be slower. You will have a harder time engaging in the type of deep processing that allows you to draw connections and inferences—both of which are required for success on law school exams. This is why expert law students takes notes about their thoughts, and organize those notes in a manner that speeds up their writing.

The key to creating a coherent plan is to link together the pieces while you are thinking about them—rather than hoping to remember the connections while you are writing. The key components to align are the issues, law and facts. For example, a writing plan for the above hypothetical might look like this:

| Issue | Rule | Facts |
|---|---|---|
| SMJ | Compl. Div. + amt | |
| AMT in cont | 75K, g.f., complaint | Complaint not filed; but emot. Distress $ from term ill, lost job, lost spouse |
| Div. | All Ps v. all Ds | |
| of individuals | Indiv. = perm home, int. to return; new if: phys pres. +int to remain | |
| Al | phys pres. +int to remain | Conn at taping, but now To TX with childhood friend Everyone in Conn was in on it: Doc, friends, co-workers, etc. (Prob TX) |
| Bob | phys pres. +int to remain | Lifelong NY, Now in CA, 8 months, trying to sell story |
| | Like Case X b/c college student only staying in Conn if she could find job=not a definite plan | Only stay, IF sells TV story=not a definite plan |
| | But Case X plans were vague b/c find a job somewhere other than WI, which wasn't definite plan to stay in Conn | Only plan is CA, and he's been working on it 8 mos (Prob NY because plan is not definite) |
| Carla | phys pres. +int to remain | Vacation home in CA Lifelong NY (Probably NY) |
| of corp. (TV corp) | State of incorp AND state of PPB=officer direct, control, etc. | DE TV corp, produces TV, etc.; Production offices in CA (los angeles) |

It is important to distinguish between a writing plan and simply taking notes about information. The key to a writing plan is to create a map for what you plan to write. There are other means of organizing information which can be helpful during an exam—but they do not substitute for a writing plan.

For example, students can create timelines to help them make sense of factually complex questions, where the sequence of events is significant. For instance, in contract disputes, which frequently result in both parties claiming the other breached the contract first, the sequence of parties' actions and of events can be crucial. To create a timeline, draw a line and mark the earliest possible starting point at one end and the latest possible event at the other end. Then, plot each event along the timeline, identifying both the date of the event and the nature of the event, making sure that the events are correctly sequenced along the timeline. Note however, that a timeline by itself is not a writing plan; a timeline only sets out factual events—it does not link those events to issues and rules. A student wishing to use a timeline as a writing plan would need to link the events to the legal issues and rules the student planned to address.

Diagrams can also be very useful for organizing information. For example, sometimes it helps to draw out the parcels of land, locations of roads, houses, etc. in a property dispute, or, where there are multiple parties in an exam, in different capacities, to diagram the parties to a lawsuit. For the above hypothetical it might be useful to create a list of the parties' domiciles, for easy comparison, like this:

| Πs | Δs |
|---|---|
| A   TX<br>B   NY or CA?<br>C   NY or CA? | TVCorp. DE and CA |

Notice that like the timeline, such a chart is not a plan for what to write, but rather a device for organizing and evaluating information. To make this chart part of a writing plan requires associating the information with a legal issue or rule. For example, you might use the chart to plan your answer like this:

| Πs | Δs |
|---|---|
| Indv = Phys pres + intent to remain<br>A     TX<br>Left fam, etc, in CONN b/c of term ill, no spouse, no job stuf on CW,<br>Now TX w/ chldhd friend<br>B    NY or CA?<br>Lifelong NY; now CA to sell story; 8 months; not sure tming<br>C    NY or CA?<br>Lifelong NY; Lag Bch, CA vacation home | Corp=where incorp and ppb<br>TVCorp.    DE and CA<br>State of Inc.  DE,<br>Ppb—production office in LA—produced CW |

Notice how this second version connects the issues, rules and facts. These details help to create a writing plan—rather than just a chart. Making notes about the issues you spot, rules and facts you plan to use, and connections you draw along the way, and putting those notes into a usable format will help with the next two critical tasks: managing exam time and writing your answer.

## 2. Allocate and Manage Time

Law school exams almost always put time pressure on students and therefore require students to manage their exam time. Primarily, this task requires you to apportion your time based on the relative weights of the questions you are answering, and the issues you must cover. As a general rule, you should consciously make sure that you devote more time to questions and issues that count for a larger share of your grade and less on questions and issues that count for a smaller share of your grade. Generally, law students can expect that greater grading weight will be assigned to those issues requiring greater thought and more discussion and lesser grading weight will be assigned to more simple issues. Law professors allocate points based on degrees of difficulty and time required for the task. In particular, issues about which lawyers representing both parties would have a great deal to say (because the outcome is ambiguous or unclear) tend to be assigned greater grading weight. Consequently, students must apportion their time within each question, spending more time on issues most likely to bear on their final grade.

Any person who has ever participated in or watched an Easter egg hunt has an excellent metaphor for this approach. Children who ever have participated in an egg hunt know that the largest quantity of candy and the best prizes can be found in the largest plastic eggs. For this reason, children go for the "big eggs" first. Law students should do the same on exams; they should make sure they get to all the "big eggs" (the major, most difficult issues) on the exam at all costs. While the smaller issues, the little eggs, do matter, students' grades usually are made or lost on the big eggs. Before you begin writing, it is a good idea to review your writing plan and determine which issues are major and minor (where are the points are). Some students even visualize the answer they plan to write, with emphasis on the major issues.

Finally, managing time requires students to pay attention to the passage of time while they are taking the examination. For the most part, students simply need to force themselves to look at the clock periodically to confirm that they are on track. You can use your writing plan to help you assess whether you are on track; before you begin writing, it helps to look at your writing plan, and think about how much you must cover, in light of how much time you have. One tip is to think about where you hope to be when your time is half over. Draw a line on your plan/map and list the time. Monitor your progress, and at the half way mark, assess whether you are on track, or need to speed up or slow down.

If you do start to run out of time, prioritize. Make sure you communicate your analysis of the significant issues even if you have to sacrifice writing quality. A former student characterized this last minute writing style as "writing in caveman talk." Instead of writing full and erudite sentences, write using the key words of the rule, the key facts from the exam question and your analysis of those facts.

### *Don't Lead the Exam; Follow It*

It is tempting to use an essay examination as an opportunity to show the professor you have learned everything covered in the course. However, law school exams do not test everything students have studied in the course. It is also tempting under the stress of an exam to cover every step of your exam approach, and every issue on your checklist, and be unwilling to deviate from your plan regardless of what you find on the exam. But one of the skills law school exams test is your ability to identify what is in issue and what is relevant. If you discuss matters beyond what the exam question requires, you are not demonstrating these skills, you are unlikely to finish the exam in the allotted time, and you are likely to receive a reduction in your grade. The ultimate source of the topics students must discuss are dictated by the exam itself— and expert law students confine their discussion to these topics.

### *Summary:* 10 Steps for Organizing Your Essay Answer

Here is a ten-step approach that incorporates all of the recommendations from this section:

1. Write down your issues checklist
2. Read the call of the question(s)
3. Read the fact pattern to see the "big picture" (without taking notes or annotating)

RECURSIVE
4. Read the facts again, and begin to issue spot, writing issues down to create your writing plan
5. Write rule elements/policy/holdings next to applicable issue
6. Add facts, align with issue and rule elements/policy/holdings
RECURSIVE

7. Identify homeless facts, review checklist to find issue(s) raised by the homeless facts
8. Review checklist looking for any additional issues you may have missed
9. Review writing plan and determine which issues are major and minor (how are the points allocated?)
10. Be sure you've answered the call/solved the problems. Visualize the answer.

Once you have created your plan and allocated your time, you are ready to write!

## 3. Writing an Answer

The format you use for your exam answer depends on the task you are being asked to do and your professor's preferences. If the task is to discuss the policy implications of adopting a particular rule of law, or to discuss the implications of employing a particular theoretical approach, you may follow the normal writing conventions you learned as an undergraduate. However, if you are given the task of applying law to a client problem or hypothetical set of facts, you will almost certainly use some form of IRAC—a legal writing convention described in the next section.

## Using IRAC

On many, if not most, law school essay exams, and on all bar exams, your job is to evaluate the facts and determine what legal issues are presented, what legal standards (rules) should be applied to resolve the issues, and what the likely result will be when that standard is applied to the facts. To justify your prediction about what they outcome will be, you must explain the basis for your opinion, which means explaining which facts were significant to your decision, and why they were significant—much the way courts do in their opinions when they explain the basis for a decision.

A very common form of analyzing a legal problem this way is called IRAC. This term is also used as a shorthand reference for the format commonly used for writing answers to legal problems—on exams and in practice. It is extraordinarily common for law students and law professors to refer to the exam writing process as "IRACing" or "using IRAC." IRAC is a mnemonic for: Issue, Rule, Analysis/Application, Conclusion. It may help you to see it this way:

I   the legal **issue** presented

R   the **rule** (standard) that should be applied to resolve the issue

A   your **analysis** of the **application** of the standard to the facts

C   the **conclusion** you predict the court will make

When you write in IRAC format it means you:

### I: Identify the Issue

A good answer identifies each main issue, and each element, factor or other component which is in issue by signaling or labeling the issue. Issues may be identified in a number of ways—for example, as a heading involving a few key words or as a detailed sentence at the start of a paragraph. Expert law students learn their professor's preferences, and adopt those conventions in their writing.

Typically a rule or rule component is in issue when a fact from the fact pattern can be used to prove that component. Major issues are those that have plausible arguments on both sides—or some ambiguity which makes it difficult to predict with certainty how a court will resolve the issue. However, even when an issue can only be resolved in one way, many law professors would deduct points from students who omitted the issue. Law professors have two good reasons for requiring such discussions: (1) the discussion still allows the student to demonstrate analytical reasoning and understanding of the rule, and (2) in real life, a lawyer would have to prove the element to succeed in proving a claim or defense and therefore real lawyers would always analyze the issue.

### R: Recite the Legal Standard (Sometimes Known as the Rule)

After each issue, there should be a statement of the applicable legal standard you intend to apply to the facts to resolve the issue. This standard can come in the form of a statute, a rule from a case, a rule you have created from synthesizing materials, a case holding, or even a proposed premise supported by a case or cases. Here are three important things to remember about rules:

1. **Rules must be correctly stated.** Accuracy is critical—you must have each required component, nothing more, and nothing less. Legal analysis requires students to match up the facts of the hypothetical to the statement of the rule; an erroneous rule statement, therefore, will result in erroneous analysis.

2. **Rules must address what is in issue.** Demonstrate you understand what is in issue by writing only the applicable rule(s). Remember that the goal of a law school exam is not to write down everything you know; instead write what is relevant to the issues being tested.

3. **Rules should be complete, yet concise.** Law school exams are usually written so it is difficult or impossible to finish within the time allotted. Maximize your time by writing rules that are concise. Additionally, many law school professors deduct points for lack of clarity, and for grammar and spelling errors.

Finally, you should never begin discussing the facts until after you have stated the applicable rule. Arguing the justice or injustice, rightness or wrongness, fairness or unfairness of the facts or the parties' behavior, without reference to a rule (or at least to a policy that you have connected with a rule), is a poor use of exam time. These considerations are important to lawyers and to you as a person, but, if your exam task is to apply the rules as they currently exist, you need to do so. Then, if you have time, you can argue that the rules should be changed because they do not achieve a just result.

### A: Apply the Standard to Analyze the Problem

After stating the issue and the rule, you can then move to the portion of your exam where the bulk of the points (usually 2/3 to 4/5 of total points) will be awarded; it is usually called the analysis or application section. In this section, you apply the stated standard (rule) to the facts, explaining how and why the facts satisfy or negate the standard.

#### Explaining the Legal Significance of Facts

Good exam answers always include good explanations as to why each referenced fact is legally significant—why the fact tends either to prove the existence or non-existence of the required standard. They link facts to the particular requirement of the rule, explaining why the fact makes it less or more likely a court would conclude that the element is or is not met. Another way to understand this process is that you are slotting the facts of the hypothetical under the elements to which they relate, and then you are explaining why those facts are significant. Excellent legal analysis, in short, involves explaining the significance of significant facts. In other words, it requires that you:

1. Identify a fact (or set of facts) which satisfy or negate the rule
2. State whether the fact satisfies or negates the rule
3. Explain why the fact (or set of facts) you selected satisfies or negates the rule[2]

Here is an example of a sentence which does each of these things:

> Carla does not intend to remain in California because she is a lifelong New York resident who is staying at her vacation home while she is in California, and vacation homes are places to visit, not places to permanently reside. Once her "vacation" is over, Carla will likely return to New York, the state where she has resided her entire life because that is what a person does when a "vacation" is over—returns to their home.

This may help you to see each of the requirements:

| | |
|---|---|
| 1. Identify a fact (or set of facts) which satisfy or negate the rule: | lifelong New York resident who is staying at her vacation home while she is in California |
| 2. State whether the fact satisfies or negates the rule: | does not intend to remain (an element of domicile) |
| 3. Explain why the fact (or set of facts) you selected satisfies or negates the rule: | vacation homes are places to visit, not places to permanently reside; she will return to the state where she has resided her entire life because that is what a person does when a "vacation" is over—returns to their home |

As you can see, explaining why a fact (or set of facts) is significant may require you to draw inferences from the facts or to use a reasonable explanation that you create based on your own experience. On some occasions however, no explanation of how the fact satisfies or negates the rule is required, because it will be clearly evident from the fact itself that the rule is satisfied or negated. For example:

Carla is physically present in California because she is currently living in her California vacation home.

| | |
|---|---|
| 1. Identify a fact (or set of facts) which satisfy or negate the rule: | living in her vacation home in California |
| 2. State whether the fact satisfies or negates the rule: | is physically present (an element of domicile) |
| 3. Explain why the fact (or set of facts) you selected satisfies or negates the rule: | [none needed because it is self-evident from the identified fact] |

---

2. Thanks to our colleague, Lisa Blasser, for identifying this process.

As you hopefully can see, law school exams require you to explain your reasoning rather than assuming the reader will know what is in your mind. It is like "showing your work" in math. You must demonstrate that you have done each step in the thinking process (i.e., you understand why each fact is significant) by explaining it in your answer, even if it seems obvious to you. In other words, the "answer" on a law school exam is really the analysis, not the conclusion.

### Avoiding Common Errors

There are four common errors law students make when using facts:

#### 1. Reciting Facts

If you merely state facts, without connecting them to rules of law or explaining their significance, it does not constitute legal analysis. Here is an example of fact reciting:

> Al was led to believe he had been fired from his job, his wife was leaving him and that he had a terminal illness. Al was so distraught over his friends' and loved ones' conduct that he moved to Texas to live with a childhood friend who had not participated in the game show ruse. Therefore, Al is physically present in Texas and intends to remain there, so he domiciled in Texas.

This answer would receive little credit, because on a law school exam, you must analyze, and not just recite, the facts. In your answer, never state a fact without a rule or holding with which to analyze that fact. In addition, you should almost always follow that fact statement with an analysis of whether that fact satisfies the requirements reflected in the rule. Here is an example which connects the facts and law:

> Although Al lived in Connecticut at the time of the taping of the show, he moved to Texas to live with a childhood friend who had not participated in the game show ruse, so he is now is physically present in Texas. Additionally, given that he left his friends and family in Connecticut because of what they did to him, he is not likely to return to Connecticut, where all the people who tricked him into believing horrible things still reside. He likely no longer trusts his doctor, who was probably involved in duping him into believing he was terminally ill. His employer and co-workers were probably involved in his believing he was out of a job, and his spouse and family were probably involved in convincing him his spouse was leaving. If everyone you trusted essentially betrayed you, and you left the state to get away—you probably aren't coming back. He most likely plans to stay in Texas, with his friend who did not participate in the ruse, i.e., he intends to remain there, which would make him domiciled in Texas.

*Tip: You can avoid fact reciting by connecting the law and facts.*

#### 2. Ignoring Facts

A student who does not use all of the facts which support an argument, or who ignores facts which do not support arguments, rather than discrediting or using those facts for counter arguments, usually has incomplete analysis, or misses issues—

thereby losing valuable points. For example, the following paragraph makes use of the facts that Carla is a lifelong resident of New York, and moved to her California vacation home:

> Carla does not intend to remain in California because she is a lifelong New York resident who is staying at her vacation home while she is in California, and vacation homes are places to visit, not places to permanently reside. Once her "vacation" is over, Carla will likely return to New York, the state where she has resided her entire life because that is what a person does when a "vacation" is over—returns to their home.

However, it ignores the fact that she left New York to "get away from it all." Notice how this paragraph makes use of that fact—and improves the student's analysis, by considering and making a counter argument:

> On the other hand, Carla left New York to "get away from it all," meaning to get away from having been subjected to her employer, spouse, medical providers and others being part of a ruse to make her believe a variety of horrible, but untrue facts. To get away from this, she would presumably have to leave New York, where it all happened, and where she would not want to return. She owns another home in California, and while that home was her vacation home when she lived in New York, it is where she is choosing to reside even when she is not on vacation.

> *Tip: Carefully consider each fact in the fact pattern, to avoid ignoring facts.*

### 3. Misstating Facts

Sometimes, during the stress of an examination, students will "see" facts that are not in the fact pattern, or misread facts. Other times, students may draw factual inferences which are not supported by the fact pattern. For example:

> TVCorp's headquarters, which is its principal place of business, is in Los Angeles, so it is a citizen of California.

Because the fact pattern does not tell you where the company has its headquarters, nor does it provide sufficient facts to make this determination, this is an unreasonable inference to draw. Instead, by using the facts that are in the fact pattern, and explaining how the missing information would impact the analysis, you can avoid misstating information. For example:

> TVCorp produced Cruel World, and has production offices, which presumably means it is in the business of producing and distributing TV shows (and potentially other things, like movies). Since its production work, which appears to be the activities of the corporation, is done in its Los Angeles offices, it indicates that this is where its activities are coordinated and controlled. Without more information it is difficult to say for certain, but TVCorp's principal place of business is probably in Los Angeles, so it is most likely a citizen of California.

*Tip: Read carefully and use the exact facts stated in the fact pattern.*

### 4. Summarizing Key Facts

While it is sometimes appropriate to summarize the significance of facts, summarizing the actual key facts rather than using each one to support a point can lead to incomplete legal analysis. For example, the following paragraph does not adequately convey the reasons for the conclusion:

> Al moved to Texas because his friends and family made him believe terrible things, which is why Al plans to stay in Texas.

By leaving out the specific reasons for his move, namely that the "terrible things" they made him believe were that he was terminally ill, lost his spouse and his job, the analysis does not convey the strength of his reasons for moving — and misses an opportunity to persuade the reader to adopt the writer's conclusion. Imagine making an argument to a judge or jury. Which argument is more likely to persuade them — one that summarizes what happened, or one which explains all of the key facts? Compare the sentence above, with this one:

> Al left his friends and family in Connecticut because they tricked him into believing he was terminally ill, he was out of a job, and his spouse left him, none of which were true. If everyone you trusted — your spouse, family, doctor and friends made you believe you were going to die soon from an illness, and in the meantime be unemployed and divorced, and you left the state to get away from the people who did it — you probably aren't coming back. Al most likely plans to stay in Texas, with his friend who did not participate in the ruse, i.e., he intends to remain there, which would make him domiciled in Texas.

The second paragraph gives the reader (or judge or jury) a reason to believe the writer's conclusion — which makes it more persuasive, and better legal analysis.

*Tip: Use the key words from the fact pattern.*

## Arguing Both Sides

Law school exams test students' ability to develop and evaluate the arguments reasonable lawyers might make in response to hypothetical fact patterns; consequently, the exams provide sufficient information for good students to develop persuasive arguments on behalf of all parties involved in the fact pattern. However, *this does not mean* students must do so for every element. Arguments need to be made as though they will be read or heard by a judge or jury. If you could not make the argument with a straight face to a judge or jury, it should not be made in an exam answer.

When you make arguments for both sides, you should separate these arguments. Avoid what is sometimes called "ping-ponging," meaning your writing bounces back and forth from one party to another like the ball in a game of ping-pong. For each issue, or sub-issue, make the argument for one party, or from one perspective, and once you are done, make the counter argument. For example:

Carla does not intend to remain in California because she is a lifelong New York resident who is staying at her vacation home while she is in California, and vacation homes are places to visit, not places to permanently reside. Once her "vacation" is over, Carla will likely return to New York, the state where she has resided her entire life because that is what a person does when a "vacation" is over—returns to their home.

On the other hand, Carla left New York to "get away from it all," meaning to get away from having been subjected to her employer, spouse, medical providers and others being part of a ruse to make her believe a variety of horrible, but untrue facts. To get away from this, she would presumably have to leave New York, where it all happened, and where she would not want to return. She owns another home in California, and while that home was her vacation home when she lived in New York, it is where she is choosing to reside even when she is not on vacation.

---

**PAUSE. THINK. ACT.** Review the practice exams you've written. Have you made any of these common errors? Redraft your answers to correct the problems.

---

### C: Craft a Conclusion

Often law school fact patterns are written so that the likely outcome is very unclear. This means there will be very good arguments that the result could go either way. Your job on a law school exam is to articulate both arguments and then make a prediction as to which one is likely to win (and why). In other words, the correct answer on law school exams is usually, at best, a prediction of how a court would rule and, often, even a moderate degree of certainty as to how a court would actually resolve all the issues on the exam is impossible. This is why many law school professors will tell you that your actual conclusion rarely matters—because the answers are not clear, there is not a single correct answer. Still, it is important for you to make a prediction, and for that prediction to logically flow from your analysis.

## Identifying IRAC

Below is a sample answer to the "Cruel World" fact pattern, written in IRAC format. Each section of the paper is numbered, and each of the numbered sections represents one or more of the concepts addressed in the previous section of this text. After you have identified the concepts which appear in each section, check your answers against the answers in the Appendix G.

---

| 1 | <u>Will the federal court have subject matter jurisdiction (SMJ)?</u> |
|---|---|
| 2 | Federal courts have limited jurisdiction and can only hear certain types of cases. Federal district courts have original jurisdiction over all civil actions where the amount in controversy exceeds the sum or value of $75,000.00, exclusive of interests and costs, |

and where there is complete diversity, meaning the matter is between citizens of different states.

**3**  ## Amount in Controversy

**4**  The amount in controversy is determined from what is claimed in the complaint. Usually all that is necessary is a good faith allegation that the amount of damages exceeds the sum of $75,000.

**5**  Here, the complaint is not yet filed, however A, B and C's suit will be based on a claim for damages for pretty extreme conduct — making someone believe they were terminally ill, meaning they were going to die, and that they lost their spouse and job would cause pretty serious emotional injury to anyone, and it is reasonable to assume the damages for that emotional injury will be higher than $75,000. While it does not say exactly what happened to Bob and Carla, they both fled the state where they had been lifelong residents, which suggests the things they were led to believe were also, as the facts state, horrible and untrue, and caused substantial emotional injury. Therefore, A, B and C will be able to make a good faith allegation in their complaint that they have damages in excess of $75,000, and so the amount in controversy requirement will be satisfied.

**6**  ## Complete Diversity

**7**  Complete diversity requires that every plaintiff be of diverse citizenship from every defendant. It does not require that every party be of diverse citizenship from every other party. There are several issues with regard to the parties' citizenship.

**8**  ### State Citizenship of an Individual — Domicile

**9**  The state of citizenship of a natural person depends on the permanent home to which she intends to return. A new state citizenship may be established by (1) physical presence and (2) the intention to remain in the state, i.e., no present intent to go elsewhere.

**10**  ### A's Citizenship

**11**  Although Al lived in Connecticut at the time of the taping of the show, he moved to Texas to live with a childhood friend who had not participated in the game show ruse, so he is now physically present in Texas. Additionally, given that he left his friends and family in Connecticut because of what they did to him, he is not likely to return to Connecticut, where all the people who tricked him into believing horrible things still reside. He likely no longer trusts his doctor, who was probably involved in duping him into believing he was terminally ill. His employer and co-workers were probably involved in his believing he was out of a job, and his spouse and family were probably involved in convincing him his spouse was leaving. If everyone you trusted essentially betrayed you, and you left the state to get away — you probably aren't coming back. He most likely plans to stay in Texas, with his friend who did not participate in the ruse, i.e., he intends to remain there, which would make him domiciled in Texas.

**12**      <u>B's Citizenship</u>

**13**      Bob is currently physically present in California because he is there trying to sell his story to producers to turn it into a made for TV movie. However, although Bob has been in California for the past eight months, he does not necessarily intend to remain there, because he only plans to remain there if he is able to negotiate the rights to turn his story into a TV movie — which is far from a sure thing as evidenced by the fact that Bob has already been in California for 8 months and his idea has not yet been picked up.

**14**      This is similar to <u>Case X</u>, where the court held a person's domicile does not change until they have a definite plan to remain in a new state. In that case, a person moved from Wisconsin to Connecticut to attend college. Although the student did not plan to return to Wisconsin, and planned to find a job upon graduation, potentially in Connecticut, the court held that the student did not have a definite plan to remain, because it was not clear whether she would find a job in Connecticut, and until it was clear and she had a definite plan to remain, her domicile would not change. Similarly, here Bob does not have a definite plan to remain. He plans to sell his story, but it is not clear whether he will, and until it is clear that he will sell the story, and that he is staying in California, he has not established a new domicile.

**15**      On the other hand, Bob has already been in California for eight months, which indicates he is persistent and plans stay in California for a long time trying to sell the

**16**      movie, which means he has present intent to remain at least for the foreseeable future. Also, he does intend to stay in California if the TV moving deal goes through. Thus, he does have some present intent to remain in California, even if it is conditional intent. This is different from <u>Case X</u> where the student planned to find a job somewhere other than Wisconsin, but Connecticut was only one of the options — making it less definite that Connecticut would be the state where she would stay. Her plans were more vague than Bob's plan to sell his movie to producers — which he has been working on for eight months.

**17**      Most likely the court will conclude that because Bob remaining in California is still contingent on his TV movie selling, the same way the student's plan to stay in Connecticut in <u>Case X</u>, was contingent on her finding a job there, it is not a definite enough plan to remain for the purposes of establishing a new domicile. Since Bob is a lifelong New York resident and his present intent is at best unclear, it is likely the court will conclude he is a New York resident, absent some change in his intent (i.e., someone in California decides to buy the rights to his story).

**18**      <u>C's Citizenship</u>

**19**      Carla does not intend to remain in California because she is a lifelong New York resident who is staying at her vacation home while she is in California, and vacation homes are places to visit, not places to permanently reside. Once her "vacation" is over, Carla will likely return to New York, the state where she has resided her entire life because that is what a person does when a "vacation" is over — returns to their home.

**20**  On the other hand, Carla left New York to "get away from it all," meaning to get away from having been subjected to her employer, spouse, medical providers and others being part of a ruse to make her believe a variety of horrible, but untrue facts. To get away from this, she would presumably have to leave New York, where it all happened, and where she would not want to return. She owns another home in California, and while that home was her vacation home when she lived in New York, it is where she is choosing to reside even when she is not on vacation.

**21**  The court will likely conclude Carla, who has not indicated she is moving to California permanently, does not yet have the required intent to remain and is still domiciled in New York.

**22**      <u>State of Citizenship of a Corporation</u>

**23**  For diversity purposes, a corporation is a citizen of every state where it is incorporated and also of the state in which it has its principal place of business.

**24**      <u>State of Incorporation</u>

**25**  TVCorp is incorporated in Delaware, therefore it is a citizen of Delaware.

**26**      <u>Principal Place of Business</u>

**27**  A corporation's principal place of business is the place where a corporation's officers direct, control and coordinate the corporation's activities.

**28**  TVCorp produced Cruel World, and has production offices, which presumably means it is in the business of producing and distributing TV shows (and potentially other things, like movies). Since its production work, which appears to be the activity of the corporation, is done in its Los Angeles offices, it indicates that this is where the activities are coordinated and controlled. Without more information, it is difficult to say for certain, but TVCorp is probably also a citizen of California.

**29**  Since A is a citizen of Texas, B may be a citizen of California or New York, C is most likely a citizen of New York, and TVCorp is a citizen of Delaware and probably California, there is a problem because complete diversity requires that every plaintiff be of diverse citizenship from every defendant, and potential plaintiffs B and/or C may be a citizen of the same state as Defendant TVCorp — California. Therefore, the court's subject matter jurisdiction hinges on whether B's physical presence and conditional intent to remain in California are sufficient to establish citizenship, whether C is planning to remain in California, and whether TVCorp's principal place of business is in California. Given that B's intent is unclear at best, the court will likely conclude he does not have sufficient intent to remain in California and will find he is a New York citizen. C is probably a New York citizen as well because all she has done is stay in her vacation home. If so, even if TVCorp's principal place of business in is California, there is complete diversity and the court will have subject matter jurisdiction.

**30**  Finally, diversity of citizenship must exist at the time the suit is instituted. It is not defeated if, after commencement of the action, a party later becomes a citizen of the same state as one of his opponents. Therefore, if the court finds Bob is a citizen of New

York and then sometime after the litigation is commenced, he sells his made for TV movie, decides to relocate to California and thus becomes a resident of California, diversity is not destroyed. The same is true if Carla decides she want to stay permanently, rather than just for an extended vacation.

---

**PAUSE. THINK. ACT.** What have you learned about IRAC from reading this sample answer? How is this writing format and style different from other writing you have done? Why do you think this format is important for legal writing?

---

### Writing Conventions

Law professors often refer to exam writing as requiring students to objectively analyze the issue; this assertion is correct in the sense that the student must analyze the facts without letting emotion interfere with the analysis, and must consider the facts from both sides' perspectives. The writing is also persuasive, however, because the author's goal is to convince the reader that the author has correctly analyzed the facts and has accurately predicted how a court would decide the issue.

There are conventions of legal writing that make it easier for the reader to know what the writer is doing. For example, when transitioning from the rule statement to the analysis, the phrases "In the present case," "Under these facts" or "Here" signal to a legally trained reader that a student's analysis is about to begin. The phrase "On the other hand" signals that the writer is about to consider another perspective (or a different party's side of the argument). The phrase "In (Case Name) the court" signals that the writer is about to discuss a particular court opinion (the named case).

---

**PAUSE. THINK. ACT.** dentify the legal writing conventions used in the sample answer above.

---

### Abusing and Overusing IRAC

The IRAC formula is described above as only "commonly used" because dozens of law school professors tell their students that they hate IRAC (however, notwithstanding professorial statements of disdain for IRAC, exams that include paragraphs written in the IRAC form, where it is appropriate to do so, often receive good marks). The dislike many law professors feel for IRAC stems not really from proper uses of IRAC, but, rather, from how students abuse and overuse IRAC. In other words, what law professors who complain about IRAC are really saying is that they dislike poor, thoughtless uses of the IRAC formula. For example, here are some common student errors:

- **Using IRAC when the exam does not call for application of law to fact.** Some exam questions require students to analyze which of two or more rules a court should apply to the parties' dispute rather than how a court would apply a particular rule to the parties' dispute. Some exam questions require students to analyze whether a particular rule is good public policy. IRAC is not a tool for analyzing questions of what law to apply or of deciding whether a particular rule is good public policy.

- **Giving equal time or attention to the "I", "R", "A" and "C".** The "I", "R" and "C" are necessary components, but they are not as heavily weighted as the "A" because the A is where a student demonstrates understanding of the material and the ability to apply concepts to future problems. This does not mean you can ignore the "I", "R" and "C", because, for example, you cannot do the A(nalysis) unless you spot the I(ssue) and know the correct R(ule) that will be applied. Rather, it means that you should spend the most time on the A section because it is where you will demonstrate that you can do more than recite the law; it is where you demonstrate you can use the law to resolve the issues—in the fact pattern and in future cases involving clients. In fact, the analysis portion of IRAC counts for 2/3 to 4/5 of students' grades; it therefore should be that much more extensive than the other portions, which is why most of this section is devoted to writing that portion of the IRAC.

- **Writing one IRAC per exam or one IRAC per broad issue.** Each legal concept should be addressed separately. For example, if the issue is whether there is diversity jurisdiction, you would be required to consider several narrower issues to address that broad issue (namely the domicile of each party, and the amount in controversy). Note that each of these narrower issues might require consideration of even narrower issues; for example the issue of domicile might require consideration of whether a party was physically present in a state, and whether they intend to remain in that state. Each of these issues requires a separate IRAC. For example, using the above hypothetical and sample answer, you can see the structure looks something like this:

### Federal Court Jurisdiction?
Rule establishing potential basis for jurisdiction (diversity jurisdiction)

#### Diversity jurisdiction?
Rule for diversity jurisdiction (complete diversity of Ps and Ds and amount in controversy)

##### Complete Diversity (no P same **domicile** as any D)
Rule for individual domicile
Application of stated rule to Al
Conclusion re: Al's domicile

Application of stated rule to Bob
Conclusion re: Bob's domicile

Application of stated rule to Carla
Conclusion re: Carla's domicile

Rule for corporation's domicile
Application of stated rule to TVCorp
Conclusion re: TVCorp's domicile

Conclusion re: Complete Diversity

**Amount in controversy?**
Rule for amount in controversy
Application of stated rule
Conclusion re: amount in controversy

Notice that the structure of this answer is really: IR IR IRAC AC AC RAC C IRAC. The IRACs (and ACs) for domicile form the "A" of the broader issue of complete diversity; the IRACs for complete diversity and amount in controversy form the "A" for the issue of diversity jurisdiction. As you can see, the term IRAC includes a number of different structural variations.

- **Failing to adapt the IRAC format to the professor and exam.** Even among faculty who use or require IRAC, there are variations with respect to what is required. For example, the "I" may require stating the issue broadly (e.g., is D negligent?), and then stating each of the narrow issues required to resolve that broader issue (e.g., Did D owe P a duty? What was the standard of care? Was D's conduct a breach of the standard of care? etc.). This might be the case where facts in the fact pattern indicate each of these narrower issues requires consideration. On the other hand, the "I" may only require stating a very narrow issue (Does a manufacturer of insulation products containing asbestos have a duty to protect the family members of its workers from injury from asbestos?). This might be the case where only that issue is contained in the call, or where a professor expects you to limit your discussion on exams to the aspect of the case that is most likely to be contested. Some professors prefer issues in the form of a question, while others might allow you to use a word or phrase to identify an issue (e.g., breach of duty). Some might want the issue in the form of a heading, and some might want it in the form of a sentence at the start of the paragraph addressing the issue. It is important to understand that these are all variations of the same task—stating the issue. Similar variations exist for the "R." For example, the "R" might consist of the words from a statute, a rule statement from a case, a broad or narrow holding from a case, or a rule or holding that represents several synthesized cases (which might require you to articulate holdings, facts and rationales to explain the "rule"). While it might frustrate you at first, becoming comfortable with the skill of responding to individual faculty preferences will prepare you for practice, because judges will often have differing preferences (for example, some judges like for you to two-hole punch documents delivered to their chambers, or to deliver a filed copy of any motions directly to their courtrooms). Also, lawyers must adapt their format to fit the circumstances, which is why it is useful to learn to adapt your IRAC format to fit the task you are given on an essay exam.

- **Labeling the pieces of the IRAC.** Some students literally write: "Issue: The issue in this case is …" IRAC works best as a guide inside your head, not as a set of labels for each of the paragraphs or sentences in your essay.

- **Ignoring all other principles of writing, organization and exam taking.** Some students, for example, never actually respond to the question posed by the exam. Some students fail to include transition sentences between sections to explain the connections, or fail to use introductions. IRAC, at best, summarizes a large part of what makes for effective exams, but good writing also helps make for good exams.

Avoiding these pitfalls, and following the steps outlined above will help you do all of the things you need to do to succeed in applying rules to facts: stating the rules, identifying all of the relevant facts, drawing factual inferences, arguing both sides, explaining every step of your reasoning, and reaching and justifying a conclusion. But **to learn to do this, you must practice.**

Applying rules to facts is a new skill and therefore students must frequently practice it if they wish to master it. Nearly all first-year law students have a hard time applying a rule to a set of facts if they have not practiced applying that particular rule. Consequently, expert law students, particularly in their first year of law school, make sure they practice applying each rule they study.

## 4. Multiple Choice Exams

Most professors design law school multiple-choice questions to test your knowledge and understanding of the rules. In this way they are very different from multiple choice questions which appear on standardized tests—which are usually designed to measure aptitude, not knowledge and application of that knowledge. For this reason, there are fewer "tricks" to doing well at law school multiple choice tests. Instead, to do well, you must focus on knowing and understanding the law—and how it applies.

Just like law school essays, law school multiple choice questions usually begin with a story (a set of hypothetical facts) and the law student's job is to sort through the facts of that story, identify the legal issues raised by those facts, apply the law to those facts and draw a conclusion. For this reason, many of the same skills which apply to law school essay testing also apply to law school multiple choice testing.

### An Approach to Multiple Choice Questions

Below is a sample fact pattern for a multiple choice question. In this section, we will use this fact pattern to illustrate the process for answering a multiple choice question, and to compare the similarities and differences between answering law school multiple choice and law school essay questions.

## Sample Question

Olivia was enraged at Anna. She rushed to Anna's home, broke down the door, and found Anna preparing dinner for Duke. She immediately said: "Anna, I am going to kill you!" Anna knew that Olivia had been convicted of attempted murder several years ago, and she became frightened when Olivia took out a gun and pointed it at her. Anna could have easily darted for the open door and evaded Olivia, but instead she lunged at Olivia with the knife in her hand and stabbed Olivia to death. Unknown to Anna, Olivia's gun was not loaded.

Does Anna have a valid argument for self-defense?

Like law school essays, law school multiple choice questions are usually a hypothetical fact pattern which ends with a question you are expected to analyze. And just like law school essays, this is where you should begin.

### a. Begin with the Call of the Question

The question at the end of multiple choice fact patterns usually will help you narrow the topics you should consider. Reading the call first helps you orient your thinking to the applicable rule. You are then in a better position to identify relevant information when you read the fact pattern and more easily organize the information you are reading. For the sample question, the call is specifically about self-defense, so this is either a Tort or Criminal Law question, about self-defense.

### b. Read the Facts Carefully

Like essays, facts in a multiple choice question drive you toward the issue. Reading carefully helps you correctly answer reading comprehension questions and it helps you spot issues and identify relevant irrelevant facts. As you read the facts, your first goal should be to identify the central issue—the narrow issue the question is addressing.

### c. Identify the "Central Issue"

Sometimes the call is very specific and you can identify the central issue from the call. Many times, however the call will narrow your focus, but will not give the precise sub-issue that is being tested. You will often need to read the facts to find the precise "central issue." For example, with the sample question, the larger, over-arching issue is self-defense, but the narrower "central issue" is whether Anna had a duty to retreat before using self-defense. The facts that should tip you off to this issue are: "Anna could have easily darted for the open door and evaded Olivia." If you did not spot these facts, and identify them as signaling the central issue, it may be because you did not yet know the law. Like law school essay exams, issue spotting on multiple choice exams requires you to possess excellent knowledge of the law. This knowledge of the law is what helps you to spot critical facts, and understand why they are included in the fact pattern. This is why it is so important to know the materials well. To do so, use studying methods that actively test your knowledge of the rules, such as applying what you know to practice problems.

### d. Recite and Apply the Rule

Once you identify the central issue, you should recite the applicable rule—meaning the specific rule or sub-rule, or exception to the rule, which precisely applies to the central issue. Here are the rules pertaining to self-defense. Try to identify the precise rule you need to solve the problem in the sample problem:

> A defendant has the burden to prove self defense; she must establish (1) she used reasonable force; (2) she actually believed force was necessary; (3) it was reasonable to believe force was necessary; and (4) she used force to prevent unlawful and immediate harm. Generally, reasonable force is force that is not intended or likely to cause death or serious bodily harm. The force used must be force that is objectively reasonable under the circumstances and no more force than is necessary to prevent or avert the threat of immediate harm. The reasonableness of the amount of force used is to be determined in the light of all the facts and circumstances of the case, which may include: the relative age, size, and strength of the parties, their reputations for violence, who was the aggressor, the degree of physical harm reasonably feared, and the presence or absence of weapons. To justify the use of deadly force, a person must be in imminent danger of death or serious bodily harm, or reasonably and actually believe she is in imminent danger of death or serious bodily harm.
>
> Defendant must also prove that she subjectively (actually and honestly) believed that force was necessary. It must also be reasonable for her to have believed such force was necessary—which is measured objectively, but from her subjective standpoint. In other words, it is possible to prove self-defense if a reasonable person in the same circumstances would have believed force was necessary. Finally, defendant must prove she used force to stop or avert an immediate threatened harm. Force may not be used for revenge, retaliation or as a preemptive strike. In the majority of jurisdictions, there is no duty to retreat before using force, even if the defendant can safely retreat without using force. In a minority of jurisdictions, a defendant must retreat before using deadly force, where it is safe to do so. In every jurisdiction a defendant is not required to retreat in her own home before using any force, even deadly force.

Once you have identified the precise rule, re-read the facts and apply the rule to the facts.

It is important to recite the rule and apply it to the facts, before you consider the answer choices. If you read the answer choices, hoping the answer will become clear to you, you are likely to be disappointed. Law school professors write very good distracters (the plausible but incorrect choices on multiple choice exams), designed to take advantage of common errors in law student thinking and understanding of the law. If you know the law, including the nuances and how it applies, and you apply the law to the facts to reach a conclusion, before looking at the answers, you are far less likely to be distracted. In other words, by being proactive (and deciding on your answer based on application of the rule you have recited and applied), rather than reactive (by trying to find an answer by reading the choices), you are less likely to be swayed by a good but incorrect choice.

### e. Reword the call if necessary

Sometimes the call will ask you for the "least correct" answer, or the "best defense," or it may use a double negative or be confusing in some other way. In such cases, it is important for you to reword the call so it is clear to you what you are looking for, before you begin to choose an answer. For example, you might reword a call which asks for the "least correct" answer to: "I'm looking for the worst answer."

### f. Look for the Correct Answer

After you apply the rule to the facts, your job is to decide the answer to the central issue (and the call).

After you have an answer to the central issue of the sample question, read on.

The part of the rule you need is this: In every jurisdiction, a defendant is not required to retreat in her own home before using any force, even deadly force. This is because the central issue is the duty to retreat, and the first line of the fact pattern tells you they were in Anna's home. If you missed this critical fact, it is a good reminder that you need to read very carefully, and pay attention to important details.

Now that you have spotted the central issue, recited the rule, and applied the rule to the facts, you can decide what the answer is—and then look for it. If you see it, circle it. Here is the quesion with answer choices:

### Sample Question

Olivia was enraged at Anna. She rushed to Anna's home, broke down the door, and found Anna preparing dinner for Duke. She immediately said: "Anna, I am going to kill you!" Anna knew that Olivia had been convicted of attempted murder several years ago, and she became frightened when Olivia took out a gun and pointed it at her. Anna could have easily darted for the open door and evaded Olivia, but instead, she lunged at Olivia with the knife in her hand and stabbed Olivia to death. Unknown to Anna, Olivia's gun was not loaded.

Does Anna have a valid argument for self defense?

a) Yes, because Anna had an honest and reasonable belief that her life was being threatened.

b) Yes, because Anna was not required to retreat.

c) No, because she had a reasonable opportunity to escape.

d) No, because her mistake of fact was not reasonable.

The answer here is "b"; because Anna was in her home, she does not have a duty to retreat. Although "a" is a correct statement of the law, it does not resolve the central issue—the duty to retreat, and ignores that in some circumstances, she would have that duty even if her belief was honest and reasonable. This illustrates why it is important to read and analyze each choice even if the first answer seems correct. Most law school tests and the bar exam require students to select the "best" answer. The term "best" suggests that more than one answer may be correct, and your task is to select the best correct answer. Moreover, a later answer may cause you to reconsider your original inclination. Again, this is why it is important to identify the central issue (the duty to retreat, in one's home) and be sure your answer resolves that issue—because often, the distractor will be correct, and resolve the broader issue (self defense).

### g. Eliminate Incorrect Answer Choices

Sometimes the answer choices will not reflect your analysis, or resolve what you thought was the central issue; sometimes the answer choices may even raise new legal issues. In such cases, if a new rule or aspect of the rule is raised, recite the applicable rule and apply the new rule or aspect of the rule to the facts to determine whether the answer is correct.

With difficult questions, start by eliminating the answers you are fairly certain are incorrect. For some very hard questions, the answer may not jump out. To make progress with such questions, you need to start by eliminating the answers you know to be incorrect. Then, you need to do your best to select from the remaining answers.

### h. Select the Best Choice and Move On

If you do not know the answer, make an educated guess. Do not skip confusing questions; rather, select an answer, circle the question or make a note to yourself in case there is time to come back to it at the end of the exam. Then move on to the next question. The time pressure on multiple-choice tests is significant. Students have, on average, less than two minutes to answer each question. Students therefore do not have time to linger over any one question. Once you have answered all the questions, however, you can take the time for greater reflection and contemplation, and then go back to the question(s) you've circled at the end if time permits. Be sure you aren't thinking about the previous question when you begin the next question—devote your mental energy to answering the question in front of you. Do the best you can for each question and then let it go!

## Improving Performance

To improve performance on multiple choice exams, a student must first identify and understand the reasons for poor performance. Below are some of the most common reasons for poor performance on multiple choice exams.

## 1. Inadequate Reading Comprehension

One of the most common problems on law school multiple choice questions is a failure to read carefully. This makes sense—because of the time pressure. Students typically have about two minutes per question, and the fact patterns can sometimes be long. You must learn to read quickly and carefully—a difficult skill to master. Some common reading comprehension problems include misreading the call, missing important factual details, assuming facts which are not present, letting your mind wander and failure to remember what you've read. If you have reading comprehension issues, you may need to slow down, make notes, underline key words, or even clear your head—by taking a walk or getting a drink of water, or closing your eyes and taking a deep breath.

## 2. Knowing the Basics, but Not the Details of the Law

Multiple choice questions frequently misstate the law you have learned or the holding of a case you studied. Such questions can be tricky; the misstatements included as wrong answers are likely to be based on common student errors or confusion, and the correct answer may depend on recall of what you perceive to be minor points. Questions also test exceptions to rules, and exceptions to the exceptions—in other words, they go far beyond the basics, which requires you to know and study the many nuances of the rule, not just the basic rule or the words of the rule.

## 3. Difficulty Spotting the Central Issue

In a set of answers each choice can correctly state (and even correctly apply) the law, but only the correct answer identifies and resolves the central issue raised by the facts. Sometimes a failure to spot the central issues is tied to not knowing the details of the rule; if you don't know the rule, it will be near impossible to spot the significant facts, which give rise to the central issue.

## 4. Relying on Instinct or Intuition

Some students substitute their own judgment or practical experience for the black letter law, relying on instinct rather than application of the law to the facts. Others, who have a previous history of being good at multiple choice questions, may fail to understand the level of study that is required and may want to rely on their instincts because they do not have detailed knowledge of the law. Others "fight the question," meaning they have trouble accepting the facts as they are given in the question—they may not want to accept that someone can drive reasonably after drinking a case of beer, or that an unconscious person could shoot someone. Others have trouble distancing themselves from the facts of the problem, and may be tricked by the facts because they are not willing to choose answers that seem unfair, or deprive severely injured persons of recovery or allow dangerous criminals to "go free". What each of these have in common is a failure to recite the applicable rule, and apply it dispassionately, to the facts given (even if those facts seem strange, unreasonable or even impossible).

## 5. Anxiety or Panic

The stress of a law school exam—essay and multiple choice—can cause students to perform more poorly than they otherwise would have performed. Some techniques for dealing with such stress are described in the next section.

## 6. Inadequate Practice, Review and Reflection

One of the most effective ways to improve performance on multiple choice exams is through deliberate practice, review and reflection. Engaging in deliberate practice, review and reflection allows you to identify your weaknesses and strengths and build knowledge of the rules and how they are applied. This section describes one way you can engage in this type of process.

After you have completed a set of multiple choice questions, review each question to determine whether you got it correct for the right reasons. If you got it wrong, or you got it "right" because of a lucky guess, read the answer explanation for the correct choice, your choice, and others you thought were plausible. Next, read the question again, looking at the call and the facts; your goal is to compare your current thinking with prior thinking—to know what your reasoning was when you made the original choice, so you can "fix" it. Keep track of the reasons you make incorrect choices. For example, the chart on the next page lists the common reasons for selecting an incorrect answer. By using a chart such as this, you can more easily see common reasons for poor performance. To help you select the most appropriate reasons, here are some questions you can ask yourself:

*You may be **missing important details** if any of the following are true:*
- Are you noticing facts for the first time?
- Did you overlook significant words?
- Did you miss relationships (LL/T, parent/child, buyer/seller)?
- Did you miss amounts, dates, quantities, ages?
- Did you miss states of mind—intended, decided, mistaken, deliberate?

*You may be have **added or assumed a fact not present** if any of the following are true:*
- Did you read something into the problem that wasn't there?
- Did you draw an inference when there was an answer that didn't need such an inference?

*You may have **other reading comprehension** issues if any of the following are true:*
- Did you confuse the parties?
- Did your mind wander?
- Did you need to re-read because you couldn't remember what you had read?

*Did you know and apply the **applicable rule**?*
- Did you disregard an important exception?
- Were you able to summon the correct rule?
- Did you recite the correct rule before you looked at the options?
- Did you apply the rule correctly?
- Have you missed the rule before?

*Did you have trouble **identifying the central issue**?*
- Did your answer resolve the main, but not the narrower central issue?
- Did you miss a significant fact or other detail?
- Did you miss the issue because you didn't know the applicable rule? (check that box too)

**INSTRUCTIONS:** Next to each question, select the appropriate choice (correct, incorrect, lucky guess). If your answer was incorrect or a lucky guess, check the box which best describes the reason for your choice. In addition to selecting the reasons for choosing an incorrect answer, you should also list the topic or subject matter and central issue of the question (so you can keep track of particular subjects which give you difficulty). You may also want to track the times you are able to eliminate two of the four choices, but still select the incorrect choice—so you can begin to determine the cause of this problem.

| Q # | GOT IT RIGHT | LUCKY GUESS | GOT IT WRONG | Did not ID central issue | Did not know rule | Missed important detail | Assumed facts not present | Tricked by facts | Reading comp | Other (explain) | Down to 2, picked wrong | Specific topic and explanation |
|---|---|---|---|---|---|---|---|---|---|---|---|---|
|  |  |  |  |  |  |  |  |  |  |  |  |  |
|  |  |  |  |  |  |  |  |  |  |  |  |  |
|  |  |  |  |  |  |  |  |  |  |  |  |  |
|  |  |  |  |  |  |  |  |  |  |  |  |  |
|  |  |  |  |  |  |  |  |  |  |  |  |  |
|  |  |  |  |  |  |  |  |  |  |  |  |  |
|  |  |  |  |  |  |  |  |  |  |  |  |  |
|  |  |  |  |  |  |  |  |  |  |  |  |  |

A complete chart, which you may reproduce as often as necessary, is contained in Appendix H.

Once you have finished completing the chart (or engaging in some other form of review which involves tracking the reasons for your selections), reflect on your performance. For example, ask yourself the following:

1) Did you know the law? If not, why? Do you need to do further study and review of this area?

2) Did you spot the central issue? If not, why? Did you know the law? Did you miss critical facts?

3) Do you continually make the same type of errors? Why? What can you do to address the problem?

4) Are certain topics or subjects more challenging than others? Is there a particular area of law you need to review?

You should also keep track of what you learn about the law, or anything else you learn and want to remember. For example, you might want to make flashcards and review them periodically.

This process requires you to do practice problems, review your performance with an eye toward identifying strengths and weaknesses, and to reflect on what to do to improve future performance. For this reason, it is what expert law students do to succeed on multiple choice examinations.

## 7. Managing Stress

Almost all students experience some exam stress. In fact, a moderate amount of stress, well managed, may actually improve performance by helping students stay focused and on task. Thus, the discussion below focuses only on techniques for dealing with excessive, debilitating exam stress—the type of stress that may cause students to perform more poorly than they otherwise would have performed. Below are techniques for dealing with exam stress:

- *Recalling past success:* When you start to feel anxious, recall a time when you succeeded at a difficult task. Invoking self-efficacy by recalling past successes helps reduce stress because it helps you remember that you can and should succeed on the exam.

- *Overlearning:* As explained above, overlearning is a powerful tool for dealing with exam stress. Overlearning increases confidence and usually produces early success on exams thereby increasing your self-confidence.

- *Reframing:* Students experiencing extreme exam stress often obsess about the exam and the possibility of failure. Reframing involves redirecting this stress; instead of worrying about the exam, you strive to substitute an alternative mental state, one that will replace this debilitating doubt and fear. For example, some students have had success imagining themselves to be excited about the exam and by thinking of the exam as an opportunity to show off what they have learned. Other students find it helpful to make themselves angry about the exam and to adopt an "attack the exam" mental focus. These seemingly irreconcilable mental states have one thing in common that explains why they work. In both situations, the student is substituting productive sets of strong emotions for unproductive exam stress emotions.

- *Plan ahead, and follow your plan:* Systematic guides, such as exam checklists and approaches, give students tools for staying on task instead of focusing on their exam stress.

- *Focus on the positive:* Positive self-talk allows students to focus on what is going well; when you catch yourself doing something well and change your focus to what is going right—rather than what might go wrong—you calm your anxiety.

- *Put it in perspective:* While law school exams are important, they are not a matter of life and death. The most meaningful things in life, such as family, friends, health, etc., are never resolved during three-hour exams. Moreover, high law school grades do not predict success in legal practice or in life and low law school grades do not predict failure. In short, while preparing earnestly for examinations is an incredibly valuable, rewarding task, worrying about exam results serves no purpose. Students who focus on what they can control, their effort and preparation, and then celebrate the fact that they have done their best are less anxious about law school exams.

- *Free write:* Spend a few minutes writing down all of the things that are causing you to worry. By putting them down on paper you free your mind to think about other things, rather than hold on to the negative, anxiety producing thoughts.

- *Take a deep breath:* Taking deep, slow breaths, focusing on taking air in through the nose and breathing out through the mouth can help you relax.

- *Learn a relaxation technique:* Meditation can slow the heart rate, lower blood pressure and improve focus. Mindfulness meditation involves gently re-directing oneself away from competing thoughts, such as exam stress, and focusing, instead, on the single thing, e.g., one's breathing. Progressive relaxation, tensing and then relaxing, one-by-one, every muscle from the toes to forehead distracts from anxiety.

A few students do not need to use any of these techniques or need to use only one of them. Many students, however, use several of these techniques at once, and still others use them all. The key to avoiding or minimizing stress is planning how you will deal with it well *before* the exam.

---

**PAUSE. THINK. ACT.** What will you do if you feel anxious before or during a law school exam? Which of the above techniques will you use? Why did you select the technique(s)?

### Getting "Unstuck"

Even students who are usually calm during exams or who have used one or more of the above techniques to calm themselves before an exam still get stuck during an exam. There are three keys to getting unstuck. First, you can use one of the above techniques to get yourself unstuck. The relaxation and meditation techniques, in particular, are effective tools for getting unstuck. Second, focus on the fact that each exam question is an opportunity. Consider only the exam question in front of you at the moment and avoid looking backwards at questions you already answered or looking forward at what is coming up ahead. Finally, set a time limit, say four minutes, to getting unstuck. If you cannot get unstuck in those four minutes, move on to the next issue or question. You are likely to do better on the current question or issue after you have been away from it for a while.

### Avoid the Crazy-Makers

In the minutes before the exam, try to avoid getting into a discussion of what you have learned or what will be on the exam. In the minutes after the exam, try to avoid torturing yourself with a post-mortem of what you and others wrote in your exam answers. Do your best, stay calm and remember, when it is all over, no one asks the lawyer who has just won a big case what grade she got in her contracts (or any other) class.

---

**PAUSE. THINK. ACT.** In light of what you have read in this chapter, what do you need to do to prepare for your upcoming examinations?

---

# Chapter 10

# Managing Law School Stress

When you experience law school stress, you should know that you are not alone. While nearly all law students regard law school as stimulating, most also experience it as stressful. If you feel stress during your first year in law school, you are in the majority. This discussion is not offered to scare you or to try to dissuade you from law school. The goal of this book is to give you a set of tools that will allow you to both enjoy and succeed in law school, and to help you understand the sources of law school stress and how you can better deal with them.

## Thinking *and* Feeling

Many students experience stress because of the emphasis on learning to think in a way that encourages or even requires students to ignore their passions, ideals, personal feelings and emotional reactions. This emphasis has the unintended effect of making students believe that their sense of justice, of right and wrong, is irrelevant. As a result, some students come to believe they have to sacrifice parts of themselves to do well in law school.

This belief is incorrect. Rather than striving to ignore your sense of justice, use your gut reactions to help you become a better law student and lawyer. There is no doubt that students who acknowledge their reactions, and even argue with judges' opinions in the cases they read, get higher law school grades than their peers who simply accept court assertions without question.

Similarly, try to convert those gut reactions into legal arguments; for example, in all bodies of law, fairness is an important public policy. If a rule or case will produce an unjust result, develop an argument that the rule or case either should not be applied or should be overruled.

## Adapting to Law School Teaching Methods

The nature of law school teaching produces stress. Students are on the spot in class, are expected to learn vicariously and, ultimately, must take much more responsibility for their own learning than they ever have taken in their lives. Moreover, most students are not told that they must learn vicariously or teach themselves. At the same time, there is a disconnect between the way many law school professors teach (which involves listening and speaking) and the way most law school professors test (which almost exclusively involves writing). Students must learn a good deal of material on their own, with little or no feedback, and figure out on their own how to improve, or suffer the consequence: poor grades. Add to that the reality that first year grades are critical, and students are often graded on a curve, and you can see how the first year of law school can easily turn into a stressful experience.

By reading this book, and adopting the strategies described in each chapter, you will know what to expect and you will learn not only how to teach yourself, but also how to get the help you need when you cannot learn vicariously or on your own.

## Adapting to Law School Testing Methods

Law school is an educational culture shock, particularly for students who attend law school right out of college. In many college courses, particularly those in the social science areas, much of the learning involves memorizing and much of the tests demand little more than regurgitation of learned material. In law school, students must memorize and be able to regurgitate even larger amounts of material, yet this regurgitation does not ensure even passing grades. Such knowledge, while essential to success on law school examinations and papers, is insufficient to achieve success, because law school exams and papers require *application* of the knowledge. By reading this book, you will develop an approach to learning that greatly increases the likelihood that you will develop those application skills.

Next, law school exams, particularly in the first year, emphasize and reward only one of the many skill sets required by lawyers — legal analysis — and usually only via demonstrating that skill in writing, in a highly structured, specialized manner. While lawyers agree that great lawyers are skilled at legal analysis, lawyers also agree that great lawyers possess many other skills. Take a look at the list below. The list is a partial statement of the skills commonly possessed by great lawyers.

- Strategic thinking
- Emotional intelligence
- Legal analysis
- Reading comprehension
- Impromptu public speaking
- Rehearsed public speaking
- Listening
- Empathy
- Workload management
- Factual investigation
- Questioning other people
- Brainstorming solutions to problems
- Selecting from among possible solutions to problems
- Negotiating
- Researching

- Helping people in conflict work out compromises
- Sound judgment
- Making connections with people
- Identifying connections among ideas
- Passion

It is easy to assume that, if you do not get grades that place you at the top of your law school class, you will not be a good lawyer. As the above list reveals, that assumption is false.

---

**PAUSE. THINK. ACT.** Which skills on this list do you already possess? Write down the reasons you believe these skills will make you a good lawyer. When you feel stressed or discouraged, look back at what you have written, to remind yourself that even if you are struggling with one skill, you have other valuable skills that you will be able to employ in the future.

---

Finally, law school exams and papers are much harder than college exams. Law school exams and papers demand significant skills, and the skills these exams and papers demand are ones many (perhaps most) students did not possess before they came to law school. On law school exams and papers, students must be able to identify previously unseen problems by type, draw analogies, apply rules and cases and predict outcomes in disputes their professors (experts in the subject area) have designed not to have obvious outcomes. To succeed in law school thus requires a willingness to work hard at challenging tasks, to persevere through the inevitable struggles and failures, and to view such struggles and failures as a necessary part of the learning process. By adopting a growth mindset and optimistic attribution style, as described in Chapter 2, you can respond to setbacks in a positive and constructive way.

## Adapting to the Law School Workload

Law school requires a significant amount of challenging work. Many students come to law school having succeeded in college without having had to work very hard. The difficulty of the work, combined with the quantity of work can be daunting. Many law students devote as much as 50 hours per week to their studies. For this reason, finding balance between school work and other interests is crucial, and developing the time management skills addressed throughout this book will improve the quality of your law student life. If you master the skills in this book, you will be the kind of student who works smarter, and is able to successfully manage the workload.

# Adapting to Law School Grading Policies

Law Schools attract high achievers. Many law school students are very competitive. Many are used to succeeding in their educational and other endeavors. Most quickly discover that all of their peers in law school also have always succeeded. Add to this that in many law schools, students are graded against each other, on a curve. This can cause students to isolate themselves or others, and to view learning as a competitive rather than collaborative process.

In addition, some employers give enormous weight to students' law school grades, which increases the grade pressure on students. This causes many students to constantly focus on how well they are doing in law school: rather than on their motivations for being in law school: to join the profession.

First, you should know that five years after students graduate, law school grades become irrelevant; clients do not chose their lawyers based on the lawyers' law school grades but, rather, based on their qualities as lawyers and as people. Many of the most rewarding jobs held by lawyers are much less grade-dependent. Moreover, law school grades, and higher salaries, do not correlate with happiness after graduation.

While there is no doubt that this book is designed to help students get good grades in law school, its ultimate purpose is to help students *learn well* in law school and for the rest of their lives. Remember what drew you to law school. Measure your performance by how well you have learned, and by what you will do with that learning in the future to meet your goals.

# Dealing with Stress

If you do find yourself feeling anxious or depressed, here are a few suggestions:

- **Avoid turning to alcohol or drugs for solace.** As I am sure you know, neither alcohol nor drugs will actually make you feel better, but both can cause considerable harm. If you do find yourself using alcohol or drugs inappropriately, please get help.

- **Do things that make you happy.** Sometimes you can get so caught up in the work of law school that you forget everything else. What did you like to do before law school — Read? Run? Binge watch a TV series? When is the last time you did something for pure enjoyment? If the answer is: before law school, it's probably time to bring some balance back into your life. Schedule time to do something that brings you joy or pleasure.

- **Find a healthy outlet.** Time with friends and family can be an excellent outlet for relieving stress. So can exercise.

- **Try Mindfulness.** Mindfulness practices can improve your well-being, and help you reduce worry and rumination, which can contribute to depression and anxiety. Websites like www.headspace.com can help you get started.

- **Avoid people who add to your anxiety or depression.** Some students act as if they prefer the feeling of stress. After every exam, they feel a need to discuss everything they believe you should have addressed, and they feel unconcerned about their effect on you or whether they may be wrong. Other students focus on what is bothering them and lose sight of the good things in their lives. Choose to be with people who choose to be happy.

- **Get help.** Do not simply assume that it's ok to be unhappy; most campuses have a student counseling center and have great expertise in helping students deal with these issues. You can also see the academic support person at your law school—they are usually a great resource.

- **Try meditation.** For some students, meditation can be a wonderful alternative to feeling stress.

- **Retrain your thinking.** As described in Chapter 2, you can train yourself to be an optimist by viewing bad events as temporary, as isolated to particular circumstances, and as something you can overcome by effort and your abilities. Dr. Martin Seligman's *Learned Optimism* is a wonderful resource that you can use to train yourself to adopt an optimistic attribution style, and to react differently to stressful events.

---

**PAUSE. THINK. ACT.** What will you do when you feel stressed? Which of the strategies described above do you think will work for you? What can you do now to reduce or eliminate potential sources of law school stress?

---

# Chapter 11

# A Chapter for the Family and Friends of Law Students

Law students: we encourage you to ask all the significant people in your lives to read this chapter—it will make your adjustment to law school and their adjustment to living with a law student much easier.

*Dean Schwartz co-authored this chapter with his wife, Dr. Stacey Hunter Schwartz. Stacey has particular expertise relevant to the matters discussed in this chapter. She has a Ph.D. in counseling psychology from the University of Southern California School of Education, and was a college dean. Stacey and Mike met while he was in law school, and they are still happily together today.[1]*

## Introduction

We have written this chapter solely for the significant people in law students' lives—their husbands, wives, partners, sons, daughters, parents, grandparents and others. Law school can be hard not only on law students, but also on the important people in law students' lives! We have written this chapter for you, the significant others of law students, because we would like the primary readers of this book, law students, to do well in law school without sacrificing their relationships with you. Law students do better in law school when they do not have to worry about their personal relationships. We also believe having a loved one in law school need not result in relationship strife but can, in fact, bring you closer. To achieve both these goals, you need to know more about what law students experience in law school, know how their experiences can alter your relationship, and know what you can do to use law school to strengthen what you have.

Almost everyone has heard or seen something that purports to explain what law school is like for new law students. The first year of law school has been depicted in movies, television shows, novels and other books. Many people also hear things about law school from family, friends and acquaintances, even from people who have never been to law school and have no idea what law school is really like. Many of these re-

---

1. Dr. Schwartz has granted express permission for the inclusion of her ideas in this book.

ports bear little resemblance to the modern law school experience, having been over-blown for dramatic purposes.

This chapter therefore begins by describing the law school process in a way that makes sense to non-law students, to people who really do not know what law students go through in law school and even for those who have some familiarity with law school but have not seen law school in its current form. The chapter explains law school by focusing on the five characteristic difficulties that first-year law students encounter: (1) the difficult and enormous workload required by law school, (2) their law professors' expectations, (3) the law schools' testing and grading practices, (4) the changes in how students think and analyze problems produced by law school, and (5) the stress produced by all these issues.

The chapter then addresses how these difficulties and other matters relating to law school can alter your relationship with the law student in your life and suggests what you can do to preserve and even strengthen your relationship.

# The Five Characteristic Difficulties Encountered by New Law Students

There is a reason why the first year of law school has been the focus of so much literary interest: the first year of law school is incredibly challenging and therefore emotionally difficult. Most law students experience their first year as the most difficult and stressful educational experience of their lives. In fact, it is that difficulty and stress that prompted me to write this book in the first place.

This section explains the things that make law school so hard, so famous and so much a trap for the fearful.

## Law School Workload

First-year law students take two types of courses. "Doctrinal" or "Casebook" courses focus on the law applicable to specific subject areas regarded as crucial, such as contract law, criminal law and constitutional law. The word doctrine, in fact, is a synonym for the "rules of law." "Skills" courses focus on teaching law students lawyering skills, such as legal research and legal writing. These labels, however, are somewhat misleading, because students learn law in their skills courses (because the students must research and use law in their legal writing papers), and students learn skills in their doctrinal classes (because success in doctrinal courses depends on students' ability to do legal reasoning, to be able to **apply** the legal rules the students are studying and not simply **know** the words of the rules).

While the focus and emphases of the two types of courses are different, both make huge time demands on law students. In fact, law students' workloads are considerably greater than the workloads of undergraduates or those attending many other, but not all, types of graduate schools. During the regular part of each semester of law school, law students are expected to devote three to four hours outside of class for every hour they are in class. Thus, a full-time law student taking a typical 15-unit class load, should be studying at least 45 hours per week and as many as 60 hours per week. In the weeks immediately before their examinations, those numbers get even higher.

Most law students do not find it difficult to fill the 45–60 hours. The law school reading load is quite heavy. For **each** of their doctrinal classes (full-time students typically take four such courses per semester whereas part-time students take two such courses per semester), students must read at least 60 pages and, sometimes, in excess of 100 pages per week. Moreover, the print in law school textbooks is tiny, and law school texts include almost no pictures, charts or graphs.

The reading is also very dense, particularly for new law students, who, because of their unfamiliarity with legal materials, must frequently use law dictionaries while they are reading. Students often compare the experience to learning a new language. The concepts addressed in these reading assignment are very difficult. Most students have to read their assignments multiple times to fully understand what they have read. In other words, legal materials cannot be read in the same way one might read a novel or newspaper; law students cannot skip or otherwise ignore the many unfamiliar words they encounter. Rather, law students must quickly become experts in this new language and become adept at using it.

Classroom experiences in doctrinal classes often do not help students increase their understanding. Many law students report that their classroom experiences often leave them more confused rather than less confused. Their professors assume the students have understood this difficult reading and focus on testing students' ability to evaluate and use what they have learned. The professors call on students individually and ask each selected student to apply what he or she has learned to a new legal problem. These new problems are difficult for new law students because the problems require the students to use materials with which they may not yet be comfortable, because the problems often do not have a clear, right answer, and because the problems require the students to use a skill, legal reasoning, that the students are still learning. Moreover, many law professors never let their students know whether they have correctly analyzed the problems. Instead, if a student seems to have correctly analyzed a problem, the professor asks the student to answer an even more challenging question.

In addition, most law professors, unlike college instructors, seldom lecture. Instead, they devote most of every class session to asking students questions about their reading material. Students must infer what they need to know from those discussions and from their peers' responses. This teaching technique is stressful on students, not in small part because most law students experience anxiety about being asked questions in front of 70 or so of their new peers. In fact, for some law students, the fear of being called upon next is so great that they have a hard time focusing on what their peers or the professor is saying.

The reading and classroom teaching for the legal research and writing courses tends to be more straightforward. The work, however, often proves at least as difficult and time consuming. For their legal research and writing courses (both full-time and part-time law students typically take one such course per semester), students must write multiple lengthy papers (as many as seven or eight ten-page papers in a 14-week semester), most of which require extensive research and highly technical citation and word processing formats. Legal research, while similar to other types of research, has its own, unique techniques and materials. One of the biggest challenges to new law students is that it can be difficult to know when one is finished researching. New legal researchers often have no choice but to stop researching even though they feel as if they would surely find the answer for which they are looking if they just searched a little longer. Even after they have finished their research, students must go back and check to make sure, for each source they have used in their papers, that the source has not been changed by a more recent statute or case. This process itself can be painstaking. Finally, excellent content is not enough; students must make sure their papers have flawless grammar, punctuation, paragraphing and word usage. Professors assume students have written and re-written their papers multiple times.

## Law Professors' Expectations

As the previous section suggests, law professors expect a great deal of their students. First, by choosing to use questions to teach the material and skills, law professors are assuming their students possess considerable and well-developed learning skills. In any given class, most professors ask questions of 6–10 students; in other words, law professors assume the other 50–90 students in the class can learn "vicariously" by watching their peers answer the questions. Second, they also assume their students can learn what they need to learn from the reading, on their own, outside of class. Finally, many law school instructors do not do much to teach the students the skills the students need to do well on their exams. Rather, they devote class discussions to questions of what lawyers call "policy." Policy refers to the reasons underlying the law, the reasons why courts and legislators enact one rule of law instead of another. Law professors, in effect, ask students to learn for themselves how to think like lawyers.

Law professors also expect students to prepare diligently for every class session. In college, many students do not prepare for class at all and do most of the course reading, if at all, only shortly before their examinations. Law students who fail to prepare for class not only are unable to learn what they need to learn during class, but also may get in trouble with their professors.

Finally, law professors expect their students to be able to memorize enormous quantities of information. Typically, students must memorize 40 or so pages of dense outlines for each of their courses. The students must develop these outlines on their own during the course of the semester, and students taking five classes must memorize four or five such outlines.

## Law School Testing and Grading Practices

*How are law students tested?* Law school final examinations are unique. To prepare themselves, law students, as noted above, must memorize an enormous amount of material in the short time before their examinations. At the same time, they must prepare themselves to deal with examinations that often are only vaguely connected to their classroom discussions. These examinations often are the only basis on which law professors assign grades for an entire semester's worth or even an entire year's worth of work. And the exams are hard. Law school exams almost always have no "right" answer and often last three or even four hours.

While law school classroom discussions often focus on "policy," most law school essay exam questions are unlike the classroom discussions and unlike, at least in some important aspects, anything the students will have to do when they become practicing lawyers. The exams are unlike the classroom discussions because the exams focus on the application of the rules and cases the class has studied to new hypothetical factual situations significantly unlike other factual situations they have studied over the course of the semester or year. Thus, classroom discussions often fail to prepare students for their final exams, and, even in courses where there is some congruity between the classroom discussion and the final examination, the actual final examination questions are nevertheless significantly different from the hypotheticals the students have discussed in class. Law professors justify this testing approach by asserting that they are assessing the extent to which their students are able to think under pressure and apply what they have learned.

Exam questions are unlike what lawyers do because the questions are often factually intricate in ways unlike law practice questions. Additionally, while many law practice problems are more complicated than law school exam questions, lawyers have three years of law school training before they actually have to deal with such questions and, in most instances, have the benefit of a supervisor to talk through the most challenging issues. Most significantly, practitioners have months or even years to fully think through law practice problems whereas law students have an hour or, at most, a day to analyze the legal issues on their examinations.

Finally, law school examinations are intellectually challenging. On most law school examinations, there is no "right" answer to the question; rather, students must determine the kinds of arguments lawyers who would handle such a dispute would be likely to make and must assess the persuasiveness of those arguments. This assessment is particularly difficult because law professors design their exams so that the likely result in the hypothetical dispute is unknown or at least uncertain, even to the professor! Thus, an excellent law school examination answer is not one that correctly decides who would win the hypothetical dispute described in the question, but, instead, one that makes plausible arguments for each of the parties described in the hypothetical. In fact, one of the most highly regarded books written about law school exams is called *Getting to Maybe*.[2] This title reflects the common law professor goal that the ultimate answer to a law school examination should be "maybe."

*How are law school examinations graded?* Law school grading is not really unusual; it is merely stingy. While most graduate students' grades are higher than their college grades, law students' grades typically are one-half to one full grade point lower. Consequently, law students, nearly all of whom excelled in college, are often stunned by their first set of law school grades. This result is particularly stunning to outside observers, because law schools get some of the very best college students. Thus, the competition for grades is very stiff. Some students who were "A students" in college must learn to feel proud of "C" grades.

Law school grades can be particularly confusing to law students. Law students often incorrectly predict their results on examinations. These predictive inaccuracies occur because law students assume that, if they felt the exam was easy, they must have done well, and, if they felt the exam was hard, they must have done poorly. In many instances, however, struggling with an exam reflects the fact that the student correctly perceived its actual difficulty, and a lack of struggle may reflect a failure to recognize the complexity and difficulty of the examination questions. Moreover, law students often assume that, if they have memorized the material perfectly, they are certain to do well on their examinations. However, as explained above, while law school examinations require excellent memorization, excellent grades on examinations depend on the extent to which the student's exam answer also reflects excellent, thoughtful analysis and convincing argumentation.

## How Law School Changes People

In general, all graduate school experiences change people. In fact, because of the changes wrought by graduate school, more than one-half of all marriages do not survive having one spouse obtain a graduate degree. Law school produces a particular set of changes that can be challenging to you.

First, law school causes students to become more analytical. Lawyers must be able to find flaws in their opponents' legal arguments. Law students learn this skill by criticizing court opinions and by having their professors criticize their arguments. This skill is like a newly-developed muscle for new law students; they often cannot help but flex their new critical skills in their interactions with their peers and significant others. You significant others, however, are unlikely to appreciate these critiques. Who would want someone in their lives to change from being kind and supportive to being critical?

Second, having been subjected to critical questioning and having witnessed it in all their classes, law students are more likely to question things they hear and read. They are less likely to accept matters at face value and more likely to insist that you

---

2. Michael Fischl & Jeremy Paul, Getting to Maybe (1999).

make sense to them. In their classes, their professors have insisted they understand the rationale underlying every court and legislative decision. This process causes some law students to search for rationales with equal vigilance in all aspects of their lives.

Third, in the competitive environment typical of law school, where higher grades lead to the more highly compensated (but not necessarily better) employment opportunities, many law students become highly competitive. The competition is invigorating for some law students but depressing and upsetting for others.

Finally, as the next section explains, for all the reasons detailed above and more, most law students experience considerable stress.

## Law School Stress

For all of the reasons discussed above, most law students experience considerable stress, particularly in their first year of law school. In particular, the difficulty and amount of work required, the pressure to succeed, the competitiveness of the law school environment, and the teaching methodology commonly used by law professors combine to produce a high level of stress. Considering also the high cost of graduate education and the students' and his or her loved ones' expectations, it is easy to see why law school puts great stress on law students' personal relationships. The key for loved ones is to recognize this fact, to try to be supportive, and to be forgiving.

# Challenges to Your Relationship and What You Can Do to Make Things Better

## Problems and Solutions Applicable to All Loved Ones

As you are reading this chapter, you may be doubting the decision your loved one made to go to law school. But you probably thought that it was a good idea for the student to go to law school at the time he or she applied. You also probably want to be supportive and certainly do not want to interfere with your law student's studies. But, what does being supportive really mean? This section explores the challenges you will be facing and suggests some solutions.

*Problems Caused by Not Understanding.* One major potential problem is not understanding all of the issues described above. Many law students have performed poorly in law school because they and their loved ones did not understand how law school changes things. They had no idea what the law students would experience, and, as a result, they put pressure on the law students to continue doing what the students did before law school. Struggling students often report that their loved ones expect them to devote the same amount of time and effort to familial obligations as they devoted prior to law school. The loved ones also put excessive pressure on the law students by expecting them to achieve the same grades in law school that the students had obtained in the past.

Your choice to read this chapter suggests you care about helping the law student in your life succeed. What you do with this information, however, remains completely within your control; you can act on this knowledge or ignore it. We hope, obviously, that knowing what to expect helps you not only accept what will be happening but also to find ways to be supportive.

***Problems Caused by Law Students' Lack of Time and Energy.*** Another problem is the dramatic decrease in time the student will be spending with you. Law students have little time and even less energy to devote to their relationships. Understanding this fact, however, does not replace what you have lost. You will find that the law student in your life will need to miss some family gatherings, such as holiday parties or Sunday dinners. The law student may fail to call on birthdays or other special occasions or to return phone calls for several weeks. Even when they do call, your law student may have little time to talk.

Recognizing these limitations, of course, does not equate to enjoying them. It does help to know, however, that law school is a three- or four-year experience, not a lifetime sentence. Law students' lack of time does not reflect a lack of priorities, but, rather, a shifting of priorities to meet new demands. Law students' lack of attentiveness does not reflect a lack of interest or caring, but only a lack of time and energy. There's nothing personal involved.

Instead of becoming angry, you can support the law student in your life by volunteering to take over or help with chores. Offer to act as a liaison to groups of friends or family so that the law student can maintain relationships with others without devoting time to communicating with them individually. Ask the law student in your life to name convenient times to discuss conflicts, to socialize with friends and family, or to perform necessary tasks. Most importantly, do not make your law student's lack of availability become an issue in your relationship. The law student in your life would rather be with you than study but must study. Don't try to induce guilt in students who may already feel guilty about their neglect of relationships.

Supportive family members and friends do not second-guess the amount of time the law student in their lives spends studying by saying things like, "You must have studied enough by now. Don't you think you're being obsessive? Exams are still several weeks away." They recognize that proper preparation takes a great deal of time and all semester- or year-long. Try offering to help by saying things like, "Would you like me to run through your contracts flashcards with you?"

***Problems Caused by Law Students' High Level of Stress.*** Competitive pressure, fatigue, deadlines, and performance anxiety all have the potential to put people in a bad mood. Try combining all these stressors for weeks on end! With such a combination of stressors, it is easy for law students to forget why they signed up for law school in the first place and, more significantly, there's some risk the law student in your life will take out her or his frustrations on you.

Supportive family members try not to let grumpy or even hostile comments from students bother them. Put the blame where it belongs — the pressure on the law students is to blame. (Of course, do not tolerate emotional or physical abuse.) Instead of being defensive and hurt if your law student acts grouchy, reframe his or her outbursts or depressive behavior by responding with remarks like, "I know that you're under a tremendous amount of stress right now. Please let me know tonight when might be a better time to talk to you." Ask, "What can I do to help?"

## Problems and Solutions Applicable to Spouses and Significant Others

Have you ever tried to be in a partnership with someone who does not pull his or her weight? If you measure your partner's participation in your relationship as you have done in the past, you have a formula for resentment. Instead, you will have to view law school studies as a project for your partnership. When you have taken out the umpteenth bag of trash or again have had to be the parent who helps your daughter with a school project, you may feel deserted. You will have to remind yourself that you wanted the person to go to law school in the first place, and you will have to remember the ultimate goal—a law school degree.

You may also resent all the time the law student spends with study group partners and even resent the bonds these students share. They are sharing a unique, emotional experience, and you are bound to feel like an outsider, maybe even jealous. Be sure to communicate these feelings to your spouse at an appropriate time in a calm, not accusatory manner. You want this experience to help your relationship grow, too, and expressing such feelings honestly can bring you closer together.

Consider productive alternatives to jealousy. Offer to make or buy dinner or lunch for the study group so you can meet and get to know everyone. While you are eating, ask the study group members about their lives and goals. But, when the meal is over, leave the room and let them get back to their studies.

As law school continues, so will your life. You will encounter your own challenges and joys. You may feel yourself slipping away emotionally from the ever-absent law student, and you may need to establish a support system for yourself. However, take care to include the law student in your important decisions and tell him or her about what is going on in your life, even if you have to schedule an appointment to do so.

## Conclusion

It is impossible, of course, to describe every challenge you and the law student in your life will face over the next few years. Relationships are often difficult, and law school makes things harder. At the same time, it also can make things better. The law student in your life is following a dream of bettering his or her life. Law school requires only three or four years; looking backward, we believe that you will regard your investment of time, effort and patience as an excellent one. Loved ones who support law students receive a level of appreciation you cannot now imagine, end up improving their relationships, and help the law students in their lives attain a better, richer life.

*If your loved one is a law student, you may want to think about these questions:*

1.  Why did the law student in your life decide to go to law school?

2.  Why do you want the law student in your life to go to law school?

3.  What are your normal expectations of the law student in your life in terms of daily chores, emotional support, time with you in person, phone calls to you, income, etc.? Which of these expectations are you willing to give up to support the law student in your life?

4.  What are you willing to do to support the law student in your life?

*You may also want to read the following resources:*

Lawrence S. Krieger, *What We're Not Telling Law Students—And Lawyers—That They Really Need to Know: Some Thoughts Toward Revitalizing the Profession from Its Roots*, 13 J. L. & HEALTH 1 (1999).

Bridget A. Mahoney, *Distress Among the Legal Profession: What Law Schools Can Do About It*, 15 NOTRE DAME J.L. ETHICS & PUB. POL. 307 (2001).

*Making Docile Lawyers: An Essay on the Pacification of Law Students*, 111 HARV. L. REV. 2027 (1998).

Cathleen A. Roach, *A River Runs Through It: Tapping into the Information Stream to Move Students from Isolation to Autonomy*, 36 ARIZ. L. REV. 667 (1994).

# Appendix A

# Answers to Exercise 2-1

The correct answers are shown in the table below. The following answers are debatable:

2-1.1 might also be classified as implicating memorization, organization and problem-solving (because students, ultimately, will have to organize and memorize what they learn from these cases and then use that information to solve the problems on their examination).

2-1.2 arguably also implicates organization because students will have to organize the results of their legal research.

| Question No. | Course | Week | Topic(s) | Assignment | Learning Tasks Implicated (check each task implicated) |
|---|---|---|---|---|---|
| 2-1.1 | Contracts | Week 5 | Damages for Breach of Contract | *Hawkins* (pp. 3–7); *Sullivan* (pp. 7–8); *Groves* (pp. 11–18); Peevyhouse (pp. 19–22); Johnson (pp. 22–25); Dix Construction (pp. 36–39) | ✓ Reading Comprehension<br>☐ Research<br>✓ Synthesis<br>☐ Problem Solving<br>☐ Memorization<br>☐ Organization<br>✓ Concept Learning<br>✓ Principle Learning<br>☐ Legal Writing |
| 2-1.2 | Legal Research and Writing | Week 7 | Objective Memorandum | Research the issues raised in the client letter distributed in class and prepare an objective memo analyzing the issues | ✓ Reading Comprehension<br>✓ Research<br>✓ Synthesis<br>✓ Problem Solving<br>☐ Memorization<br>☐ Organization<br>✓ Concept Learning<br>✓ Principle Learning<br>✓ Legal Writing |
| 2-1.3 | Torts | Week 15 | Final Examination | None | ☐ Reading Comprehension<br>☐ Research<br>☐ Synthesis<br>✓ Problem Solving<br>✓ Memorization<br>✓ Organization<br>✓ Concept Learning<br>✓ Principle Learning<br>☐ Legal Writing |

# Appendix B

# Michael Hunter Schwartz & Adrian J. Walters, *Contracts: A Context and Practice Casebook* 316–22 (2d ed. 2015)

This appendix contains a sample reading assignment in the form of a portion of the table of contents and selected pages from CONTRACTS, A CONTEXT AND PRACTICE CASEBOOK, SECOND EDITION. The pages for the assignment are highlighted in the table of contents.

# Contracts

*A Context and Practice Casebook*

SECOND EDITION

**Michael Hunter Schwartz**
William H. Bowen School of Law
University of Arkansas at Little Rock

**Adrian Walters**
IIT Chicago-Kent College of Law

CAROLINA ACADEMIC PRESS
Durham, North Carolina

---

# Contents

CONTENTS

CONTENTS

2. Assume that, at the time the county first repudiated the contract, Luten Bridge had already entered into subcontracts under which it would be liable for breach of contract if it refused to go forward. Assume also that Luten Bridge could not fully predict how much it would have to pay in damages to those subcontractors if it were to repudiate those contracts. If Luten Bridge determined that the cost of finishing the bridge would only be a thousand dollars more than it would have to pay in damages to the subcontractors, could Luten Bridge recover the full contract price if it finished the bridge?

### Exercise 6-12: *Parker*

The next case, *Parker v. Twentieth Century-Fox Film Corp.*, also address the avoidability rule. *Parker* involves an employment contract in a specialized field, movie making, and involves a famous actress (although you will not see her screen name in the opinion). As you read the case, consider the following:

1. The starting point for an award of benefit-of-the-bargain damages in the employment context is the full contract price, not a FMV-contract price differential. Why?

2. Explain the sense in which the case involves an application of the avoidability rule.

3. The *Parker* court states and relies on a specific avoidability rule. What is that rule?

4. The dissenting opinion in *Parker* seems to criticize at least part of the majority's analysis as too superficial.

a. Which aspect of the majority's analysis is superficial? In other words, what step of applying rules did the majority omit?

b. Develop a proper analysis of your own. Your analysis should include identifying each difference between the two offers of employment and arguing why each difference is legally significant.

## Parker v. Twentieth Century-Fox Film Corp.

### 3 Cal. 3d 176, 474 P.2d 689 (1970)

Burke, Justice. Defendant Twentieth Century-Fox Film Corporation appeals from a summary judgment granting to plaintiff the recovery of agreed compensation under a written contract for her services as an actress in a motion picture. As will appear, we have concluded that the trial court correctly ruled in plaintiff's favor and that the judgment should be affirmed.

Plaintiff is well known as an actress, and in the contract between plaintiff and defendant is sometimes referred to as the "Artist." Under the contract, dated August 6, 1965, plaintiff was to play the female lead in defendant's contemplated production of a motion picture entitled "Bloomer Girl." The contract provided that defendant would pay plaintiff a minimum "guaranteed

6 · CONTRACT DAMAGES　　　　317

compensation" of $53,571.42 per week for 14 weeks commencing May 23, 1966, for a total of $750,000. Prior to May 1966 defendant decided not to produce the picture and by a letter dated April 4, 1966, it notified plaintiff of that decision and that it would not "comply with our obligations to you under" the written contract.

By the same letter and with the professed purpose "to avoid any damage to you," defendant instead offered to employ plaintiff as the leading actress in another film tentatively entitled "Big Country, Big Man" (hereinafter, "Big Country"). The compensation offered was identical, as were 31 of the 34 numbered provisions or articles of the original contract.[1] Unlike "Bloomer Girl," however, which was to have been a musical production, "Big Country" was a dramatic "western type" movie. "Bloomer Girl" was to have been filmed in California; "Big Country" was to be produced in Australia. Also, certain terms in the proffered contract varied from those of the original.[2] Plaintiff was given one week within which to accept; she did not and the offer lapsed. Plaintiff then commenced this action seeking recovery of the agreed guaranteed compensation.

The complaint sets forth two causes of action. The first is for money due under the contract; the second, based upon the same allegations as the first, is for damages resulting from defendant's breach of contract. Defendant in its answer admits the existence and validity of the contract, that plaintiff complied with all the conditions, covenants and promises and stood ready to complete the performance, and that defendant breached and "anticipatorily repudiated" the contract. It denies, however, that any money is due to plaintiff either under the contract or as a result of its breach, and pleads as an af-

---

1. Among the identical provisions was the following found in the last paragraph of Article 2 of the original contract: "We (defendant) shall not be obligated to utilize your (plaintiff's) services in or in connection with the Photoplay hereunder, our sole obligation, subject to the terms and conditions of this Agreement, being to pay you the guaranteed compensation herein provided for."

2. Article 29 of the original contract specified that plaintiff approved the director already chosen for "Bloomer Girl" and that in case he failed to act as director plaintiff was to have approval rights of any substitute director. Article 31 provided that plaintiff was to have the right of approval of the "Bloomer Girl" dance director, and Article 32 gave her the right of approval of the screenplay. Defendant's letter of April 4 to plaintiff, which contained both defendant's notice of breach of the "Bloomer Girl" contract and offer of the lead in "Big Country," eliminated or impaired each of those rights. It read in part as follows:

> The terms and conditions of our offer of employment are identical to those set forth in the "Bloomer Girl" Agreement, Articles 1 through 34 and Exhibit A to the Agreement, except as follows:
>
> 1. Article 31 of said Agreement will not be included in any contract of employment regarding "Big Country, Big Man" as it is not a musical and it thus will not need a dance director.
>
> 2. In the "Bloomer Girl" agreement, in Articles 29 and 32, you were given certain director and screenplay approvals and you had preapproved certain matters. Since there simply is insufficient time to negotiate with you regarding your choice of director and regarding the screenplay and since you already expressed an interest in performing the role in "Big Country, Big Man," we must exclude from our offer of employment in "Big Country, Big Man" any approval rights as are contained in said Articles 29 and 32; however, we shall consult with you respecting the director to be selected to direct the photoplay and will further consult with you with respect to the screenplay and any revisions or changes therein, provided, however, that if we fail to agree ... the decision of ... (defendant) with respect to the selection of a director and to revisions and changes in the said screenplay shall be binding upon the parties to said agreement.

firmative defense to both causes of action plaintiff's allegedly deliberate failure to mitigate damages, asserting that she unreasonably refused to accept its offer of the leading role in "Big Country."

Plaintiff moved for summary judgment under Code of Civil Procedure section 437c, the motion was granted, and summary judgment for $750,000 plus interest was entered in plaintiff's favor. This appeal by defendant followed.

The familiar rules are that the matter to be determined by the trial court on a motion for summary judgment is whether facts have been presented which give rise to a triable factual issue. The court may not pass upon the issue itself. Summary judgment is proper only if the affidavits or declarations in support of the moving party would be sufficient to sustain a judgment in his favor and his opponent does not by affidavit show facts sufficient to present a triable issue of fact. The affidavits of the moving party are strictly construed, and doubts as to the propriety of summary judgment should be resolved against granting the motion. Such summary procedure is drastic and should be used with caution so that it does not become a substitute for the open trial method of determining facts. The moving party cannot depend upon allegations in his own pleadings to cure deficient affidavits, nor can his adversary rely upon his own pleadings in lieu or in support of affidavits in opposition to a motion; however, a party can rely on his adversary's pleadings to establish facts not contained in his own affidavits. [Citation omitted.] Also, the court may consider facts stipulated to by the parties and facts which are properly the subject of judicial notice. [Citations omitted.]

As stated, defendant's sole defense to this action which resulted from its deliberate breach of contract is that in rejecting defendant's substitute offer of employment plaintiff unreasonably refused to mitigate damages.

The general rule is that the measure of recovery by a wrongfully discharged employee is the amount of salary agreed upon for the period of service, less the amount which the employer affirmatively proves the employee has earned or with reasonable effort might have earned from other employment.[4] [Citations omitted.] However, before projected earnings from other employment opportunities not sought or accepted by the discharged employee can be applied in mitigation, the employer must show that the other employment was comparable, or substantially similar, to that of which the employee has been deprived; the employee's rejection of or failure to seek other available employment of a different or inferior kind may not be resorted to in order to mitigate damages. [Citations omitted.]

In the present case defendant has raised no issue of reasonableness of efforts by plaintiff to obtain other employment; the sole issue is whether plaintiff's refusal of defendant's substitute offer of "Big Country" may be used in mitigation. Nor, if the "Big Country" offer was of employment different or inferior when compared with the original "Bloomer Girl" employment, is there an issue as to whether or not plaintiff acted reasonably in refusing the substitute offer. Despite defendant's arguments to the contrary, no case cited or

---

4. Although it would appear that plaintiff was not discharged by defendant in the customary sense of the term, as she was not permitted by defendant to enter upon performance of the "Bloomer Girl" contract, nevertheless the motion for summary judgment was submitted for decision upon a stipulation by the parties that "plaintiff Parker was discharged."

which our research has discovered holds or suggests that reasonableness is an element of a wrongfully discharged employee's option to reject, or fail to seek, different or inferior employment lest the possible earnings therefrom be charged against him in mitigation of damages.[5]

Applying the foregoing rules to the record in the present case, with all intendments in favor of the party opposing the summary judgment motion—here, defendant—it is clear that the trial court correctly ruled that plaintiff's failure to accept defendant's tendered substitute employment could not be applied in mitigation of damages because the offer of the "Big Country" lead was of employment both different and inferior, and that no factual dispute was presented on that issue. The mere circumstance that "Bloomer Girl" was to be a musical review calling upon plaintiff's talents as a dancer as well as an actress, and was to be produced in the City of Los Angeles, whereas "Big Country" was a straight dramatic role in a "Western Type" story taking place in an opal mine in Australia, demonstrates the difference in kind between the two employments; the female lead as a dramatic actress in a western style motion picture can by no stretch of imagination be considered the equivalent of or substantially similar to the lead in a song-and-dance production.

Additionally, the substitute "Big Country" offer proposed to eliminate or impair the director and screenplay approvals accorded to plaintiff under the original "Bloomer Girl" contract, and thus constituted an offer of inferior employment. No expertise or judicial notice is required in order to hold that the deprivation or infringement of an employee's rights held under an original employment contract converts the available "other employment" relied upon by the employer to mitigate damages, into inferior employment which the employee need not seek or accept. [Citation omitted.]

Statements found in affidavits submitted by defendant in opposition to plaintiff's summary judgment motion, to the effect that the "Big Country" offer was not of employment different from or inferior to that under the "Bloomer Girl" contract, merely repeat the allegations of defendant's answer to the complaint in this action, constitute only conclusionary assertions with respect to undisputed facts, and do not give rise to a triable factual issue so as to defeat the motion for summary judgment. [Citations omitted.]

In view of the determination that defendant failed to present any facts showing the existence of a factual issue with respect to its sole defense—plaintiff's rejection of its substitute employment offer in mitigation of damages—we need not consider plaintiff's further contention that for various reasons, including the provisions of the original contract set forth in footnote 1, ante, plaintiff was excused from attempting to mitigate damages.

---

5. Instead, in each case the reasonableness referred to was that of the efforts of the employee to obtain other employment that was not different or inferior; his right to reject the latter was declared as an unqualified rule of law. Thus, *Gonzales v. Internat. Assn. of Machinists, supra,* 213 Cal. App. 2d 817, 823–24, 29 Cal. Rptr. 190, 194, holds that the trial court correctly instructed the jury that plaintiff union member, a machinist, was required to make "such *efforts* as the average (member of his union) desiring employment would make at that particular time and place" (italics added); but, further, that the court *properly rejected* defendant's *offer of proof of the availability of other kinds of employment* at the same or higher pay than plaintiff usually received and all outside the jurisdiction of his union, as plaintiff could not be required to accept different employment or a nonunion job....

The judgment is affirmed.

Sullivan, Acting Chief Justice (dissenting). The basic question in this case is whether or not plaintiff acted reasonably in rejecting defendant's offer of alternate employment. The answer depends upon whether that offer (starring in "Big Country, Big Man") was an offer of work that was substantially similar to her former employment (starring in "Bloomer Girl") or of work that was of a different or inferior kind. To my mind this is a factual issue which the trial court should not have determined on a motion for summary judgment. The majority have not only repeated this error but have compounded it by applying the rules governing mitigation of damages in the employer-employee context in a misleading fashion. Accordingly, I respectfully dissent.

The familiar rule requiring a plaintiff in a tort or contract action to mitigate damages embodies notions of fairness and socially responsible behavior which are fundamental to our jurisprudence. Most broadly stated, it precludes the recovery of damages which, through the exercise of due diligence, could have been avoided. Thus, in essence, it is a rule requiring reasonable conduct in commercial affairs. This general principle governs the obligations of an employee after his employer has wrongfully repudiated or terminated the employment contract. Rather than permitting the employee simply to remain idle during the balance of the contract period, the law requires him to make a reasonable effort to secure other employment.[1] He is not obliged, however, to seek or accept any and all types of work which may be available. Only work which is in the same field and which is of the same quality need be accepted.[2]

Over the years the courts have employed various phrases to define the type of employment which the employee, upon his wrongful discharge, is under an obligation to accept. Thus in California alone it has been held that he must accept employment which is "substantially similar" (citations omitted); employment "in the same general line of the first employment," [citation omitted]; "equivalent to his prior position" [citation omitted]; "employment in a similar capacity," [citations omitted]; employment which is "not ... of a different or inferior kind." [Citation omitted.]

For reasons which are unexplained, the majority cite several of these cases yet select from among the various judicial formulations which contain one particular phrase, "Not of a different or inferior kind," with which to analyze this case. I have discovered no historical or theoretical reason to adopt this phrase, which is simply a negative restatement of the affirmative standards set out in the above cases, as the exclusive standard. Indeed, its emergence is an exam-

---

1. The issue is generally discussed in terms of a duty on the part of the employee to minimize loss. The practice is long-established and there is little reason to change despite Judge Cardozo's observation of its subtle inaccuracy. "The servant is free to accept employment or reject it according to his uncensored pleasure. What is meant by the supposed duty is merely this: That if he unreasonably reject, he will not be heard to say that the loss of wages from then on shall be deemed the jural consequence of the earlier discharge. He has broken the chain of causation, and loss resulting to him thereafter is suffered through his own act." *McClelland v. Climax Hosiery Mills* (1930) 252 N.Y. 347, 359, 169 N.E. 605, 609 (concurring).

2. This qualification of the rule seems to reflect the simple and humane attitude that it is too severe to demand of a person that he attempt to find and perform work for which he has no training or experience. Many of the older cases hold that one need not accept work in an inferior rank or position nor work which is more menial or arduous. This suggests that the rule may have had its origin in the bourgeois fear of resubmergence in lower economic classes.

ple of the dubious phenomenon of the law responding not to rational judicial choice or changing social conditions, but to unrecognized changes in the language of opinions or legal treatises. However, the phrase is a serviceable one and my concern is not with its use as the standard but rather with what I consider its distortion.

The relevant language excuses acceptance only of employment which is of a different kind. [Citations omitted.] It has never been the law that the mere existence of differences between two jobs in the same field is sufficient, as a matter of law, to excuse an employee wrongfully discharged from one from accepting the other in order to mitigate damages. Such an approach would effectively eliminate any obligation of an employee to attempt to minimize damage arising from a wrongful discharge. The only alternative job offer an employee would be required to accept would be an offer of his former job by his former employer.

Although the majority appear to hold that there was a difference "in kind" between the employment offered plaintiff in "Bloomer Girl" and that offered in "Big Country" (opn. at p. 10), an examination of the opinion makes crystal clear that the majority merely point out differences between the two films (an obvious circumstance) and then apodictically assert that these constitute a difference in the kind of employment. The entire rationale of the majority boils down to this: that the "mere circumstances" that "Bloomer Girl" was to be a musical revue while "Big Country" was a straight drama "demonstrates the difference in kind" since a female lead in a western is not "the equivalent of or substantially similar to" a lead in a musical. This is merely attempting to prove the proposition by repeating it. It shows that the vehicles for the display of the star's talents are different but it does not prove that her employment as a star in such vehicles is of necessity different in kind and either inferior or superior.

I believe that the approach taken by the majority (a superficial listing of differences with no attempt to assess their significance) may subvert a valuable legal doctrine.[5] The inquiry in cases such as this should not be whether differences between the two jobs exist (there will always be differences) but whether the differences which are present are substantial enough to constitute differences in the kind of employment or, alternatively, whether they render the substitute work employment of an inferior kind.

It seems to me that this inquiry involves, in the instant case at least, factual determinations which are improper on a motion for summary judgment. Resolving whether or not one job is substantially similar to another or whether, on the other hand, it is of a different or inferior kind, will often (as here) require a critical appraisal of the similarities and differences between them in light of the importance of these differences to the employee. This necessitates a weighing of the evidence, and it is precisely this undertaking which is forbidden on summary judgment. [Citation omitted.]

---

5. The values of the doctrine of mitigation of damages in this context are that it minimizes the unnecessary personal and social (*e.g.*, nonproductive use of labor, litigation) costs of contractual failure. If a wrongfully discharged employee can, through his own action and without suffering financial or psychological loss in the process, reduce the damages accruing from the breach of contract, the most sensible policy is to require him to do so. I fear the majority opinion will encourage precisely opposite conduct.

This is not to say that summary judgment would never be available in an action by an employee in which the employer raises the defense of failure to mitigate damages. No case has come to my attention, however, in which summary judgment has been granted on the issue of whether an employee was obliged to accept available alternate employment. Nevertheless, there may well be cases in which the substitute employment is so manifestly of a dissimilar or inferior sort, the declarations of the plaintiff so complete and those of the defendant so conclusionary and inadequate that no factual issues exist for which a trial is required. This, however, is not such a case.

It is not intuitively obvious, to me at least, that the leading female role in a dramatic motion picture is a radically different endeavor from the leading female role in a musical comedy film. Nor is it plain to me that the rather qualified rights of director and screenplay approval contained in the first contract are highly significant matters either in the entertainment industry in general or to this plaintiff in particular....

I cannot accept the proposition that an offer which eliminates any contract right, regardless of its significance, is, as a matter of law, an offer of employment of an inferior kind. Such an absolute rule seems no more sensible than the majority's earlier suggestion that the mere existence of differences between two jobs is sufficient to render them employment of different kinds. Application of such per se rules will severely undermine the principle of mitigation of damages in the employer-employee context.

I remain convinced that the relevant question in such cases is whether or not a particular contract provision is so significant that its omission create employment of an inferior kind. This question is, of course, intimately bound up in what I consider the ultimate issue: whether or not the employee acted reasonably. This will generally involve a factual inquiry to ascertain the importance of the particular contract term and a process of weighing the absence of that term against the countervailing advantages of the alternate employment. In the typical case, this will mean that summary judgment must be withheld.

In the instant case, there was nothing properly before the trial court by which the importance of the approval rights could be ascertained, much less evaluated. Thus, in order to grant the motion for summary judgment, the trial court misused judicial notice. In upholding the summary judgment, the majority here rely upon per se rules which distort the process of determining whether or not an employee is obliged to accept particular employment in mitigation of damages.

I believe that the judgment should be reversed so that the issue of whether or not the offer of the lead role in "Big Country, Big Man" was of employment comparable to that of the lead role in "Bloomer Girl" may be determined at trial....

---

### Exercise 6-13: *Parker* Revisited

1. Imagine you are a lawyer for Twentieth Century-Fox. The president of the company informs you that the company has decided not to produce "Bloomer Girl" notwithstanding its contract with MacLaine. The company has not yet

# Appendix C

# Jeffrey Ferriell, *Understanding Contracts* 572–74 (4th ed. 2018)*

## §[A] MITIGATION IN EMPLOYMENT CONTRACTS[178]

The mitigation principle applies with equal force in employment contracts. To recover for her lost salary, a wrongfully discharged employee must make reasonable efforts to pursue alternative employment of a substantially similar character.[179] Sums spent in seeking alternative employment are recoverable.[180] Amounts that the employee could have earned in a job of similar character are deducted from the damages if the substitute work is refused. On the other hand, the employee does not have to accept employment of a different or inferior character.

This point is illustrated by the well-known decision in Parker v. Twentieth Century-Fox Film Corp.[181] The plaintiff, better known as the actor Shirley MacLaine, was discharged from her contract to star in a movie musical *Bloomer Girl*. She later turned down the lead in the Western drama *Big Country, Big Man* and sued to recover the salary she had been promised for appearing in *Bloomer Girl*. The court determined that playing the female lead in a dramatic Western was inferior as a matter of law to her lead role in the musical review for which she had been originally engaged. MacLaine, the court ruled, was entitled to the $750,000 salary she had been promised.[182] As those familiar with her career know, several years later MacLaine played the "different and inferior" lead female role in the Western drama, *Two Mules for Sister Sara*, co-starring Clint Eastwood.

While the differences between the two types of roles would not seem to warrant the California court's conclusion, other differences, such as MacLaine's discretionary rights over both the script and the director in *Bloomer Girl*, as well as the strong like-

---

178. Mary Joe Frug, *Re-Reading Contracts: A Feminist Analysis of a Contracts Casebook*, 34 Am. U. L. Rev. 1065, 1114–25 (1985); Victor P. Goldberg, *Bloomer Girl Revisited or How to Frame an Unmade Picture*, 1998 Wis. L Rev. 1051; Richard J. Gonzalez, *Satisfying the Duty to Mitigate in Employment Cases: A Survey and Guide*, 69 Miss. L.J. 749 (1999).

179. Lee v. Scotia Prince Cruises Ltd., 828 A.2d 210 (Me. 2003).

180. *E.g.*, Mr. Eddie, Inc. v. Ginsberg, 430 S.W.2d 5 (Tex. Civ. App. 1968). See Restatement (Second) of Contracts § 347 cmt. c & illus. 3 (1981).

181. 474 P.2d 689 (Cal. 1970).

182. These were 1966 dollars. Adjusted for inflation, her salary would have been approximately $5 1/2 million in 2017.

lihood that the movie was loosely based on the life of a Civil War-era women's rights activist,[183] may justify the result.[184]

In cases involving other discharged employees, courts have ruled that alternative employment as a teacher is not an adequate substitute for a job as a school principal, even though the salary is the same.[185] Likewise, working as a kitchen manager in a restaurant, which involves physical labor, is different and inferior to work as a general restaurant manager, which involves different duties.[186]

Wrongfully discharged employees are also required to make a reasonably diligent effort to secure another job. For example, a college teacher who delayed her effort to find a new teaching position, and who even then did little more than check the local classified ads, without seeking the assistance of an employment agency or submitting her résumé to available trade journals, was precluded from receiving her lost wages, even though the employer had not proven the availability of alternative employment.[187] A discharged employee who makes no reasonable effort to secure alternative employment cannot recover his or her lost wages, even if he or she removed herself from the labor market for personal reasons.[188] However, an employee is not required to look for or accept even substantially similar employment in a geographically distant location.[189]

Amounts the employee could have earned are deducted only to the extent that the alternative available employment was incompatible with performance under the contract in question. In *Soules v. Independent School District No. 518*,[190] a teacher who was wrongfully discharged from her part-time position, and subsequently turned down a full-time teaching job for less pay, lost only one-half of the salary from the alternative job, because only half of it was incompatible with her part-time position with the school district that fired her.[191]

Amounts an employee actually earned are deducted from his or her damages, provided that the person could not have reasonably held both jobs simultaneously.[192] Such earnings are deducted even if the alternative employment requires duties com-

---

183. *See* Mary Joe Frug, RE-READING CONTRACTS: A FEMINIST ANALYSIS OF A CONTRACTS CASEBOOK, 34 AM. U.L. REV. 1065, 1114–25 (1985).

184. *See also* Victor P. Goldberg, *Bloomer Girl Revisited or How to Frame an Unmade Picture*, 1998 WIS. L. REV. 1051 (regarding the "pay-or-play" clause in the *Bloomer Girl* contract)

185. *E.g.*, Williams v. Albemarle City Bd. of Educ., 508 F.2d 1242 (4th Cir. 1974).

186. Feges v. Perkins Rests., Inc., 483 N.W.2d 701, 709 (Minn. 1992).

187. Sellers v. Delgado Coll., 902 F.2d 1189 (5th Cir. 1990).

188. Miller v. Marsh, 766 F.2d 490 (11th Cir. 1985). *But see* Thorkildson v. Ins. Co. of N. Am., Co., 631 F. Supp. 372 (D. Minn. 1986).

189. Hadra v. Herman Blum Consulting Eng'rs, 632 F.2d 1242, 1246 (5th Cir. 1980); Hubbard Broad., Inc. v. Loescher, 291 N.W.2d 216 (Minn. 1980); Punkar v. King Plastic Corp., 290 So. 2d 505 (Fla. Dist. Ct. App. 1974); William H. Danne Jr., Annotation, *Nature of Alternative Employment Which Employee Must Accept to Minimize Damages for Wrongful Discharge*, 44 A.L.R.3d 629 (1972).

190. 258 N.W.2d 103 (Minn. 1977).

191. *See also* Marshall v. Mardels, Inc., 1978 U.S. Dist. LEXIS 16565 (E.D.N.Y. July 17, 1978).

192. *E.g.*, Marshall Sch. Dist. v. Hill, 939 S.W.2d 319 (Ark. Ct. App. 1997).

pletely different from or inferior to those in the contract with the defendant.[193] After all, dollars actually received are perfect substitutes from those promised by the breaching employer. Thus, an employee who takes a different or inferior job must deduct her earnings from the damages she can recover in her "wrongful discharge" suit against her former employer.[194]

Government benefits, such as unemployment compensation and social security benefits, have received disparate treatment.[195] Some courts have reduced the injured employee's damages by the amount of any unemployment compensation benefits the employee received.[196] However, Social Security disability[197] and retirement benefits[198] have been treated differently because, unlike unemployment benefits, the employer's contribution to Social Security is not affected by the number of claims made by its employees.[199] The distinction has also been based on the greater likelihood of a windfall to the employee if amounts received as unemployment compensation are not deducted from the recovery.[200]

When an employee breaches, the employer must take reasonable steps to seek and employ someone to provide the services that were to have been performed by the breaching employee. The fact that the substitute had better qualifications than the breaching employee does not impair the employer's ability to recover for the additional salary that had to be paid to the substitute, where the employer has taken reasonable steps to hire someone with qualifications that are comparable to those of the employee who left.[201] Employers who fail to make reasonable efforts to find a substitute are unable to recover for losses they claim to have suffered as a result of the breaching employee's premature departure.

---

193. S. Keswick, Inc. v. Whetherholt, 293 So. 2d 109 (Fla. Dist. Ct. App. 1974).

194. *Id.*; Marshall Sch. Dist. v. Hill, 939 S.W.2d 319 (Ark. Ct. App. 1997).

195. *See generally* John G. Fleming, *The Collateral Source Rule and Contract Damages*, 71 Calif. L. Rev. 56 (1983).

196. Corl v. Huron Castings, Inc., 544 N.W.2d 278 (Mich. 1996). *Accord* Masterson v. Boliden-Allis, Inc., 865 P.2d 1031 (Kan. Ct. App. 1993).

197. Seibel v. Liberty Homes, Inc., 752 P.2d 291 (Or. 1988).

198. Filter v. City of Vernonia, 770 P.2d 83 (Or. 1989); State ex rel. Stacy v. Batavia Local Sch. Dist. Bd. of Educ., 829 N.E.2d 298 (Ohio 2005).

199. Filter v. City of Vernonia, 770 P.2d 83 (Or. 1989).

200. *Id.*; Dehnart v. Waukesha Brewing Co., 124 N.W.2d 664 (Wis. 1962).

201. *E.g.*, Handicapped Children's Educ. Bd. v. Lukaszewski, 332 N.W.2d 774 (Wis. 1983).

# Appendix D

# Answers to Chapter 5 Case Brief Matching Exercise

Parker (Plaintiff/Appellee/Actress-Employee); Twentieth Century Fox Corp. (Defendant/Appellant/Movie Studio-Employer)

Parker (Plaintiff/Appellee/Employee) filed suit for breach of contract. Plaintiff moved for summary judgment. The motion was granted and the lower court awarded Parker a judgment in the amount of the agreed compensation under her written contract with Twentieth Century Fox Corp. (Defendant/Appellant/Employer); Defendant appealed. Appellate court concluded trial court correctly ruled in plaintiff's favor. Lower court judgment affirmed.

[T]he measure of recovery by a wrongfully discharged employee is the amount of salary agreed upon for the period of service, less the amount which the employer affirmatively proves the employee has earned or with reasonable effort might have earned from other employment. However, before projected earnings from other employment opportunities not sought or accepted by the discharged employee can be applied in mitigation, the employer must show that the other employment was comparable, or substantially similar, to that of which the employee has been deprived; the employee's rejection of or failure to seek other available employment of a different or inferior kind may not be resorted to in order to mitigate damages.

**Heading**

**Parties**

**Procedural History**

**Facts**

**Question Presented**

**Holding**

**Rule**

**Reasoning**

Parker is entitled to summary judgment and award of her guaranteed compensation because she did not have to mitigate her damages by accepting Defendant's offer for a role in a different movie genre, filmed in a different location, which impaired or eliminated her rights to director and screen play approval because that offer was different and inferior to the original offer.

Where an employer breaches an employment contract, the employee will be entitled to the amount she would have earned under the contract, minus the amount the employer proves she could have made from other comparable or substantially similar employment. An employee does not have to accept a different or inferior offer of employment to mitigate her damages under an employment contract when the employer breaches that contract.

Whether Plaintiff employee's damages from Defendant-employer's breach of contract should be reduced because Defendant-employer's substitute offer of employment for a role in a movie of a different genre, which was to be filmed in a different location was comparable or substantially similar to the role offered to the Plaintiff-employee in the employment contract such that Plaintiff's refusal to accept the new offer was an unreasonable refusal to mitigate her damages.

A straight dramatic role in a western taking place in an opal mine, to be filmed in Australia is not the equivalent of or substantially similar to the lead in a song and dance production, to be filmed in Los Angeles and calling on the actress' talents as a dancer. And an offer eliminating or impairing director and screenplay approvals is inferior. Since the substitute role was different and inferior, Parker is not required to accept it to mitigate her damages. It would be unfair to allow an employer to breach a contract and then not have to pay for the breach by offering employment different from what they contracted to do—an employer would have no incentive to abide by the contract.

Plaintiff, Parker, an actress, entered a contract to play the female lead in a musical called Bloomer Girl, which was to be filmed in Los Angeles, California. Parker was "guaranteed compensation" amounting to $750,000. Under the contract, Parker also had the right to approve the film director, the dance director and the screenplay. Defendant Fox, the movie studio, decided not to make the film, and notified Parker they were not going to comply with the contract. Fox offered Parker a role for the same compensation, in a dramatic western called Big Country, Big Man, to be filmed in Australia. The new offer did not give Parker approval over the director or screenplay. Parker did not accept the offer. Parker filed an action seeking recovery of the guaranteed compensation.

*Parker v. Twentieth Century-Fox Film Corp.*, 3 Cal. 3d 176 (1970).

Parker is entitled to damages from Defendant's breach of the employment contract because an employee does not have to accept a different or inferior offer of employment to mitigate their damages resulting from an employer's breach of an employment contract.

269

# Appendix E

# Self Assessment Worksheet

## Step 1: Issues

_____ **Answer identifies all of the issues and sub-issues**

_____ Answer is missing the following issues/subissues:

_____

_____

For each missed issue—why did you miss the issue?

_____

_____

_____

_____

_____ Answer does not use headings for each of the issues identified in the rubric/sample answer

_____ Each issue is not addressed in a separate paragraph (issues are blended together)

_____ Issues are not covered in the same order as the rubric/sample answer, and order was important

_____ Missing issues are not in essay approach/outline

_____ Missing issues are not in issues checklist

_____ Answer raises non issues:

_____

_____

_____

## Step 2: Headings

_____ **Answer uses heading similar in style, content and frequency to rubric/sample answer**

_____ Answer does not have sufficient headings

_____ Answer contains inappropriate headings such as "issue", "rule", "analysis" or "conclusion"

_____ Answer does not flag key issues and sub issues with headings

## Step 3: Organization

_____ **Answer is organized in an orderly and logical manner, and follows order in rubric/sample answer**

_____ Answer does not follow organization in rubric/sample answer, but is still well organized (explain why):

_____

_____

_____

_____

_____ Answer is not organized in an orderly and logical manner (explain what should be improved):

_____

_____

_____

_____

## Step 4: Rule Statements

_____ **Rule statements are accurate and complete (received full credit), and in the appropriate place**

_____ Rule statements are incomplete for the following issues:

_____

_____

_____

_____

_____ Rule statements are inaccurate for the following issues:

_____

_____

_____

_____

_____ Rule statements are unnecessarily lengthy/contain info for which points were not allotted in rubric, or more than what is stated in sample answer

_____ Rule statements are not set out immediately after each issue heading

_____ Rule statements for issues and sub-issues are written in one section and are not located with the appropriate issue/sub-issue

## Step 5: Facts

\_\_\_\_\_ **Answer uses all of the applicable facts for each issue/does not summarize, recite or ignore facts**

\_\_\_\_\_ Answer does not use critical facts as listed in rubric/sample answer

\_\_\_\_\_ Answer does not use all of the applicable facts for the following issues/sub-issues (list issues/sub-issues and missing facts):

_____

_____

_____

_____

_____

\_\_\_\_\_ Answer recites facts, but does not link facts to the law

\_\_\_\_\_ Answer summarizes facts rather than using each fact

\_\_\_\_\_ Answer ignores important facts

\_\_\_\_\_ Answer misstates facts

## Step 6: Seeing Both Sides

\_\_\_\_\_ **Answer includes more than one perspective where appropriate**

\_\_\_\_\_ Answer does not include more than one perspective where appropriate

\_\_\_\_\_ Answer includes more than one perspective where only one was appropriate

## Step 7: Conclusions

\_\_\_\_\_ **Conclusions are logically consistent with analysis**

\_\_\_\_\_ **Conclusions are accurate where only one conclusion was appropriate**

\_\_\_\_\_ Answer does not reach a conclusion

\_\_\_\_\_ Answer concludes without performing analysis

\_\_\_\_\_ Conclusion is stated before analysis, rather than at the end of the analysis

## Step 8: Format

\_\_\_\_\_ **Answer is properly formatted**

\_\_\_\_\_ Answer is not in same order as the rubric/sample answer

\_\_\_\_\_ Headings are not used for the issues highlighted in the rubric/sample answer

\_\_\_\_\_ Headings do not match the style (one word, sentence, etc.) and content of rubric/ sample answer

\_\_\_\_\_ Answer does not leave space between paragraphs and/or headings

_____ Answer does not use IRAC structure or other required structure (explain what is wrong/ missing):

_____

_____

_____

_____

_____Answer contains grammar, spelling and/or typographical errors


## Reflection:

Be as specific as possible. The more specific your response, the greater the chance you will improve from this reflection.

My greatest strength on this essay was:

_____

_____

_____

_____

_____

_____

_____

_____

_____

_____

_____


My critical weakness on this essay was:

_____

_____

_____

_____

_____

_____

_____

_____

_____

_____

I am going to improve by:

_____

_____

_____

_____

_____

_____

_____

_____

_____

_____

_____

_____

# Appendix F

# Group Contract

## Team Guidelines[1]

Names (and contact information) of Team Members:

_____

_____

_____

_____

_____

_____

_____

We agree that the following attributes help us learn from each other and work effectively as a team:

_____

_____

_____

_____

_____

_____

_____

We agree that each of us will make our best efforts to employ these attributes for the benefit of our team. We also agree to abide by the following team rules:

_____

_____

_____

_____

_____

_____

_____

We agree that these rules are subject to change if the team so decides.

---

1. Based on forms and guidelines from our colleague Sophie Sparrow.

We agree to the following the consequences for any member of the team who does not meet the team guidelines or follow team rules:

_____

_____

_____

_____

_____

_____

_____

_____

Sample team criteria you may wish to include:

- Everyone is responsible for the success of the team and its members
- Listen to other team members
- Be receptive to and respectful of others' thoughts/input
- Be patient with others' process and learning
- Be prepared - put in a good faith effort
- Be proactive in addressing problems
- Contribute to discussions
- Don't hide behind the laptop
- Communicate with team about absences and other team-related tasks
- Have a sense of humor
- Be on time
- Work for the team
- Be willing to apologize
- Don't monopolize or dominate the team discussion
- Take turns leading the team

# Appendix G

# Answers to IRAC Example (*pages 215–219*)

1. Heading for Main issue
2. Rule for Main issue (notice it does not contain rules for the sub-issues)
3. Heading for sub-issue 1
4. Rule for sub-issue 1
5. Analysis and conclusion for sub-issue 1 (conclusion is final sentence of paragraph)
6. Heading for sub-issue 2
7. Rule for sub-issue 2
8. Heading for sub-sub issue 2a
9. Rule for sub-sub-issue 2a
10. Heading for analysis of sub-sub issue 2a as it pertains to A's Citizenship
11. Analysis of sub-sub issue 2a as it pertains to A's Citizenship
12. Heading for analysis of sub-sub issue 2a as it pertains to B's Citizenship
13. Analysis of sub-sub issue 2a as it pertains to B's Citizenship
14. Applying precedent to analyze sub-sub issue 2a, as it pertains to B's Citizenship
15. Counter argument analysis of sub-sub issue 2a as it pertains to B's Citizenship
16. Distinguishing case to analyze sub-sub issue 2a as it pertains to B's Citizenship
17. Conclusion for sub-sub issue 2a as it pertains to B's Citizenship
18. Heading for analysis of sub-sub issue 2a as it pertains to C's Citizenship
19. Analysis of sub-sub issue 2a as it pertains to C's Citizenship
20. Counter argument analysis of sub-sub issue 2a as it pertains to C's Citizenship
21. Conclusion for sub-sub issue 2a as it pertains to C's Citizenship
22. Heading for sub-sub issue 2b
23. Rule for sub-sub-issue 2b
24. Heading for sub-sub issue 2b(i)
25. Analysis and conclusion for sub-sub issue 2b(i)
26. Heading for sub-sub issue 2b(ii)
27. Rule for sub-sub issue 2b(ii)
28. Analysis and conclusion for sub-sub issue 2b(ii) (conclusion is final sentence of paragraph)
29. Conclusion for sub-issue 2 and main issue
30. Complete IRAC for new, minor issue

# Appendix H

# MBE Practice Chart

| Q # | GOT IT RIGHT | LUCKY GUESS | GOT IT WRONG | Did not ID central issue | Did not know rule | Missed important detail | Assumed facts not present | Tricked by facts | Reading comp | Other (explain) | Down to 2, picked wrong | Specific topic and explanation |
|---|---|---|---|---|---|---|---|---|---|---|---|---|
| | | | | | | | | | | | | |
| | | | | | | | | | | | | |
| | | | | | | | | | | | | |
| | | | | | | | | | | | | |
| | | | | | | | | | | | | |
| | | | | | | | | | | | | |
| | | | | | | | | | | | | |
| | | | | | | | | | | | | |
| | | | | | | | | | | | | |
| | | | | | | | | | | | | |
| | | | | | | | | | | | | |
| | | | | | | | | | | | | |
| | | | | | | | | | | | | |
| | | | | | | | | | | | | |
| | | | | | | | | | | | | |
| | | | | | | | | | | | | |

# References

## Chapter One

K. Anders Ericsson & P. Ward, *Capturing the Naturally Occurring Superior Performance of Experts in the Laboratory: Toward a Science of Expert and Exceptional Performance*, 16 Current Dir. Psych. Science 346 (2007).

Benedict Carey, *How we Learn: The Surprising Truth About When, Where and Why it Happens* (2015).

Peggy A. Ertmer & Timothy J. Newby, *The Expert Learner: Strategic, Self-Regulated and Reflective*, 24 INSTRUCTIONAL SCIENCE 1 (1996).

Gerald F. Hess, *The Legal Educator's Guide to Periodicals on Teaching and Learning*, 67 UMKC L. REV. 367 (1998).

Barbara K. Hofer, Shirley L. Yu & Paul R. Pintrich, *Teaching College Students to Be Self-Regulated Learners* in SELF REGULATED LEARNING: FROM TEACHING TO SELF-REFLECTIVE PRACTICE 57 (D.H. Schunk, B. Zimmerman, eds. 1998).

Reinhard W. Lindner & Bruce Harris, *Self-Regulated Learning: Its Assessment and Instructional Implications*, 16 EDUCATIONAL RESEARCH QUARTERLY 29 (1992).

Bridget Murray, *Getting Smart About Learning Is Her Lesson*, 29 APA MONITOR (April 1998).

James R. P. Ogloff, David R. Lyon, Kevin S. Douglas & V. Gordon Rose, *Annual Nebraska Survey & Survey of Legal Education: Article More Than "Learning to Think Like a Lawyer:" The Empirical Research on Legal Education*, 34 CREIGHTON L. REV. 73 (2000).

Paul R. Pintrich, *Understanding Self-Regulated Learning* in UNDERSTANDING SELF-REGULATED LEARNING 3 (P. Pintrich, ed. 1995).

Paul R. Pintrich, David A.F. Smith, Teresa Garcia & Wilbert J. McKeachie, *Reliability and Predictive Validity of the Motivated Strategies for Learning Questionnaire*, EDUCATIONAL AND PSYCHOLOGICAL MEASUREMENT, #53, 83–92 (1993).

Gregory Schraw & David W. Brooks, *Helping Students Self-Regulate in Math and Science Courses: Improving the Will and the Skill*, retrieved from http://www.ccci.unl.edu/chau/SR/Self Reg. html.

Bruce C. Howard, Steven McGee, Regina Shia & Namsoo Shin Hong, *The Influence of Metacognitive Self-Regulation and Ability Levels on Problem Solving* (American Educational Research Association 2001), http://www.google.com/search?q=cache:0h2dcIIZS0Y:www.cet.edu/research/papers/regulation/AERA2001BHsral.pdf++College+and+achievement+%22self-regulate%22&hl=enhttp://www.cet.edu/research/papers/regulation/AERA2001BHsral.pdf.

Claire E. Weinstein and Richard E. Mayer, *The Teaching of Learning Strategies*, in HANDBOOK OF RESEARCH ON TEACHING(M.C. Wittriock, ed. 1986).

Claire E. Weinstein & Gretchen Van Mater Stone, *Broadening Our Conception of General Education: The Self-Regulated Learner*, 81 NEW DIRECTIONS IN COMMUNITY COLLEGES 31 (1993).

Barry J. Zimmerman, *Developing Self-Fulfilling Cycles of Academic Regulation: An Analysis of Exemplary Instructional Models* in SELF REGULATED LEARNING: FROM TEACHING TO SELF-REFLECTIVE PRACTICE 1 (D.H. Schunk, B. Zimmerman, eds.1998).

# Chapter Two

Albert Bandura & Dale H. Schunk, *Cultivating Competence, Self-Efficacy, and Intrinsic Interest Through Proximal Self-Motivation,* 41(3) JOURNAL OF PERSONALITY AND SOCIAL PSYCHOLOGY 586 (1981).

John P. Barker & Joanne P. Olson, *Medical Students' Learning Strategies: Evaluation of First-Year Changes,* http://www.msstate.edu/org/mas/ejour2.html.

Deborah L. Butler, *A Strategic Content Learning Approach to Promoting Self-Regulated Learning by Students with Learning Disabilities* in SELF REGULATED LEARNING: FROM TEACHING TO SELF-REFLECTIVE PRACTICE 160 (D.H. Schunk, B. Zimmerman, eds. 1998).

Charles S. Carver & Michael F. Scheier, *Optimism, Pessimism, and Self-regulation* in OPTIMISM AND PESSIMISM: IMPLICATIONS FOR THEORY, RESEARCH, AND PRACTICE (Edward C. Chang Ed. 2001).

Benedict Carey, *How we Learn: The Surprising Truth About When, Where and Why it Happens* (Random House 2015).

Martin M. Chemers, Li-tze Hu & Ben F. Garcia, *Academic Self-Efficacy and First-Year College Student Performance and Adjustment,* 93(1) JOURNAL OF EDUCATIONAL PSYCHOLOGY 55 (2001).

Arthur L. Costa & Lawrence E. Lowery, TECHNIQUES FOR TEACHING THINKING (1989).

Stephen R. Covey, THE SEVEN HABITS OF HIGHLY EFFECTIVE PEOPLE (1989).

Carol Dweck, MINDSET, THE NEW PSYCHOLOGY OF SUCCESS (2008)

Peggy A. Ertmer & Timothy J. Newby, *The Expert Learner: Strategic, Self-Regulated and Reflective,* 24 INSTRUCTIONAL SCIENCE 1 (1996).

Friedrich Fåsterling, *Attributional Retraining: A Review,* 98(3) PSYCHOLOGICAL BULLETIN 495 (1985).

Teresa Garcia, *The Role of Motivational Strategies in Self-Regulated Learning* in UNDERSTANDING SELF-REGULATED LEARNING 29 (P. Pintrich, ed. 1995).

Anastacia S. Hagan & Clare Ellen Weinstein, *Achievement Goals, Self-Regulated Learning and the Role of the Classroom Context* in UNDERSTANDING SELF-REGULATED LEARNING 43 (P. Pintrich, ed. 1995).

Barbara K. Hofer, Shirley L. Yu & Paul R. Pintrich, *Teaching College Students to Be Self-Regulated Learners* in SELF REGULATED LEARNING: FROM TEACHING TO SELF-REFLECTIVE PRACTICE 57 (D.H. Schunk, B. Zimmerman, eds. 1998).

William Y. Lan, Teaching Self-Monitoring Skills in Statistics in Self-Regulated Learning: From Teaching to Self-Reflective Practice 86 (1998).

William Y. Lan, The Effects of Self-Monitoring on Students' Course Performance, Use of learning Strategies, Attitude, Self-Judgment Ability, and Knowledge Representation, 64(2) Journal of Experimental Education 101 (1997).

Robert W. Lent, Steven D. Brown & Kevin C. Larkin, *Self-Efficacy in the Prediction of Academic Performance and Perceived Career Options* 33(3) JOURNAL OF COUNSELING PSYCHOLOGY 265 (1986).

Reinhard W. Lindner & Bruce Harris, *Self-Regulated Learning: Its Assessment and Instructional Implications,* 16 EDUCATIONAL RESEARCH QUARTERLY 29 (1992).

Mark Morgan, Self-Monitoring of Attained Subgoals in Private Study, 77(6) Journal of Educational Psychology 623 (1985).

Karen D. Multon, Steven D. Brown & Robert W. Lent, *Relationship of Self-Efficacy Beliefs to Academic Outcomes: A Meta-Analytic Investigation,* 38(1) J COUNSELING PSYCHOLOGY 30 (1991).

Bridget Murray, *Getting Smart About Learning Is Her Lesson,* 29 APA MONITOR (April 1998).

Bridget Murray, Teaching Students How to Learn: College Students Often Struggle to Find Effective Learning Strategies, But Professors Can Help, Monitor on Psychology, Volume 31, No. 6, June 2000 http://www.apa.org/monitor/jun00/howtolearn.html.

Frances O'Tuel & Ruth K. Bullard, DEVELOPING HIGHER ORDER THINKING IN THE CONTENT AREAS K—12 50 (1993).

Daniel H. Pink, DRIVE, THE SURPRISING TRUTH ABOUT WHAT MOTIVATES US (2009)

Paul R. Pintrich, *Understanding Self-Regulated Learning* in UNDERSTANDING SELF-REGULATED LEARNING 3 (P. Pintrich, ed. 1995).

Corie Rosen, *Creating the Optimistic Classroom: What law Schools Can Learn from Attribution Style Effects,* 42 McGeorge L. Rev. 319 (2011).

Corie Rosen, *The Method and the Message,* 2 Nev. Law Journal (2012).

Martin Seligman, FLOURISH, A VISIONARY NEW UNDERSTANDING OF HAPPINESS AND WELL-BEING (2011)

Martin Seligman, LEARNED OPTIMISM, HOW TO CHANGE YOUR MIND AND YOUR LIFE (2006)

Stephen Stoynoff, *Self-Regulated Learning Strategies of International Students: A Study of High- and Low-Achievers,* COLLEGE STUDENT JOURNAL 329 (1997).

Frank Van Overwalle & Machteld De Metsenaere, *The Effects of Attribution-Based Intervention and Study Strategy Training on Academic Achievement in College Freshmen,* 60 BRITAIN JOURNAL OF EDUCATIONAL PSYCHOLOGY 301–304, 305–308 (1990).

Claire E. Weinstein & Richard E. Mayer, *The Teaching of Learning Strategies,* in HANDBOOK OF RESEARCH ON TEACHING(M.C. Wittriock, ed. 1986).

Claire E. Weinstein & Gretchen Van Mater Stone, *Broadening Our Conception of General Education: The Self-Regulated Learner,* 81 NEW DIRECTIONS IN COMMUNITY COLLEGES 31 (1993).

Timothy Wilson & Patricia Linville, 49(1) JOURNAL OF PERSONALITY AND SOCIAL PSYCHOLOGY, 287 (1985).

Philip H. Winne & A.F. Hadwin, *Studying as Self-Regulated Learning* in METACOGNITION IN EDUCATIONAL THEORY AND PRACTICE 279 (D.J. Hacker, J. Dunlosky and A.C. Graesser, eds. 1997).

Christopher A. Wolters, *Self-Regulated Learning and College Students' Regulation of Motivation,* 90(2) JOURNAL OF EDUCATIONAL PSYCHOLOGY 224 (1998).

Robert E. Wood & Edwin A. Locke, *The Relation of Self-Efficacy and Grade Goals to Academic Performance,* 47 EDUCATIONAL AND PSYCHOLOGICAL MEASUREMENT 1013 (1987).

Barry J. Zimmerman, *A Social-Cognitive View of Self-Regulated Academic Learning,* 81 JOURNAL OF EDUCATIONAL PSYCHOLOGY 329–339 (1989).

Barry J. Zimmerman, *Developing Self-Fulfilling Cycles of Academic Regulation: An Analysis of Exemplary Instructional Models* in SELF REGULATED LEARNING: FROM TEACHING TO SELF-REFLECTIVE PRACTICE 1 (D.H. Schunk, B. Zimmerman, eds. 1998).

Barry J. Zimmerman, Sebastian Bonner & Robert Kovach, DEVELOPING SELF-REGULATED LEARNERS: BEYOND ACHIEVEMENT TO SELF-EFFICACY(1996).

Barry J. Zimmerman & Andrew S. Paulsen, *Self-Monitoring During Collegiate Studying: An Invaluable Tool for Academic Self-Regulation* in NEW DIRECTIONS IN COLLEGE TEACHING AND LEARNING: UNDERSTANDING SELF-REGULATED LEARNING 13 (No. 65:1995).

Barry J. Zimmerman, *Developing Self-Fulfilling Cycles of Academic Regulation: An Analysis of Exemplary Instructional Models* in SELF REGULATED LEARNING: FROM TEACHING TO SELF-REFLECTIVE PRACTICE 1 (D.H. Schunk, B. Zimmerman, eds. 1998).

# Chapter Three

Robin A. Boyle & Rita Dunn, *Teaching Law Students Through Individual Learning Styles*, 62 ALB. L. REV. 213 (1998).

Gerald F. Hess & Steve Friedland, TECHNIQUES FOR TEACHING LAW (1999).

M.H. Sam Jacobson, *A Primer on Learning Styles: Reaching Every Student*, 25 SEATTLE UNIV. L. REV. 139 (2001).

Marty Peters, JURIS TYPES (2007)

Vernellia R. Randall, *The Myers-Briggs Type Indicator, First-Year Law Students and Performance*, 26 CUMBERLAND L. REV. 26 (1995).

Paul D. Tieger & Barbara Barron-Tieger, DO WHAT YOU ARE (3d ed. 2001).

# Chapter Four

### For reading speed:

http://www.readingsoft.com/

http://www.spreeder.com/

http://web.mst.edu/~gbert/SpeedReader/read.html

### For grammar and writing:

http://coregrammarforlawyers.com/ (requires purchase)

http://www.englishgrammar.org/exercises/

https://owl.english.purdue.edu/exercises/2/

http://www.quickanddirtytips.com/grammar-girl

### For an introduction to the state and federal court systems (legal civics):

http://www.law.northwestern.edu/law-school-life/studentservices/orientation/documents/Orientation-Reading-Slocum-Ch_022.pdf

https://system.uslegal.com/state-courts/

http://www.fjc.gov/public/pdf.nsf/lookup/U.S._Legal_System_English07.pdf/$file/U.S._Legal_System_English07.pdf

# Chapter Five

Lisa Christensen, *Legal Reading and Law School Success: An Empirical Study*, 30 SEATTLE U. L. REV. 603 (2007)

Laurel Currie Coates, *Beating the Odds: Reading Strategies of Law Students Admitted Through Alternative Admissions Programs*, 83 IOWA L. REV. 139, 158–159 (1997).

Arthur L. Costa & Lawrence E. Lowery, TECHNIQUES FOR TEACHING THINKING (1989).

Dorothy H. Deegan, *Exploring Differences Among Novices Reading in a Specific Domain: The Case of Law*, 30 READING RESEARCH QUARTERLY 154, 163 (1995).

Peter Dewitz, *Conflict Of Laws Symposium: Reading Law: Three Suggestions for Legal Education*, 27 U. TOL. L. REV. 657 (1996).

Elizabeth Fajans & Mary R. Falk, *Against the Tyranny of Paraphrase: Talking Back to Texts*, 78 CORNELL L. REV. 163 (1993).

Anastasia S. Hagan & Claire Ellen Weinstein, *Achievement Goals, Self-Regulated Learning and the Role of the Classroom Context* in UNDERSTANDING SELF-REGULATED LEARNING (P. Pintrich, ed. 1995).

Barbara K. Hofer, Shirley L. Yu & Paul Pintrich, *Teaching College Students to Be Self-Regulated Learners* in SELF-REGULATED LEARNING: FROM TEACHING TO SELF-REFLECTIVE PRACTICE 57, 76 (1998).

Mary A. Lundeberg, *Metacognitive Aspects of Reading Comprehension: Studying Understanding in Legal Case Analysis*, 22 READING RESEARCH QUARTERLY 407–415 (1987).

Ruth Ann McKinnney, READING LIKE A LAWYER: TIME-SAVING STRATEGIES FOR READING LAW LIKE AN EXPERT (2005).

Frances O'Tuel & Ruth K. Bullard, DEVELOPING HIGHER ORDER THINKING IN THE CONTENT AREAS K–12 50 (1993).

Patricia L. Smith & Tillman J. Ragan, INSTRUCTIONAL DESIGN (1999).

Paul T. Wangerin, *Learning Strategies for Law Students*, 52 ALB. L. REV. 471 (1988).

Claire E. Weinstein & Richard E. Mayer, *The Teaching of Learning Strategies* in HANDBOOK OF RESEARCH ON TEACHING (M.C. Wittrock, ed. 1986).

B.Y.L. Wong, *Self-Questioning Instructional Research: A Review*, 55 REVIEW OF EDUCATIONAL RESEARCH 227 (1990).

Barry J. Zimmerman, Sebastian Bonner & Robert Kovach, DEVELOPING SELF-REGULATED LEARNERS: BEYOND ACHIEVEMENT TO SELF-EFFICACY (1996).

## Chapter Eight

K. Anders Ericsson, et. al, *The Role of Deliberate Practice in the Acquisition of Expert Performance*, 100 Psych. Rev'w (1993).

K. Anders Ericsson & P. Ward, *Capturing the Naturally Occurring Superior Performance of Experts in the Laboratory: Toward a Science of Expert and Exceptional Performance*, 16 Current Dir. Psych. Science 346 (2007).

Jennifer M. Cooper, *Smarter Law Learning: Using Cognitive Science to Maximize Law Learning* 44 Capital U. L. Rev, ____ (2016). Available at SSRN: http://ssrn.com/abstract=2501128 or http://dx.doi.org/10.2139/ssrn.2501128

Peter C. Brown, Henry L. Roediger, and Mark A. McDaniel, *Make It Stick: The Science of Successful Learning.* (HUP 2014).

Benedict Carey, *How we Learn: The Surprising Truth About When, Where and Why it Happens* (Random House 2015).

Joshua Foer, *Moonwalking with Einstein: The Art and Science of Remembering Everything* (Penguin 2011).

Sophie M. Sparrow and Margaret Sova McCabe, *Team-Based Learning in Law* (January 16, 2012), available at SSRN: http://ssrn.com/abstract=1986230 or http://dx.doi.org/10.2139/ssrn.1986230

Vernellia R. Randall, *Increasing Retention and Improving Performance: Practical Advice on Using Cooperative Learning in Law Schools*, 16 T.M. COOLEY L. REV. 201 (1999).

Clifford S. Zimmerman,*"Thinking Beyond My Own Interpretation:" Reflections on Collaborative and Cooperative Learning Theory in the Law School Curriculum*, 31 ARIZ. ST. L.J. 957 (1999).

## Chapter Nine

Benedict Carey, *How we Learn: The Surprising Truth About When, Where and Why it Happens* (2015).

Carol Dweck, MINDSET, THE NEW PSYCHOLOGY OF SUCCESS (2008)

# Chapter Ten

Authentic Happiness, University of Pennsylvania, www.authentichappiness.sas.upen.edu

Rebecca Flanagan, *Lucifer Goes to Law School: Towards Explaining and Minimizing Law Student Peer-to-Peer Harassment and Intimidation*, 47 Washburn L. J. 453 (2008).

Humanizing Legal Education, http://www.law.fsu.edu/academic_programs/humanizing_law school.html

Lawrence S. Krieger, *What We're Not Telling Law Students—And Lawyers—That They Really Need to Know: Some Thoughts Toward Revitalizing the Profession from Its Roots*, 13 J. L. & Health 1 (1999).

Bridget A. Mahoney, *Distress Among the Legal Profession: What Law Schools Can Do About It*, 15 Notre Dame J.L. Ethics & Pub. Pol. 307 (2001).

*Making Docile Lawyers: An Essay on the Pacification of Law Students*, 111 Harv. L. Rev. 2027 (1998).

Paula J. Manning, *Understanding the Impact of Inadequate Feedback: A Means to Reduce Law Student Psychological Distress, Increase Motivation and Improve Learning Outcomes*, 43 Cumberland L. Rev. ___ (2013) *available at:* http://ssrn.com/author=1758309

Ruth Ann McKinney, Depression And Anxiety In Law Students: Are We Part Of The Problem And Can We Be Part Of The Solution? 8 Legal Writing: J. Legal Writing Inst. 229 (2002).

Cathleen A. Roach, *A River Runs Through It: Tapping into the Information Stream to Move Students from Isolation to Autonomy*, 36 Ariz. L. Rev. 667 (1994).

Corie Rosen, *Creating the Optimistic Classroom: What law Schools Can Learn from Attribution Style Effects*, 42 McGeorge L. Rev. 319 (2011).

Corie Rosen, *The Method and the Message*, 2 Nev. Law Journal (2012).

Martin Seligman, Learned Optimism, How to Change Your Mind and Your Life (2006)

Martin Seligman, Flourish, A Visionary new Understanding of happiness and Well-Being (2011)

Kennon M. Sheldon and Lawrence S. Krieger, *Does Legal Education Have Undermining Effects on Law Students? Evaluating Changes in Motivation, Values, and Well-Being*, 22 Behav. Sci. & Law 261 (2004).

Kennon M. Sheldon and Lawrence S. Krieger, *Understanding the Negative Effects of Legal Education on Law Students: A Longitudinal Test and Extension of Self Determination Theory*, 33 Personality & Soc. Psychol. Bull. 883 (2007)

# Index